COMPANY LAW IN THE EUROPEAN COMMUNITIES

COMPANY LAW IN THE EUROPEAN COMMUNITIES

Third edition

ROBERT R PENNINGTON LL D

Solicitor
Professor of Commercial Law
University of Birmingham

FRANK WOOLDRIDGE LL M PhD

Senior Lecturer in Law
University of Birmingham

Oyez Longman

© Oyez Longman Publishing Limited 1982
Norwich House, 11/13 Norwich Street
London EC4A 1AB

ISBN 0 85120 638 7

First published 1962
Second edition 1970
Third edition   1982

Formerly entitled *Companies in the Common Market*

Set in Times by Vantage Photosetting Co. Ltd,
London and Southampton
and printed in Great Britain by
Biddles Ltd, Guildford and King's Lynn

PREFACE

It is now twelve years since the second edition of this book appeared under the title of *Companies in the Common Market*. Since that time four countries (including the UK) have joined the original six member states of the European Communities and the law of the original six member states governing companies has changed radically. It is therefore appropriate that a new edition of this work, giving an up-to-date picture of the company legislation in all the Common Market countries (other than the UK), should now appear. The work of preparing a new edition has been undertaken mainly by Dr Frank Wooldridge, one of the co-authors. Professor Pennington has been prevented, by his commitments as Dean of the Faculty of Law at the University of Birmingham over the last three years, from taking as active a part in drafting the text as he would have wished. Both authors, however, have revised the text thoroughly and accept joint responsibility for its accuracy and completeness.

The purpose of this book remains that of the first two editions, namely, to present a synoptic view of company law in each of the other member states of the European Communities in a form and manner which will be useful to the British lawyer and businessman. The book does not pretend to deal with the details of the systems of national law exhaustively, but constitutes an introductory guide to the relevant law with sufficient detail to enable the lawyer or businessman to comprehend the main facets of national company law and to see the principal differences between those systems and the UK law governing companies.

This edition is unavoidably considerably longer than the two earlier editions in view of the rapid expansion over the last twelve years of the volume of national legislation governing companies, and also because of the addition of chapters dealing with the company laws of Denmark, Greece and Ireland. For this reason it has been necessary to omit the concluding chapters of the second edition dealing with the conflict of laws aspects of Western European Company law and the harmonisation of company legislation by directives issued by the Council of Ministers of the European Communities. This latter topic has now become a subject in its own right, and the reader is referred to the standard works on the directives and draft directives which have so far been issued. These directives are, however, mentioned incidentally in this book in connection with the effect they will have on the existing company legislation of the member states.

The law is stated in this edition as it stood on 1 April 1982.

Robert R Pennington
Frank Wooldridge

September 1982

CONTENTS

ABBREVIATIONS

So far as possible the abbreviations used in the text are those used conventionally in the particular Member State. The abbreviations of company names are listed on the contents page and appear in the main headings within each chapter. The following abbreviations have also been used:

Germany
BGH   *Bundesgerichtshof* (Federal Supreme Court)
RG   *Reichsgericht* (Imperial Supreme Court)
BGHZ   *Entscheidungen des Bundesgerichtshofes in Zivilsachen* (decisions of the Federal Supreme Court)
RGZ   *Entscheidungen des Reichsgerichts in Zivilsachen* (decisions of the Imperial Supreme Court)

France
D   *Dalloz*
DP   *Dalloz périodique*
S   *Sirey*
Gaz Pal   *Gazette du Palais*
J Soc   *Journal des sociétés civiles et commerciales*

Italy
Foro ital   *Foro italiano*
Giur ital   *Giurisprudenza italiana*
Dir fall   *Diritto fallimentare*

Netherlands
HR   *Hooge Raad* (Netherlands Supreme Court)
NJ   *Nederlandsche Jurisprudentie*

Belgium
Trib comm   *Tribunal de commerce* (commercial court of first instance)
Rev prat soc   *Revue pratique des sociétés*

European Communities
OJ   Official Journal of the European Communities

CHAPTER 1

WEST GERMANY

German law recognises six forms of commercial association, namely: the commercial partnership (*offene Handelsgesellschaft*); the limited partnership (*Kommanditgesellschaft*) (similar to the UK limited partnership formed under the Limited Partnerships Act 1907); the silent partnership (*stille Gesellschaft*), which is similar to the relationship created under our Partnership Act 1890, s 2(3)(*d*), where a person lends money to the proprietor of a business in consideration of a share of the profits; the incorporated public company (*Aktiengesellschaft*); the incorporated private company (*Gesellschaft mit beschränkter Haftung*); and the incorporated public company whose directors are personally liable for its debts (*Kommanditgesellschaft auf Aktien*). All these commercial associations are subject to the German Commercial Code, but the latter three are principally governed by special statutes, the *Aktiengesellschaft* (AG) and the *Kommanditgesellschaft auf Aktien* (KGaA) by the *Aktiengesetz* of 1965 (which superseded the earlier Law of 1937), and the *Gesellschaft mit beschränkter Haftung* (GmbH) by the *GmbH Gesetz* of 1892, which underwent substantial revision in 1980.

In addition, there are civil companies (*Gesellschaft des bürgerlichen Rechts*) which are governed exclusively by the Civil Code; they are distinguished from commercial associations by their non-commercial objects, and comprise principally professional partnerships (other than brokers), agricultural partnerships and companies, and mining companies. AGs and GmbHs are treated as commercial associations irrespective of their objects (*Aktiengesetz*, § 3; *GmbH Gesetz*, § 13(3)), and so an AG which carries on mining or farming is a commercial association.

The companies which an English lawyer is most likely to encounter are the AG and the GmbH, and its variant, the GmbH & Co; and this chapter is therefore confined to them. References in this chapter to paragraphs (§§) by number are, in the first part, to paragraphs of the *Aktiengesetz* as amended and in the latter part to paragraphs of the *GmbH Gesetz* as amended.

1

The first two directives of the Council of Ministers of the European Communities on the harmonisation of company law have been implemented in Germany.

AKTIENGESELLSCHAFT (AG)

1 Formation

The first step towards incorporating an AG is for the founders, who must be at least five in number, to execute a contract for its formation (the *Satzung*, hereafter referred to as the articles of the company) before a judge or notary (§§ 2 and 23(1)). The articles contain the same subject matter as the memorandum and articles of association of an English company, but tend to be shorter because many of the matters which can be dealt with in the articles of an British company are governed by mandatory provisions of the *Aktiengesetz* which cannot be departed from by agreement. The articles of an AG must set out (§ 23(3) and (4)):

1 The name of the company, which must indicate the nature of its business and contain the word '*Aktiengesellschaft*' or the abbreviation AG (§ 4(1)), and must not be the same as that of any other undertaking registered in the same district (Commercial Code, § 30(1)).

2 The domicile of the Company (*Sitz*), that is the city or district in which it carries on business (§ 5); since 1965, the domicile can be outside West Germany.

3 The nature of the company's business.

4 The amount of the company's share capital, which must not be less than DM 100,000 (£23,600 approximately) (§ 7), and must be divided into shares (*Aktien*) each with a nominal value of DM 50 or DM 100 or a multiple of DM 100 (§ 8).

5 The nominal values of the shares, and the number of shares of each nominal value, and where applicable the classes into which the shares are divided, and the number of shares of each class.

6 Whether the shares are in registered or bearer form.

7 The numbers of members of the executive board (*Vorstand*) or the rules according to which this number is determined.

8 The newspapers in which the company will publish notices about its affairs.

If the articles do not contain any provision governing the amount of the share capital or the object of the company, or if the provisions governing the objects of the company are void (eg because they violate legal rules which are designed exclusively or primarily to protect the company's creditors or are otherwise in the public interest), the court may declare the company annulled on an application by a shareholder or director or member of the supervisory board (*Aufsichtsrat*) within three years after the company is registered (§ 275(1) and (3)). The effect of annulment is the same as if the company has been ordered to be wound up, and transactions previously entered into by it are not invalidated (§ 277(1) and (2)).

The founders must subscribe for the whole of the share capital of the company (§§ 2 and 29), but they may transfer the shares they do not wish to retain to a bank for resale to the public or to a group of investors. They may not transfer any of their shares before the company has been registered, however (§ 41(4)), and since at least a quarter of the nominal value of the shares which they have subscribed for in cash plus any stipulated share premium must be paid into a bank account in the company's name before it can be registered (§§ 36(2) and 54(3)), it means that the founders must provide at least one-quarter of the company's share capital allotted in cash out of their own pockets or with the help of a bank loan. Formerly it was possible for the founders to obtain subscriptions from other persons for that part of the company's share capital allotted for cash which they did not themselves take (AktG 1937, § 30), but this is no longer so.

Contributions in kind must consist of assets which are capable of economic assessment. A company's capital cannot be paid up by way of an undertaking to do work or perform services (§ 27(2)). Non-cash contributions must be transferred in full before the company is registered. However, if the non-cash consideration is a contractual undertaking to transfer an asset to the company, the transfer must take place within five years of registration (§ 36a(2)).

German law takes care to ensure that special privileges conferred on particular shareholders, promotion expenses and remuneration, the issue of shares for a consideration other than cash, and the acquisition of assets by the company for any consideration are brought to the attention of investors and are fairly arranged. The arrangements in respect of such matters must be set out in the articles (§§ 26 and 27), the founders must report thereon to the directors and the supervisory board (§ 32) and the latter must inquire into the arrangements and report on them, in particular, as to whether assets acquired by the company in consideration of an allotment of shares or for any other consideration are equal in value to the nominal value of the shares allotted for them, or to the other consideration given for them (§§ 33(1) and 34(2)). Additionally, and perhaps most importantly, a similar inquiry and report must be made by professionally qualified examiners appointed by the court (*Gründungsprüfer*), except where the whole of the company's share capital is allotted for cash, and none of the directors or members of the supervisory board are founders or interested in the promotion of the company (§ 33(2)–(4)). This report must describe each of the assets in question, set out the methods of valuation, and state whether the value of the consideration is at least equal to the nominal value of the shares (§ 34(2)). Similar provisions apply if the company acquires assets within two years after its registration in consideration of shares or cash amounting to more than one-tenth of its share capital, and contracts for such acquisitions require the approval of a general meeting of shareholders by a resolution passed by a three-quarters majority (§ 52). If the founders or directors intentionally or negligently cause the company harm by entering into detrimental arrangements of these kinds, they are liable to it in damages (§ 46(2)), and other persons who knowingly participate in such improper arrangements (eg allottees of shares for a consideration in kind which has been overvalued) are also liable (§ 47).

The company is incorporated as an AG by being registered in the Commercial Register kept by the district court (*Amtsgericht*) for the city or district where the company is domiciled, or if it is domiciled outside West Germany, for the district within which it has a German branch (*Zweigniederlassung*) (§§ 36(1), 41(1) and 44(1)). Before the application for registration is made, the founders appoint the first supervisory board and the first auditors of the company (§ 30(1)) and the supervisory board appoints the first directors (§ 30(4)). If the company is formed to take over the whole or part of an existing undertaking, which normally has more than 2,000 employees, or is engaged in the iron, steel or coal industries and has normally more than 1,000 employees, the founders appoint only one-half of the members of the supervisory board: this proportion is increased to two-thirds in the case of companies employing not more than 2,000 employees which are not engaged in the iron, steel or coal industries, and thus governed by the rule which has just been mentioned. When the law requires that the founders shall not appoint all the members of the first supervisory board, the members of the supervisory board appointed by the founders appoint the first executive directors and the latter ensure that the remaining members of the supervisory board are elected by the employees of the company in accordance with the rules for employee participation (see p13) (§§ 31, 97 and 98).

After these appointments have been made, the founders, directors and members of the supervisory board appointed by the founders all join in making the application for the company to be registered (§ 36(1)), and the application must be accompanied by a declaration that at least a quarter of the company's share capital allotted for cash plus the whole of any share premiums has been paid up, a statement of the powers of representation granted to the individual directors, the articles of the company, any contracts for the allotment of shares in consideration of kind and for the acquisition of assets by the company for any other consideration, an account of the promotion expenses, the documents by which the first directors and members of the supervisory board were appointed, and the reports referred to in the last paragraph (§ 37). The court examines these documents and, if it finds them in order, registers the company (§ 38). If the company sets up branch establishments in other districts, it must apply to the district courts for those districts to be registered in their Commercial Registers (§ 42). The incorporation of the company and the establishment of a branch by it must be advertised in the Federal Gazette (*Bundesanzeiger*) and at least one other newspaper (§§ 25 and 40, and Commercial Code, § 10).

The company may commence carrying on business as soon as it is registered, and may also within three months adopt contracts made on its behalf before registration, thereby becoming a party thereto in place of the person who contracts on its behalf, the consent of the other party to the contract in such circumstances being unnecessary (§ 41(3)).

2 Shares and bonds

(a) Shares

An AG has separate legal personality from its shareholders, (*Aktionäre*) and its assets alone are liable to satisfy its obligations (§ 1(1)). Its shareholders are not personally liable for its obligations, even if its membership is reduced to one shareholder; their liability is limited to the unpaid part of the nominal value or higher issue price of their shares (§ 54(1)).

Shares may not be issued at a discount, but they may be issued at a premium, and the obligation to pay the premium, like the obligation to pay their nominal value, is enforceable against the registered shareholder for the time being (§§ 9, 63(1) and 67(2)). The issue price of the shares may be made payable by the instalments specified in the terms of issue, or may be left to be called up by the board of directors. Calls are made by advertisement in the newspapers specified in the articles (§ 63(1)), and if the shareholders fail to pay a call within the time limited, the company may advertise on three occasions a further period within which they must pay it, not being less than three months from the date of the first advertisement nor less than one month from the third, and their company may forfeit their shares if the call is still unpaid (§ 64(1), (2) and (3)). New shares may be issued in place of those forfeited, and their holder is liable for the calls unpaid on the corresponding forfeited shares; nevertheless, the former holder of the forfeited shares remains liable for the whole of the issue price which is still unpaid, whether called up or not, in so far as it is not recovered from the holder of the new shares (§ 64(4)). After forfeiting shares, the company may also recover the call in arrear from former holders (§ 65(1)), but a former holder is only liable to pay calls made within two years after the registration of the transfer of shares by him (§ 65(2)). Any former holder who pays a call is entitled to the issue of new shares in place of those forfeited, credited as paid up to the same extent as they were paid up plus the amounts paid by him (§ 65(3)). Moreover, it seems that he has the first option to take up new shares, for the company is directed to sell the shares to other persons only after it has ascertained that it cannot recover the call outstanding on the forfeited shares (§ 65(3)). The foregoing rules apply in a liquidation as well as while the company is a going concern.

Shares may be in registered, or if the articles so provide, in bearer form, but until the whole issue price has been paid, the shares and letters of allotment (*Zwischenscheine*) issued in respect of them must be in registered form (§ 10). Bearer share certificates are negotiable instruments, and so the holder of a bearer certificate can enforce the company's obligations in respect of the shares: furthermore, whether he acquired the shares for value or not, a person who takes delivery of bearer shares from the original or an intermediate holder acquires a good title to them, unless he was aware that his transferor's title was defective, or unless he would have discovered that fact but for his gross negligence (Civil Code, §§ 932 and 935). In practice, all fully paid shares are in bearer form, except those of a few banks and insurance companies which avail themselves of a provision in the *Aktiengesetz* by which the articles may require transfers of registered shares to be approved by the company (§ 68(2)); this is the only restriction which the articles may place on the free transferability of shares, and shares subject to it are known as vinculated shares (*vinkulierte Aktien*). The distinction between registered shares and bearer shares is not so important in German law as it is in British law, apart from this point. Although a transferee of registered shares should apply to be registered by the company, and so far as the company is concerned the transferor alone is entitled to the shares until the transfer has been registered (§§ 67(2) and 68(3)), the beneficial title to shares may be transferred by the registered holder endorsing the share certificate in blank like a cheque and delivering it to the transferee, whereupon it becomes a negotiable instrument, and the bearer of the endorsed certificate may at any time insist on being registered by the company (§ 68(1) and (3)). The company then has to check the formal regularity of the endorsements, but is not liable to any person who claims an interest in the shares if it transpires that any of the endorsements are forged and notwithstanding this the company registers the last endorsee as holder (§ 68(4)). The same provisions apply to letters of allotment (§ 68(5)), which are therefore similar to the renounceable allotment letters of an English company. In practice, share certificates are usually deposited with banks, which hold shares of the same class as a common fund without distinction for the benefit of all the depositors, and account for dividends and other payments to them periodically, and retransfer equivalent shares to them on request: this kind of deposit must be expressly agreed to by the depositor, however (*Depotgesetz* of 1937, §§ 11 and 15).

A company may not issue shares to itself, and if it issues shares to a person who holds them on its behalf, or on behalf of a company controlled by it, or a company in which it holds a majority of the issued shares or voting rights, the subscriber is personally liable to pay the issue price, but cannot exercise any rights in respect of the shares (§ 56(1) and (3)). Furthermore, a company is in principle not permitted to acquire its own shares, except when carrying out a resolution to reduce its capital (§ 71(1) No 6). However, it may acquire its own shares where it is necessary for it to do so in order to prevent serious and imminent harm to its interests; or in order to offer the shares for sale to its employees, or those of an associated company; or for the purpose of paying compensation to minority shareholders in subsidiaries with which a control contract is being concluded, or to minority shareholders of subsidiaries which are being integrated with it (§ 71(1) Nos 1–3). A company may accept a gratuitous transfer of any of its shares, and a bank or other financial institution may acquire its own shares as purchasing commission (§ 71(1) No 4). Finally, a company may acquire its own shares as the result of a universal transfer of assets, for example on death (§ 71(1) No 5).

The nominal value of the shares acquired for the purposes specified in § 71(1) Nos 1–3, together with that of the shares previously acquired by the company and held by it must not exceed one-tenth of its share capital in total. Such an acquisition is only permitted where it can take place out of assets surplus to those required to represent the company's nominal capital plus those reserves which may not be distributed under the law or the articles, and where it takes place for the purposes specified in Nos 1, 2 and 4, it is only permitted if the shares are fully paid (§ 71(2)).

A company which is controlled by another company or a majority of whose shares or voting rights are held by another company can only hold shares in that other company if the other could hold the shares itself, and in calculating the maximum fraction of one-tenth of the other company's capital which may be acquired by it or by the first company, their respective holdings are aggregated (§ 71d).

An acquisition of shares in breach of the foregoing rules is effective but the directors are liable for any resulting loss (§§ 71(4) and 93(3) No 3). An executory contract for such an acquisition is unenforceable (§ 71(4)). A company cannot claim or exercise any rights (eg to receive dividends or to vote) in respect of shares in itself whilst it continues to hold them (§ 71b). Shares acquired in contravention of § 71(1) and (2) must be disposed of within one year or cancelled (§ 71c(1)). Where the total nominal value of the shares that the company has acquired and now holds in conformity with § 71(1) exceeds 10 per cent of the subscribed capital, the excess shares must be disposed of or cancelled within three years (§ 71c(2)). A legal transaction whereby a company provides financial assistance for the acquisition of its own shares is null and void (§ 71a(1)).

Only the profits shown in the company's annual balance sheet and amounts on account thereof (interim dividends) may be distributed to shareholders (§§ 58(5), 59 and 60). The profit is the excess of the company's assets over its liabilities shown in its balance sheet, and liabilities for this purpose include its nominal capital and reserves (§ 151(4)). A general meeting may resolve by a three-quarters majority vote to capitalise profits which have been transferred to reserve and to issue fully paid bonus shares (and, where necessary, fractional certificates) to its shareholders in proportion to their existing holdings (§§ 207(1), 212 and 213). A capitalisation issue must not affect the relationship between classes of shares (§ 216(1), and the existing proportions between voting rights attaching to different classes of shares must be maintained. The rights of third parties under existing contracts with the company are not altered by the capitalisation (§ 216(3)), so that an existing option to subscribe for unissued shares of the company will be increased in proportion to the capitalisation, and the conversion rights of the holders of convertible bonds will be proportionately augmented.

(b) Bonds

Companies may issue bonds (*Schuldverschreibungen*) in favour of a named person or to bearer, but in practice only bearer bonds are met with. Bearer bonds are negotiable instruments (Civil Code, § 793), but if they promise payment of a fixed sum, as they usually do, they are void unless the approval of the state is given (Civil Code, §§ 795 and 808a). Companies may also issue bonds which entitle their holders to convert them into shares, or to subscribe for further shares (*Wandelschuldverschreibungen*), or which entitle their holders to a payment proportionate to the dividends paid to the shareholders in addition to or in lieu of interest (*Gewinnschuldverschreibungen*). The issue of such bonds requires the approval of a general meeting of shareholders by a three-quarters majority as well as the approval of the Federal Government, and unless the shareholders' resolution waives their right, the bonds must first be offered to the shareholders in proportion to their existing holdings (§ 221(1) and (3)). Bonds may be secured on property of the company or a third person or by a guarantee given by a bank or another company, but they are very often issued without security, and then carry no priority in the event of the company's insolvency. In practice secured bonds are protected by mortgages of land (*Hypothek*) and of fixed assets such as equipment, patents and investments (*Sicherungsübereignung*). Current assets are not used as security for bonds, but trade debts are often employed as security for bank loans and overdrafts. It is theoretically possible for a company to create a floating charge over its whole undertaking, because the invalidation by the Civil Code, § 310, of contracts for the transfer or mortgage of the whole of the property a person will acquire in the future does not apply to such a contract made by an AG (§ 361(1)). In practice, however, such floating charges are not met with, because they might be considered a fraud on the unsecured creditors of the company, and might also run foul of the Civil Code, § 419, by which a transferee (including a mortgagee) of substantially the whole of the property of any person (including a company) is made personally liable for his or her debts.

If a company issues a series of 300 or more bonds whose nominal values amount to at least DM 300,000, the bondholders are entitled to appoint a representative who fulfils the same function as the trustee for debenture holders of a British company (*Schuldverschreibungsgesetz* of 1899, § 1). The representative's powers are defined by the resolution appointing him, and he may by a resolution passed by a three-quarters majority at a bondholders' meeting be given exclusive power to enforce the bondholders' rights (SchuldvG, § 14). A modification or surrender of the bondholders' rights requires their consent by the same majority vote, but the principal of the bonds cannot be cancelled or reduced without their unanimous consent, and other modifications of their rights are permitted only if necessary to enable the company to pay its current debts which are due or to avoid bankruptcy (SchuldvG §§ 11(1) and 12(2)).

(c) Dealings

The shares and bonds of an AG may be dealt in on a stock exchange which has given permission for the purpose, or in the open market, which in practice means through the agency of the banks. German stock exchanges are regulated by a special law, the *Börsengesetz*, which subjects them to state supervision. An AG may apply for permission for its shares and bonds to be dealt in on a stock exchange only after a year has elapsed from its incorporation, unless the government allows it to apply earlier (BörsG, § 41(1)). The stock exchange must ensure that the prospectus or other advertisement to be published in respect of the securities is accurate and gives all the information an investor requires to judge their value (BörsG, § 36(3)), and if a published prospectus is deficient in either of these respects, the persons who issued it and knew of the deficiency, or who would have discovered the deficiency but for their gross negligence, are liable in damages to any allottee or purchaser who is misled (BörsG, § 45(1)). There is no statutory liability for false or defective prospectuses under the *Aktiengesetz* itself, and so if an AG publishes a prospectus in respect of shares or bonds for which a stock exchange quotation is not currently sought, the liability of the company, its directors and other persons responsible for the prospectus depends on the general law of contract and delict.

3 Management and control

(a) Board of directors

The board of directors, or executive board (*Vorstand*), of an AG may consist of one or more individuals of full age and capacity appointed by the supervisory board for terms of up to five years. If the company's capital exceeds DM 3m, at least two directors must be appointed, unless the articles expressly provide for one only (§ 76). In coal, iron and steel companies employing as a general rule more than 1,000 workers and in other companies employing as a general rule more than 2,000 workers, a labour director (*Arbeitsdirektor*) who is specially responsible for the employees' interests is also necessary, and he is entitled to participate in the board's deliberations (*Mitbestimmungsgesetz* of 1951, § 12, and *Mitbestimmungsgesetz* of 1976, § 33). Retiring directors may be appointed for successive periods of up to five years, but a resolution for reappointment may not be passed by the supervisory board more than a year before the expiration of a current director's term of office (§ 84(1)).

Unless the articles otherwise provide, all the directors (*Vorstandmitglieder*) must concur in acts done on the company's behalf; if the articles permit directors to act individually, they may not permit a minority of the directors to override the majority (§ 77(1) and (2)). Furthermore the articles may permit one or more of the directors, whether named or not, to exercise all or any of the board's powers, and the board may delegate any of its powers in respect of particular transactions (eg to negotiate a contract for a particular purpose) to one or more of its number (§ 78(3) and (4)). But if an outsider deals with the whole board or a duly constituted majority or delegate, the company is responsible for their acts, whether done within the limits of their authority and in furtherance of the company's business or not, and the outsider can enforce obligations incurred by them in its name unless he is a party to a fraud practised by them on it (Civil Code, §§ 31 and 164). Moreover, third parties are not affected by restrictions on the board's powers contained in the articles, but directors who disregard restrictions imposed by the articles or by resolution of the

supervisory board or a general meeting, are personally liable to the
company for any damage it thereby suffers (§ 82(1) and (2)).

Directors may be removed from office for substantial reasons by
the supervisory board (*Aufsichtsrat*), in particular if the director has
been guilty of a breach of duty, or is incompetent to manage the
company's business or has lost the confidence of the shareholders
(§ 84(3)). The supervisory board fixes the directors' remuneration,
which may include a share of the company's profits, but if the
company's financial position deteriorates so that it would be unjust
to require it to continue to pay the remuneration which has been
fixed, the supervisory board may reduce it, but any director may
then resign on giving six weeks' notice (§§ 86 and 87(1) and (2)).
Directors may not carry on any business on their own or in partnership, whether the business competes with the company's or not, nor
may they be directors or managers of another company, nor engage
in any transaction of a sort which the company engages in, without
the consent of the supervisory board, which may only be given for a
particular undertaking, appointment or transaction, and not in the
form of a general permission. Directors must exhibit the skill and
care of ordinary conscientious business managers, and they are
liable for loss caused to the company by their failure to do so, or by
breaches of the *Aktiengesetz* or the articles; however, the company
cannot recover damages if they acted on a resolution lawfully
passed by a general meeting (a resolution of the supervisory board is
not sufficient for this purpose), but this does not protect them from
liability to the company's creditors if they have been guilty of gross
negligence (§ 93). Directors may borrow from the company or a
company controlled by it only with the consent of the first company's supervisory board, and they may borrow from a company
which controls their own company only with the consent of its
supervisory board (§ 89(1) and (2)); loans to the spouses and infant
children of directors are similarly treated, as are loans to other
companies and partnerships of which the borrowing director is a
director, manager or partner (§ 89(3) and (4)).

(b) Supervisory board

The supervisory board's function is to supervise the board of
directors, and it may at any time require a report from the directors
on any matter, inquire into the directors' conduct and the state of
the company's affairs and call general meetings; moreover, the
articles may require its consent for any class of transactions entered
into by the board, though, if its consent is refused, the board of

directors may refer the matter to a general meeting, which may substitute its consent by so resolving by a three-quarters majority (§§ 90(3) and 111(1)–(4)). Additionally, the board of directors must report to the supervisory board yearly on the business policy and the earnings prospects of the company, and quarterly on its current business and turnover, and before entering into any transaction that may substantially affect the profitability or liquidity of the company, the directors must report to the board in sufficient time for it to express its opinion (§ 90(1)). The supervisory board has the right to inspect the company's books and correspondence and to verify the state of the company's assets (§ 101(2)). Its function is limited to informing itself, advising, and consenting; it cannot take any part in managing the company's affairs except in respect of transactions between the company and its directors. It is further empowered to litigate in the company's name to enforce claims for damages against members of the board of directors for breaches of their duties (§§ 111(4) and 112).

If the company is engaged in the iron, steel and coal industries, the shareholders appoint half the members of the board, and the employees appoint the other half; the board has ten members so elected, but this number may be increased to fourteen if the company's capital exceeds DM 20m or twenty if it exceeds DM 50m. The committee is presided over by an eleventh neutral member, who is elected from outside by a complex procedure (§§ 96(1) and 101(1) and Mitbestimmungsgesetz of 1951, §§ 4–6 and 9). In companies which normally have not more than 2,000 employees, the supervisory board must have at least three members, and may have a larger number fixed by the articles which is divisible by three: the number may not exceed nine, or fifteen if the company's capital exceeds DM 3m, or twenty-one if it exceeds DM 20m (§ 95). Two-thirds of the members of the board are appointed by the shareholders in general meeting, and the other third by the company's employees over eighteen years of age by secret ballot (§§ 96(1) and 101(1) and Betriebsverfassungsgesetz of 1952, § 76).

If the company has as a rule more than 2,000 employees, and is not subject to the special rules governing the iron, steel and coal industries, the supervisory board is made up of an equal number of representatives of the company's shareholders and its employees. In the case of companies with between 2,000 and 10,000 employees, the supervisory board consists of six representatives of the shareholders, and six of the employees. In companies which employ

10,000 but not more than 20,000 persons, the supervisory board consists of eight representatives of the shareholders, and eight of the employees. Companies which employ regularly more than 20,000 persons have a supervisory board consisting of ten representatives of the shareholders, and ten of the employees (*Mitbestimmungsgesetz* of 1976, § 7(1)).

A supervisory board with six employee members must have four employee members working in the company and two trade union representatives. A supervisory board with eight employee members must have six employee members working in the company and two trade union representatives. A supervisory board with ten employee members must have seven employee representatives working in the company and three trade union representatives (§ 7(2)). The employee representatives must include at least one salaried employee, and one employee in a managerial position (§ 15).

The election of the employee representatives takes place through an electoral committee, except where the company has less than 8,000 employees, when a direct vote takes place: the employees of the latter companies may, however, adopt the electoral committee system by a simple majority vote, and employees of companies having more than 8,000 employees may by a similar majority adopt the system of direct elections (§ 39).

Where the supervisory board is elected under the *Mitbestimmungsgesetz* of 1976 the supervisory board elects its chairman from among shareholders' representatives by a resolution of its members passed by a two-thirds majority of the votes cast. If that majority cannot be obtained, a second vote must take place when a simple majority suffices. If there is no majority in favour of a particular shareholder representative, those representatives then elect the chairman from among their number, and the deputy is elected by the employee members of the board from among their number (§ 27). Decisions of the supervisory board are normally made by a majority vote. In the event of a deadlock, a second vote must be held, at which the chairman has a second or casting vote (§ 29). A two-thirds majority is necessary for the appointment of members of the board of directors. If it cannot be reached, a committee appointed from among the members of the supervisory board, of which the chairman is a member together with the deputy chairman and one representative of the shareholders and employees, must take a new vote within one month. If this committee fails to reach agreement, the appointment is decided by the casting vote of the chairman (§ 31).

Directors and managers of a company may not be members of its supervisory board (AktG, § 105(1)), nor may directors of a company controlled by it, nor directors of a company which has a director of the first company on its own supervisory board (AktG, § 100(2)). Members of the supervisory board must be natural persons, and no person may be a member of the supervisory boards of more than ten companies, including GmbHs which have such boards, but if a director of a company is a member of the supervisory board of any companies which it controls, up to five such memberships may be disregarded in determining the maximum number of supervisory boards to which he may belong (§ 100(1) and(2)). Members of supervisory boards may be appointed for a period expiring on or before the fifth annual general meeting after their appointment (§ 102), and shareholders may remove members appointed by them at any time by a resolution passed by a three-quarters majority (§ 103(1)).

(c) General meetings

A general meeting of the shareholders (*Hauptversammlung*) may only exercise the powers given them by the *Aktiengesetz* or the articles; it cannot exercise the powers of management vested in the directors, or give instructions to them (§ 119).

The directors call general meetings, but a meeting must be called on the requisition of the holders of at least one-twentieth of the company's share capital (§§ 121(2) and 122(1)). Similarly, the holders of one-twentieth of the capital, or the holders of shares with a total nominal value of at least DM1m may request matters specified by them to be put on the agenda of any general meeting (§ 122(2)). An annual general meeting must be called within the first eight months of the company's financial year to receive the report of the board of management and the supervisory board, to approve the conduct of the directors, and to declare dividends out of the previous year's profits (§§ 170(2) and (3) and 175(1)). The company's annual accounts (balance sheet and profit and loss account) must be audited by professionally qualified auditors (*Abschlussprüfer*) appointed by a general meeting, and they are then laid, together with the auditors' report and the directors' proposals for the application of the profits shown in the accounts, before the supervisory board so it may report to the shareholders (§§ 170 and 171). If the supervisory board approves the annual accounts, they do not require to be affirmatively accepted by the annual general meeting, but if the board disapproves them, or if the board of management and the supervisory board refer the accounts to the annual general meeting by agreement, the shareholders may approve or amend the accounts (§§ 172 and 173). Whether the annual general meeting approves the accounts or not, it has the disposal of the profits shown by them, and must resolve what part of them shall be paid out as dividend and what part carried forward or transferred to reserve (§ 174(1)). This power is, however, subject to the limitation that one-twentieth of the year's profits must be transferred to statutory reserve until it amounts to one-tenth of the company's capital (§ 150(2)) and to the power of the directors and the supervisory board to transfer up to half the year's profits to the free or revenue reserves until it amounts to one-half of the company's capital (§ 58(2)). Furthermore, the articles of the company may require up to one-half of the year's profits to be transferred to free reserve (§ 58(1)).

Because shares in German companies are usually in bearer form, notices calling general meetings are published in the newspapers mentioned in the articles at least one month before they are held, or if the articles require shareholders to deposit their shares with the company or to notify it if they intend to take part in the meeting, at least one month before the last day for doing this (§§ 123(1) and (2) and 124). The company must also notify individually banks and shareholders' associations which so require, or which voted as proxies at the last general meeting, and also shareholders who so require or who, being registered shareholders, were not represented by a bank at the last general meeting (§ 125(1) and (2)). When an annual general meeting has been called, the annual accounts, the directors' report and the report of the supervisory board to be laid before it must be available for inspection by any shareholder, and, at his request, a copy of these documents must be sent to him (§ 175(2) and (3)). Each fully paid share entitles its holder to vote at general meetings, and votes are cast in proportion to the nominal value of shares (§ 134(1)). The articles may, however, confer voting rights on partly paid shares, and voting rights are then exercisable in proportion to the amount paid up on all shares, whether fully or partly paid (§ 134(2)). No share may carry multiple voting rights, and no share may be issued without voting rights (§ 12), except cumulative preference shares (*Vorzugsaktien*) which may be deprived of voting rights so long as the preference dividend is not more than a year in arrear, but such shares may not exceed one-half of the issued share capital of the company, and in any case they carry voting rights on resolutions to reduce or extinguish the preference dividend attached to them, or to issue further preference shares with prior or equal ranking rights (§§ 139–141). A shareholder may vote by proxy, and a proxy appointment signed by the shareholder and lodged with the company at any time before the meeting begins is valid (§ 134(3)). Banks and shareholders' associations often act as depositaries of share certificates and vote thereon as permanent proxies, but their authority to vote must be expressed in writing signed by the shareholder, and must be renewed at fifteen month intervals if it is not to expire (§ 135(1), (2) and (9)). Depository banks and shareholders' associations which have received notification from the company of a general meeting must pass the information they have received in respect of the meeting to the shareholders they represent with their advice how to vote on the agenda and a statement of the way in which the bank or association will vote if not instructed otherwise by the shareholder (§ 128(1)–(4)). If the shareholder instructs his bank to vote in a particular way, it must carry out his instructions (§ 135(10)).

Except where the law or the articles otherwise require, resolutions are passed by a simple majority of votes cast (§ 133(1)). Certain resolutions must, however, be passed by a majority which comprises three-quarters of the capital in respect of which votes are cast; in such cases the votes of shareholders who attend in person or by proxy but abstain from voting are disregarded. The resolutions which fall into this category include resolutions amending the articles (§ 179(2)), resolutions increasing or reducing the share capital (§§ 182(1) and 222(1)), resolutions for the winding up of the company (§ 262(2)), and for the amalgamation with another AG or GmbH (§§ 340(2), 353(1), and 355(2)).

4 Provisions for the protection of shareholders and creditors

In addition to the provisions already dealt with, the interests of minority shareholders and creditors are protected in the following ways:

(1) If the annual or interim accounts of an AG show that it has suffered a loss equal to at least half its capital, the board of management must immediately call a general meeting and report the position to it (§ 92(1)). If an AG becomes insolvent or unable to pay its debts as they fall due, the directors must within three weeks petition the court to adjudge the company bankrupt or to wind up its affairs, and they must not make any payments out of its assets

except those necessary for continuing its business temporarily (§ 92(2) and (3)). A director who fails to take these steps on the company's insolvency is liable to pay its creditors the difference between what they recover out of the company's assets and what they would have recovered if the company had been made bankrupt at the proper time and no payments in respect of its debts had been made after insolvency supervened (German Supreme Court, (1939) RGZ 162 129, 142).

(2) If any person intentionally uses his influence over a company or its board of directors or supervisory board (eg as a majority shareholder) to act in a way which is detrimental to the interests of the company, he and the directors and members of the supervisory board who collaborate with him are liable in damages to the company and the shareholders who have suffered loss (§ 117(1) and (2)). If the company is insolvent, the creditors may recover damages so as to satisfy their claims, and if the company is adjudged bankrupt the damages are sued for by its trustee in bankruptcy (§ 117(5)).

(3) Any shareholder may require the board of management to provide a general meeting with such information about the company's affairs and its relations with associated undertakings as is required for proper discussion of matters on the agenda (§ 131(1)). The board may only refuse to give such information if it would be guilty of a criminal offence if it did so (eg bank directors must refuse to give information about particular customers); or if the disclosure would be likely to result in considerable harm to the company or an associated undertaking or if it relates to the acceptability of balance sheet items for tax purposes, or to the calculation of particular taxes; or if it relates to any difference between the value at which assets are entered on the balance sheet and their higher market value; or if it relates to the methods of valuation and depreciation employed in preparing the annual balance sheet, provided that the annual report explains such method sufficiently clearly to provide the fullest possible understanding of the state of the company's assets and trading position (§ 131(3)).

(4) A general meeting may appoint special examiners to inquire into matters connected with the formation or management of the company, and if it fails to do so, the holders of one-tenth of the share capital or of shares with a total nominal value of at least DM 2m may apply to the court to appoint special examiners (*Sonderprüfer*) (§ 142(1) and (2)).

(5) Claims for damages for misconduct by the founders, directors or members of the supervisory board may be brought in the

company's name if a general meeting so resolves, or if the holders of one-tenth of the share capital so require (§ 147(1)).

(6) As indicated above, at least one-twentieth of the net profit for the year, reduced by any losses carried forward from the preceding year, must be transferred to statutory reserve until the amounts transferred equal one-tenth of the share capital (§ 150(1)). Share premiums must also be credited to statutory reserve, including premiums arising on the conversion of convertible debentures into shares with a lower aggregate nominal value (§ 150(2)). No part of the statutory reserve may be distributed to the shareholders except on a reduction of capital or a liquidation, but it may be used to write off trading losses if free reserves have first been used in doing so, and if the statutory reserve exceeds one-tenth of the share capital, the excess may be used to write off trading losses or be capitalised and used to pay the nominal value of bonus shares issued to the shareholders (§ 150(3)).

(7) Amendments of the articles which alter the relationship between classes of shares to the detriment of one class require the approval of a meeting of shareholders of that class by a resolution passed by a three-quarters majority (§§ 138 and 179(3)). The same applies to increases and reductions of share capital (§§ 182(2) and 222(2)). The consent of the class of shareholders adversely affected by the alteration of the articles is necessary not only when their class rights are directly altered (eg by a reduction in the rate of preference dividend) but also when an advantage they previously enjoyed is taken away (eg when preference shareholders holding 30 per cent of a company's capital are deprived of their power to veto a certain kind of transaction which the articles originally permitted only if a general meeting gave its approval by a three-quarters majority, by the articles being altered so as to enable a general meeting to approve it by a simple majority (German Supreme Court, (1929) RGZ 125, 356)).

(8) On an increase of capital, each shareholder is entitled to subscribe for the new shares in proportion to his existing holding. He must be granted at least two weeks within which to exercise this right, which may be modified or excluded by the resolution for the increase (§ 186(1) and (3)). The same preferential subscription rights apply on the issue of convertible bonds, bonds exchangeable for shares, bonds carrying the right to subscribe for further shares, and bonds carrying the right to a share of profits (§ 221(3)).

(9) Generally speaking an AG cannot have unissued shares, because the whole of its capital must be subscribed before it can be

incorporated, and the whole of any increase in its capital must be subscribed before the increase takes effect (§§ 29, 188(3) and 189). This means that new shares cannot be issued without the consent of the existing shareholders in general meeting at the time the issue takes place. There are two exceptions to this rule. A company may increase its capital conditionally (*bedingtes Kapitalerhöhung*) to secure exchange or subscription rights on an issue of convertible bonds, to facilitate a merger of undertakings, and to secure subscription rights for the company's employees. The total capital conditionally created may not exceed one-half of the issued capital (§ 192). Secondly, the articles or a general meeting by a three-quarters majority vote may create approved capital (*genehmigtes Kapital*) not exceeding one-half of the issued capital, and permit the board of management during a period up to five years to issue shares representing approved capital to whomsoever they wish on such terms as they think fit (§§ 202–204). Approved capital is seldom created, but if the directors wish to grant options to subscribe for shares, it provides the means for doing so.

(10) Resolutions passed in general meeting may be declared invalid or annulled by the court on certain grounds, in particular on the ground that a shareholder used his vote in order to procure an advantage which is detrimental to the interests of the company or the other shareholders (§§ 241 and 243). An application for annulment may be made by any shareholder whose protest against the resolution was recorded in the minutes of the meeting, or who was not properly notified of the meeting at which the resolution was passed, or, in the specific case mentioned above, by any shareholder (§ 245).

5 Take-overs and mergers

(a) Take-overs

Take-over bids (*Übernahmeangebote*) do not occur very frequently in Germany, and they are not subject to legal regulation, but a voluntary code exists governing certain aspects of cash and exchange bids, and in particular the preparation of the bid, the contents of the offer, and the procedure which should be carried out. The Code of Practice is based upon the recommendations of the Committee of Stock Exchanges. The Minister of Finance has expressed his approval of the Code, which came into force in 1979. It is designed to ensure that all shareholders receive equal treatment by the bidder, and to discourage insider trading, which is also regulated by another Code of Practice of 1976 based on the recommendations of the Committee of Stock Exchanges and the Ministry of Finance, which were drawn up with the assistance of the banks.

(b) Mergers

The *Aktiengesetz* contains detailed rules governing mergers (§ 339 *et seq*): the rules governing mergers between private companies contained in the new Law governing such companies of 1980 are very clearly modelled on those of the *Aktiengesetz*. A merger may be carried out by one company taking over another company or companies ('merger by transfer'), or by existing companies being taken over by a newly formed company ('consolidation'). The former method may be used for the purpose of merging an AG with another AG, a GmbH or a KGaA. An AG, GmbH or KGaA may be the transferor or transferee company (§§ 354 and 355(1) and Law of 1980 amending the Law of 1892 governing public companies, § 33(1)). Mergers by consolidation are only possible between AG, AG and KGaA and between two or more GmbH (§§ 353 and 354 and Law of 1980, § 19(11)).

Shareholders in the transferor company receive shares in the transferee company or the new company. Shareholders in the transferor company or companies may be paid in cash for fractions of shares where necessary: the sum so payable must not exceed one-tenth of the nominal value of the shares to be allotted by the transferee or newly formed company (§§ 344(2), 353(2), 355(2) and 357(2) and Law of 1980, § 33(2)). In the case of a merger by transfer, the transferor company will usually have to create the shares to be allotted under the merger by effecting an increase of its capital.

The merger contract is prepared by the boards of directors of the merging companies, and it must be embodied in a notarial deed (§§ 341, 353(1) and (4) and Law of 1980, § 33(2)). The contract requires approval by general meetings of the merging companies in order that it may be effective: the required majority is three-quarters of the capital in respect of which votes are cast in the case of an AG (§§ 340 and 353(1)).

Creditors of the transferor company or companies may require security to be given by the acquiring or newly formed company for their claims, and they may notify the latter company to this effect within six months after its incorporation (§§ 347, 353(1), 354, 355 and 357, and Law of 1980, § 33(2)). The members of the board of directors and the supervisory board of the transferor company or each of the transferor companies are jointly and severally liable for any damage suffered by the company or companies, and its or their shareholders and creditors as a result of the merger. They escape such liability where they have exercised due care in the examination of the financial state of the participating companies and in the conclusion of the merger contract (§§ 349(1), 353(1), 354(2), 355(5), 357(5) and Law of 1980, § 33(4)).

When a merger by transfer is entered in the Commercial Register in respect of the transferor company, the merger is completed. Thereupon all assets and liabilities of the transferor company vest in the transferee company, and the former company is automatically dissolved (§§ 346(3), (4) Nos 1 and 2, 354(2), 355(2) and 357(2), and Law of 1980, § 33(2)). When a merger takes place by the formation of a new company, the assets and liabilities of the transferor companies vest in the new company on its registration, and the transferor companies are automatically dissolved (§§ 353(6) and 354(2)).

A merger with a company which does not have its registered office or seat in the Federal Republic of Germany is not possible. However, an operation similar to a merger may be carried out by means of the transfer of a German company's assets under § 361 in return for an allotment of a foreign company's shares.

6 Dissolution and liquidation

Under German law, 'dissolution' (*Auflösung*) of the company means that the company is put into liquidation, and the winding up of its assets follows. The rules contained in the *Aktiengesetz* are only applicable to AGs (§§ 262–274). The liquidation procedure in all cases in which bankruptcy proceedings are not instituted is the same. The rules governing the dissolution and liquidation of a GmbH are in general similar to those applicable to an AG.

(a) Dissolution

The circumstances in which an AG is dissolved are set out in §§ 262 and 396. The most important are upon the passing of a resolution for dissolution by the general meeting which must be supported by the holders of three-quarters of the capital in respect of which votes are cast (§ 262(1) No 2); upon the adjudication of the company in bankruptcy proceedings (§ 262(1) No 3); and when an adjudication in bankruptcy of the company cannot be made because the company's assets are insufficient to cover the costs of realising its assets and the bankruptcy proceedings (§ 262(1) No 4).

A company's objects can no longer be pursued upon its dissolution. It continues to exist as a legal person and retains its name during the winding up of its affairs (§ 296(6)). The provisions of the *Aktiengesetz* apply to the company during its winding up except in four respects (§ 264(2)). These are: firstly, the company ceases to carry on its undertaking and must wind up its affairs; secondly, the unpaid capital on shares in the company remains payable only to the extent that it is required to satisfy creditors; thirdly, shareholders are not entitled to the payment of dividends during the winding up, and fourthly, shares are freely transferable during the winding up.

The dissolution of the company must be entered on the Commercial Register (§ 263).

(b) Liquidation

The liquidation of the AG is carried on by its liquidators who will be the former members of its board of management, unless other persons are appointed by a resolution passed by a general meeting, or the company's articles otherwise provide (§ 265(1) and (2). Where good cause can be shown, the court is empowered to appoint and remove liquidators upon an application by the supervisory board, or by a qualified minority of shareholders whose shares amount to not less than one-twentieth of the company's capital, or have a nominal value of at least DM 1m (§ 265(3)). The appointment and removal of liquidators must be entered on the Commercial Register (§ 266).

The liquidators must prepare a balance sheet setting out the company's assets and liabilities at the beginning of the winding up (§ 270(1)). This balance sheet must be approved by a general meeting of the company, and must be published by the liquidators (§ 270(2)).

The liquidators must make three public advertisements calling on the company's creditors to submit particulars of their claims against it (§ 267). The law does not provide for any particular interval between publications.

The liquidators must complete pending business transactions, collect debts due to the company, sell all available assets, and satisfy any outstanding debts (§ 268(1)). They must finally distribute the remaining net assets amongst the shareholders (§ 271). The residual assets are distributed amongst the shareholders in proportion to the nominal value of their shares, except to the extent that the company's statutes confer preferential rights to the repayment of capital on particular shareholders (§ 271(2)). A distribution may not be made to shareholders until one year after the third publication of the advertisement calling on creditors to submit particulars of their claims (§ 272(1)).

When the distribution to the shareholders has been completed, the liquidators are required to submit final accounts to a general meeting and to notify the completion of the liquidation for registration to the Commercial Register. After this has been done, the company is struck off the register, and its legal personality is extinguished (§ 273(1)).

(c) Insolvency

When a company is unable to satisfy its debts as they fall due, or when its liabilities are in excess of its assets, the board of management must, without undue delay, apply to the court to adjudge the company bankrupt, or must apply to the court for its approval of a composition with its creditors (§ 92(2)). The same rule is applicable when it becomes evident that a company is insolvent during the course of its winding up (§ 207(2) of the Bankruptcy Law of 1877, as amended (*Konkursordnung*)).

When a company becomes unable to satisfy its liabilities as they fall due, or when its liabilities exceed its assets, the board of management may no longer make any payments to the company's shareholders and creditors (§ 92(3)). The board must on its own responsibility determine whether bankruptcy proceedings would benefit creditors, and then decide whether to institute bankruptcy or composition proceedings.

Composition proceedings are governed by the Judicial Composition Law of 1935 (*Vergleichsordnung*), as subsequently amended. The board of management makes application to the court to approve the composition (§ 2 of the Judicial Composition Law). The application must be accompanied by concrete and detailed proposals for a settlement, a list of assets and liabilities, including the names of creditors and debtors, and must set out the company's balance sheets for the last three financial years (§§ 4 and 5(2) of the Judicial Composition Law). The proposals must provide for the payment of a minimum percentage of the company's debts, which is normally 35 per cent, but which is increased to 40 per cent in certain circumstances (§ 7(2) of the Judicial Composition Law). Where the composition proposals satisfy these conditions, the court appoints a provisional administrator, and orders that the proposals should be published together with the name of the provisional administrator (§ 11(1) of the Judicial Composition Law). The court also takes all the measures which appear to it necessary to prevent disposals of the company's assets which are detrimental to its creditors (§ 12 of the Judicial Composition Law). The court then examines the proposals, and if it finds them to be fair and practicable, it orders the holding of a meeting of the creditors, and the taking of all other requisite steps, for example the appointment of a committee of creditors (§ 44 of the Judicial Composition Law). It must refuse to make such an order on a number of grounds, which are set out in detail in §§ 17 and 18. If the proposals are accepted at the creditors' meeting they still have to be approved by the court (§ 78 of the Judicial Composition Law), and its approval may be refused if the composition is inconsistent with the common interests of the creditors (§ 79 of the Judicial Composition Law). If the composition is approved by the court, it is binding on all creditors (§ 82 of the Judicial Composition Law).

Where the board's application to approve a composition is refused by the court, or where the board applies initially for the adjudication of the company as a bankrupt, bankruptcy proceedings against the company are initiated and the company is dissolved when the court orders its adjudication; the administration of its assets are placed in the hands of a trustee in bankruptcy (*Konkursverwalter*) appointed by the court. The trustee realises the company's assets and satisfies the creditors' claims so far as possible in accordance with the rules contained in the Bankruptcy Law, and under the court's supervision.

GESELLSCHAFT MIT BESCHRÄNKTER HAFTUNG
(GmbH)

The GmbH is roughly the equivalent of the British private company. There is no numerical limit on its membership, and so it may be in substance anything from a one-man business or an incorporated partnership having a handful of members to a gigantic concern run almost like an AG. Unlike the British private company however, a GmbH is not governed by the same rules as a public company subject to certain modifications, but is governed by a separate statute, the GmbH *Gesetz*. Nevertheless, the German courts apply a number of rules in the *Aktiengesetz* to GmbH by analogy, and if a GmbH is structurally similar to a partnership (ie with a small membership, and managers who are majority shareholders), the courts also apply appropriate rules of partnership law to it. For example, the German Supreme Court has held that members of a GmbH stand in a fiduciary relationship to each other, and if one is guilty of serious misconduct, the others may expel him from membership as though the company were a partnership ((1953) BGHZ 9.157). The GmbH *Gesetz* does not contain as many mandatory provisions as the *Aktiengesetz*, and this gives the founders considerable freedom to plan the structure of the company in accordance with their needs.

The principal differences between a GmbH and an AG are as follows:

(1) A GmbH may be formed by one or more persons (GmbH *Gesetz*, § 1). The articles must be executed by all the members (§ 2(1)). They must state the name of the company, which must include the words '*Gesellschaft mit beschränkter Haftung*' or the abbreviation GmbH (§ 4(2)); the district in the Federal Republic where the company will be domiciled; the nature of its business; the amount of its capital and the nominal value of the share each shareholder takes in it (§ 3(1)). The company's capital must be at least DM50,000 (£11,800 approximately) (§ 5(1)), but transitional provisions exist for companies formed, or in respect of which an application for registration was made, before 1st January 1981 when this requirement came into force (Law of 4th July 1980 amending the law governing Private Companies of 1892, § 12(1) and (2)). Each member's share must have a nominal value of DM500, or a higher amount which is a multiple of DM100 (§ 5(1)).

The company is incorporated as a GmbH by registration in the Commercial Register of the district court where it has its domicile (§§ 7(1) and 11), but this can only be done where every member has accepted his share, and if it is payable in cash, has paid up at least one-quarter of its nominal value (§ 7(2) No 1). The total amount or value contributed, including contributions in kind, must not be less than DM25,000 (§ 7(2) No 2). Transitional provisions exist for companies formed, or in respect of which an application for registration was made before 1st January 1981 (Law of 1980, § 12(1) and (2)). If a company is formed by one person only, the requirements of § 7(2) Nos 1 and 2 must be complied with, and in addition, the single individual must provide security for the payment of the remaining part of the contributions to be paid by him in cash before application for registration of the company can be made (§ 7(2)

No 3). Contributions in kind must also be made by shareholders in such a way that they are at the free disposal of the managers before an application for registration can be made (§ 7(3)).

The articles must set out the nature and value of any contributions to be made in kind in return for the issue of shares (§ 5(4) No 1). The application for the registration of the company will have to be accompanied by a report by the founders stating the essential facts supporting the adequacy of the contributions in kind. If a business enterprise is acquired by the company in return for an issue of shares, this report will have to be accompanied by a balance sheet and a profit and loss account for the two preceding years (§§ 5(4) No 2 and 8(1)).

The court must refuse to register the company if it finds that the contributions in kind are overvalued (§ 9c). If the contributions in kind are obviously overvalued, the court will be able to act on its own initiative. If there is room for doubt, it will act after consulting qualified persons. Persons who transfer an asset which is overvalued to the company in exchange for an issue of shares will be required to make a cash payment equal to the amount of the overvaluation. The material time for determining the value of the asset will be the time of registration of the company, which will be able to bring an action for the sum due to it within five years of registration (§ 9).

(2) A member may have only one share (*Geschäftsanteil*) on the formation of the company, but there is no need for shares of different members to have the same nominal value (§ 5(2) and (3)). Shares are freely transferable and transmissible on death unless the articles impose restrictions, for example that the managers' consent is required for transfers (§ 15(1) and (5)). A transfer or bequest of part of a share is possible only if the managers' consent is obtained, and the part disposed of must have a nominal value of DM 500 or a higher amount which is divisible by 100 (§ 17(1) and (4)). Transfers of the whole or part of a share must be effected by a written instrument of transfer attested by a judge or notary (§ 15(3)), and the transferee becomes the holder of the share as far as the company is concerned only when the transfer is notified to it (§ 16(1)). A share in a GmbH is not negotiable like a share in an AG, but is treated in the same way as a debt or chose in action (Civil Code, § 413). Consequently, if a share certificate is stolen, no person who derives title through the thief will acquire ownership of the share under the Civil Code, § 935.

(3) If a member of a GmbH fails to pay any instalment of the nominal value of his share at the time fixed by the articles or when

called up by resolution of a general meeting (§ 46 No 2), the managers may forfeit his share after giving him a month's notice threatening to do so if the instalment is not paid (§ 21(1) and (2)). The member and persons who were formerly registered holders of the share within the five years before the instalment fell due can be sued for the instalment, and if a former holder pays it, he is entitled to acquire the share (§§ 21(3) and 22). If the instalment cannot be recovered from the member or a former holder or by the company selling the share by public auction (§ 23), the other members of the company must make good the instalment in proportion to their existing holdings, and the forfeited share is then divided between them in the same proportions (§ 25).

(4) A shareholder who grants a loan to the company at a time when a careful businessman would instead have provided it with capital will be unable to claim repayment of the loan in bankruptcy proceedings, or in composition proceedings (*Vergleichsverfahren*) intended to avoid bankruptcy (§ 32a(1)).

(5) The company's business is conducted by one or more managers (*Geschäftsführer*) who are appointed by the articles or a resolution of the members for any desired length of time and who must be natural persons of full age and capacity (§§ 6(1)–(3) and 46 No 5). Unless the articles otherwise provide, managers must act jointly, so that a delegation of their powers to one of their number is not possible, except by appointing him an agent of the company for a particular transaction, or by a general meeting of members appointing him to be a general agent to manage the company's business (§§ 35(2) and 46(7)). On the other hand, limitations on the authority of managers to bind the company imposed by the articles do not bind outsiders dealing with the company (§ 37(2)), and so, under the provisions of the Civil Code referred to in connection with the directors of an AG, the company is bound by and responsible for all their acts to an outsider in the absence of fraud on his part. In performing their functions, managers must exhibit the skill and care of an ordinary conscientious businessman (§ 43(1)). The members in general meeting may revoke the appointment of a manager for any reason, but the articles may restrict this power to cases in which there are serious grounds for the dismissal (§ 38). Unless the articles otherwise provide, the members in general meeting may give directions to the managers as to the performance of their functions, and they are bound to conform to such directions (§ 37(1)).

(6) A GmbH which does not employ more than 500 employees

has no supervisory board, unless its articles provide for one, but if they do, the provisions of the *Aktiengesetz* apply as to its composition and powers: its members are then all elected by the members of the company and there is no employee representation (§ 52(1)). If the company employs between 500 and 2,000 employees, it must have a supervisory board, and its employees are represented on it in the same way as if it were an AG governed by the *Betriebsverfassungsgesetz* of 1952 (BVG, § 77). If a GmbH is engaged in the iron, steel or coal industry, it must have a supervisory board constructed in the same way as if it were an AG, irrespective of the number of its employees (*Mitbestimmungsgesetz* of 1951, § 3). If the company has more than 2,000 employees, but is not subject to the special rules governing the iron, steel and coal industry, it must have a supervisory board constructed in the same way as if it were an AG (*Mitbestimmungsgesetz* of 1976, § 1(1) No 1).

(7) General meetings of members of a GmbH are called by the managers (GmbH *Gesetz*, § 49(1)), but members who hold one-tenth of the company's capital may require a meeting to be called (§ 50(1)). Each member has one vote for every DM 100 capital he holds (§ 47(2)). Resolutions are passed by a simple majority vote (§ 47(1)), except resolutions for the amendment of the articles (including increases and reductions of capital), which must be passed by a majority of three-quarters of the votes cast (§ 53(1) and (2)). An annual balance sheet and profit and loss account must be drawn up by the managers (§ 41(2)) and submitted to the members in general meeting for approval (§ 46 No 1). At present the accounts of private companies do not generally require to be audited by professionally qualified auditors or published, although the Federal Government may make regulations requiring this to be done (§ 42). This power has been exercised in connection with banks. The accounts of all companies other than small companies will have to be audited by a specially qualified auditor when legislation is passed in conformity with the requirements of Directive 78/660/EEC on Company Accounts issued by the Council of the European Communities (OJL 222/11 of 14th August 1978).

A common form of private company in Germany is the GmbH & Co. This is a partnership or, more usually , a limited partnership in which the GmbH and its individual members are partners. If the partnership is a limited one (*Kommanditgesellschaft*) the GmbH is the general partner, liable without limit for the partnership debts, while its individual members are limited partners liable only to the extent of their agreed contributions (Commercial Code, § 161).

Members of a GmbH already enjoy limited liability for its debts, of course (§ 13(2)), and the real advantage of forming a GmbH & Co instead of a simple GmbH is fiscal. Only incorporated companies pay corporation tax (*Körperschaftssteuer*) and so by ensuring in the articles of the limited partnership that only a small part of its profits is paid to its general partner, the GmbH, and that the bulk of the profits go to the individual limited partners, the burden of corporation tax is minimised.

ASSOCIATED COMPANIES

The most distinctive and striking feature of the *Aktiengesetz* of 1965 is its detailed classification and regulation of the various kinds of inter-company relationship. Unlike the British Companies Act 1948, which is content to specify only one such relationship, that of holding company and subsidiary, the German legislation devotes a whole division of the *Aktiengesetz* (§ 291–338) to the different degrees of proximity which may exist between companies, ranging from integration at one extreme to mutually participating companies (ie companies holding more than a quarter of each other's issued share capital) at the other. These provisions only apply where a public company is associated with another enterprise in the manner defined, but the courts are beginning to develop rules intended to protect private companies which belong to a group.

1 Integrated companies

The closest possible form of association between companies is integration (*Eingliederung*) which may only be effected between two or more AGs. Integration does not destroy the legal personality of the integrated companies, although this may be achieved by merger (*Verschmelzung*) quite simply at any time while the integration subsists. Instead the integrated companies carry on business separately, and otherwise pursue their separate legal existences just as before integration. In practice, of course, this separateness is technical rather than real, for one of the companies will be the principal company (*Hauptgesellschaft*) of the whole group; its directors are legally empowered to instruct the boards of the other companies to take any action that the directors think fit (§ 323(1)), and conversely the principal company is liable to creditors of the integrated company jointly and severally with the latter for all its debts and liabilities incurred both before and after integration took place (§ 332(1)).

The basis for integration consists of the passing of a resolution by a general meeting of the shareholders of the company to be integrated that its integration should take place. This may be done wherever the parent company owns 95 per cent or more of the issued capital of the company involved. This resolution does not become effective until it is approved by the principal company's shareholders by a resolution passed at a general meeting; the resolution must be supported by the holders of three-quarters of the capital in respect of which votes are cast (§§ 320(1) and 319(2)). Upon the entry of integration in the Commercial Register relating to the company to be integrated, integration is completed (§§ 319(4) and 320(4)).

When all the shares in the company to be integrated are owned by the principal company, the problem of the protection of minority shareholders does not arise. However, where the principal company owns less than 100 per cent but 95 per cent or more of the issued share capital (disregarding shares held by or on behalf of the company to be integrated in itself), all the outstanding shares in the integrated company vest in the principal company on the registration of the resolution for integration (§ 320(1) and (4)). The principal company must determine the consideration to be offered to the minority shareholders before the two resolutions necessary for integration can be passed (§ 320(1)). The consideration normally takes the form of an allotment of shares in the principal company, but if that company is itself dependent on a third enterprise, the former shareholders of the integrated company must be offered the choice of being paid the value of their shares in cash, or receiving shares in the principal company (§ 320(5)). The number of shares to be allotted is ascertained by comparing the *pro rata* assets value of a share in the senior company after the integration with that of a share in the integrated company beforehand, though it appears permissible to take their average listed values if both companies are listed on the stock exchange.

Although integration is usually permanent, the law does not regard integration as an irreversible situation. The principal company may terminate it at any time by passing an ordinary resolution at a general meeting of the integrated company and the integration automatically terminates if the principal company is wound up or if it transfers any of the shares it holds in the integrated company to anyone other than its own nominees (§ 327(1)).

2 Association contracts

A somewhat looser form of association between two or more AGs may be brought about by association contracts (*Unternehmensverträge*) entered into between them. Such contracts may only be made if they are approved in advance by resolution passed at general meetings of all the participating companies (§ 293(1)). The commonest kind of contract met with in practice is the management contract (*Beherrschungssvertrag*) under which the controlling company is given the right to manage the business of the dependent company (§ 291(1)). The other important type of contract met with in Germany is the profit transfer agreement (*Gewinnabführungsvertrag*), by which the participating companies retain their managerial independence to a greater or lesser extent, but transfer the right to receive the whole of their profits to one of their number (§ 291(1)). Besides these two types of association contracts, there are other less important variants of them, namely, the profit-pooling contract (*Gewinngemeinschaft*), the contract for the partial transfer of profits (*Teilgewinnabführungsvertrag*), and the contract for the leasing or the temporary transfer of one company's business to another (*Betriebspachtvertrag*; *Betriebsüberlassungsvertrag*) (§ 292).

If a management contract is concluded, the managing company may require the management boards of the other companies to carry out its instructions in conducting their affairs, and they may not refuse to do so even if their own company would suffer loss in consequence, unless it is obvious that no advantage will accrue to the managing company, or to it and the other companies as a group (§ 308(1) and (2)). On the other hand, the directors of the managing company are under a duty to the other companies to act in good faith and to exercise the care and skill of competent businessmen in giving such instructions, and if they fail in this duty, individual shareholders and creditors of the companies, as well as the companies themselves, may sue them and the managing company for damages (§§ 309 and 310).

In the case of other kinds of association contracts between companies, German law gives no express powers of direction or control to any of the participating companies. However, if any such company is the controlling company (*herrschende Gesellschaft*) of the group, that is, if it 'can exercise a controlling influence (upon the others) directly or indirectly' (§ 17(1)), it must not use its influence so as to cause or permit harm to be suffered by the others, nor so as to cause them to enter into prejudicial transactions, unless the loss is adequately compensated by a cash payment or some other advantage (§ 311). If the controlling company breaks its duty in this respect, both it and its directors are liable in damages to the company which has suffered loss (§§ 317 and 318). These provisions as to the harmful exertion of influence by a controlling company also apply to situations where there is no contractual link between the controlling and the other companies, and it is expressly provided that if one company is the majority holding company (*mehrbesitzende Gesellschaft*) of another, that is, if it holds more than half of the issued shares of the other or can exercise more than half of the voting rights at the other's general meetings (§ 16(1)), the majority holding company is presumed to control the subsidiary, and so may be liable to it in damages if it uses powers in a manner detrimental to the subsidiary.

German law contains four special provisions for the protection of shareholders and creditors of subordinate companies in the case of management and profit transfer contracts. If the subordinate company's accounts show that it has suffered a loss during any financial year, the management or recipient company must pay it the amount of the loss except to the extent that it can be written off out of amounts transferred to free reserves during the existence of the control or profit-transfer contract (§ 302(1)). Secondly, in addition to indemnifying it against losses, the managing or recipient company must undertake in the contract with the subordinate company to pay its shareholders a fair equivalent to the dividends they would otherwise receive (§ 304(1)). This dividend must at least amount to 'the prospective average dividend which would [otherwise] be paid in respect of the shares [by the subordinate company] having regard to its previous and prospective earnings, taking depreciation and revaluations of assets into account, but making no provision for increasing its revenue reserves'; nevertheless, the managing or recipient company may satisfy its obligations by ensuring that the minority shareholders receive the dividend that they would receive if the subordinate company were merged into the managing or recipient company (§ 304(2)). Thirdly, the managing or recipient company must undertake in the contract with the subordinate company to acquire the holdings of its shareholders who require their shares to be taken off their hands within a period specified in the contract, being not less than two months after its registration (§ 305(1) and (4)). In exchange for the shares so tendered, the managing or recipient company must issue shares in itself, or if it is itself controlled by a third company, it must pay compensation in cash: the number of shares to be issued is ascertained in the same way as on an expropriation of shares in an integrated company (§ 305(1) and (3)). Finally, when a management or profit-transfer contract comes to an end, the managing or recipient company must protect existing creditors of the subordinate company by giving security for their debts or guaranteeing them (§ 303).

3 Mutually participating companies

The loosest form of association between companies (whether AG or GmbH) is participation, that is one company holding shares in another. The only situation of this kind that the law regulates, apart from those dealt with under the two headings immediately above, is where the participation is mutual (*wechselseitige Beteiligung*), that is to say where each company holds more than one-quarter of the issued shares of the other (§ 19(1)). When a company acquires more than one-quarter of the issued shares of another, it must notify that other, and cannot exercise any voting rights attached to the shares until it has done so (§§ 20(1) and (7) and 21(1) and(4)). In the case of mutually participating companies at least one of which is an AG, the company which is the first to notify its participation to the other may exercise its rights as a shareholder of the other without restriction. On the other hand, the other company, when it later gives notice of its holding, may only exercise the rights attaching to the shares it holds insofar as they do not relate to more than one-quarter of the first company's capital for the time being issued and outstanding. The principal purpose of this provision is to prevent the directors of mutually participating companies from exercising the votes on the shares that their companies hold in each other for the purpose of rendering themselves irremovable.

4 Group accounts and reports

The obligation to prepare group annual accounts and a group annual report is imposed on the board of management of a German AG with enterprises dependent on it which are under its unified management as the parent enterprise of the group (§ 329(1)). If the parent company is a GmbH or a mining association (*bergrechtliche Gewerkschaft*), group accounts must be prepared where one of its dependent enterprises is an AG (§ 28 of Introductory Law to *Aktiengesetz*). Such accounts must also be prepared where the parent enterprise of the group is one which has its head office in

Germany, and at the end of three consecutive financial years of the parent enterprise, at least two of the following conditions are fulfilled: (*a*) the total value of the assets of the group (other than indebtedness between group enterprises) exceeds DM150m; (*b*) the turnover of the group (other than dealings between group enterprises) exceeds DM250m; (*c*) the group enterprises in Germany have more than 5,000 employees (§§ 11 *et seq* of Publicity Law of 1969).

The concept of unified management is not defined in the *Aktiengesetz*. However, this statute provides that integrated companies and companies between which a management contract subsists shall be deemed to be under the unified management of the principal or managing company, and that all companies shall be deemed to be under the unified management of the company which can exercise a controlling influence over them (§§ 17(1) and 18(1)). What is important to remember, however, is that a company which holds the majority of the shares or voting rights in another company is presumed to have a controlling influence over the other (§ 17(2)), and so when the presumptions in §§ 17(2) and 18(1) are added together, a majority holding company is best advised to play safe and prepare group accounts and reports. This is always done in practice.

CHAPTER 2

FRANCE

The business associations which may be formed under French law are the general partnership (*société en nom collectif*), the limited partnership (*société en commandite simple*), the private consortium (*société en participation*), the public company (*société anonyme*), the public company where directors are personally liable for the company's debts (*société en commandite par actions*), the private company (*société à responsabilité limitée*), and a new form of association for the carrying out of pilot schemes and experiments, providing ancillary trading services and generally assisting with the expansion of the businesses of its members which was sanctioned in 1967, the commercial interest group (*groupement d'intérêt économique*). These forms of association are commercial in character, irrespective of the nature of the business or activity they carry on, with the exception of the private consortium and the commercial interest group, which are commercial associations only if they carry on one of the activities specified in the Commercial Code, arts 632 and 633 (Law on commercial companies (No 66–537) of 24th July 1966, art 1(2)). In addition to these commercial associations, it is possible to form a civil partnership (*société civile*) for non-commercial objects, and it is governed exclusively by the Civil Code and the Law of 4th January 1979.

The law governing commercial associations is now contained in the Law of 24th July 1966, except for commercial interest groups. The Law has been supplemented by a Decree of 23rd March 1967 (No 67–236), and both have been slightly amended by subsequent legislation. References in this chapter to articles by number are to articles of the Law, unless otherwise indicated or unless preceded by 'D' when they are to articles of the Decree. This chapter will deal only with public and private companies, which are the forms of business association the British practitioner is most likely to meet.

The first two directives of the Council of Ministers of the European Communities on the harmonisation of company law have been implemented in France.

SOCIÉTÉ ANONYME (SA)

1 Formation

The first step in the formation of a *société anonyme* (SA) is for the founders, who must be at least seven in number, to file draft articles of association (*statuts*) at the office of the commercial court (*tribunal de commerce*) for the locality of the company's domicile (arts 73 and 74(1)), unless the company does not intend to invite the public to subscribe for its shares or bonds. In this case, the articles are signed by the seven or more founders, and they or a notarised copy of them are filed in the commercial court together with the other documents mentioned below (art 87). A company is deemed to invite the public to subscribe for its shares or bonds if they are to be quoted immediately on a stock exchange, or if they are allotted to banks, issuing houses or stockbrokers so that they may be sold to investors (art 72).

The articles of an SA must contain the following matters (art 2 and D art 55):

1 A statement that the company will be a *société anonyme*.
2 The duration of the company, which must not exceed ninety-nine years.
3 The name of the company, which may include the personal names of any of its shareholders (art 70).
4 The address of the company's registered office, which must be in France.
5 The nature of the company's business (*objet social*), though this is never stated with the particularity of the objects clause of a British company's memorandum of association.
6 The amount of the company's share capital, which must be at least 1,500,000 F (£134,300 approximately) in the case of companies formed after 31st December 1981, the date of entry into force of the Law No 81–1162 of 30th December 1981 implementing the requirements of the Second Directive; in the case of companies formed after that date which do not invite the public to subscribe for their shares or bonds, the relevant amount is 250,000 F (£22,400 approximately); companies in existence at the date of entry into force of the Law of 1981 are given until 1st January 1985 to comply with the new requirements (art 71(1) as amended by arts 8 and 33 of Law No 81–1162); the capital must normally be divided into shares (*actions*) of a fixed nominal value not less than

100 F (£9 approximately), but exceptions exist for companies which issue shares to give effect to employees' rights to participate in the company's profits, and for companies whose shares are officially listed on a stock exchange; the capital of these companies may be divided into shares of a nominal value of not less than 10 F (art 268 and D art 206).

7 Any restriction on the free transferability of shares.

8 The names of persons to whom shares are allotted otherwise than for cash, the number of shares to be issued to them, and the value of the consideration to be given by them.

9 Any special advantages to be conferred on particular shareholders (eg benefits for having assisted in the promotion of the company).

10 The composition and powers of the board of directors or other organs of management and administration of the company.

11 Provisions as to the distribution of the company's profits.

The founders must obtain subscriptions for the whole of the company's share capital (art 75(1)). If the company invites the public to subscribe for its shares and bonds, it must publish a notice in an official publication, the *Bulletin des annonces légales obligatoires* (BALO) published as an annex to the Official Journal of the French Republic, summarising the contents of its articles, the terms on which the shares or bonds are offered and the period for which the offer is open, and this information must also appear in all prospectuses issued by the company (art 74(2) and D arts 59 and 60). Persons who subscribe for shares for cash must pay at least one-quarter of the nominal value of the shares they take to a bank or a notary, and these payments cannot be withdrawn until the company has been registered (arts 72(2), 77(1) and 83(1)). Consideration other than cash to be given for a company's shares must be furnished in full before the shares are issued (art 75(3)). After allotting all the shares and receiving the whole or part of the consideration for them, the founders call a constitutive general meeting of all subscribers for shares (*assemblée générale constitutive*) by publishing a notice in BALO and in a newspaper carrying legal notices which circulates in the locality in which the company's registered office is situated (art 79(1) and D arts 66 and 67). The meeting receives and approves a notarised declaration by the founders as to the subscriptions and payments for the shares allotted for cash (art 79(2)), and receives the report of professionally qualified examiners (*commissaires aux apports*) who have been appointed by the court on the founders' application to express their opinion on the fairness and propriety of the allotment of shares for a consideration other than cash and of any special advantages conferred on particular shareholders (art 80(1) and (2)). The constitutive general meeting must verify the subscription of all the company's shares and the payment of the requisite fraction of their nominal value, approve the draft articles of the company, and approve the allotment of shares for a consideration other than cash and the conferment of special advantages; if it does not do so, the company cannot be formed (arts 79(2) and 80(3) and 80(4)). The meeting also appoints the first directors or members of the supervisory board of the company, and its first auditors (art 79(2)). The meeting is conducted in the same way as an extraordinary general meeting, but no subscriber can cast more than ten votes, and no subscriber can vote on the approval of the allotment of shares to himself for a consideration other than cash or on the conferment on himself of special advantages (arts 83(2) and 82). After the constitutive general meeting has been held the founders execute the articles and deposit the original or a notarised copy of them at the local commercial court together with a declaration signed by them and the first directors of the company that the procedural requirements relating to the formation of the company have been fulfilled (art 6 and D arts 54 and 69). The company is registered in the commercial register kept by the court and is thereupon incorporated (art 5(1)).

If a company is formed without inviting the public to subscribe for its shares or bonds, no constitutive general meeting is held, but if shares are allotted for a consideration other than cash, or if special advantages are conferred on any shareholders by the articles, examiners are appointed by the court to report on these matters, and their report is annexed to the original or notarised copy of the articles (arts 84 and 86). The first directors or members of the supervisory board of the company and its first auditors are appointed by the articles (art 88). The articles must be signed by all the original shareholders of the company (art 87), and the articles or a notarised copy, a notarised declaration by one or more shareholders that all the shares have been subscribed and the requisite fraction of the nominal value of these allotted for cash has been paid, and a declaration by the directors that the procedural requirements relating to the formation of the company have been fulfilled are deposited at the local commercial court (arts 55 and 87 and D art 75). Upon the registration of these documents the company is incorporated (art 5(1)).

When a company has been registered in the commercial register, the official in charge of it (*greffier*) publishes a notice in BALO summarising the contents of its articles, and giving the names and addresses of its directors and members of its supervisory board (Decree in respect of the Commercial Register (No 67–237) of 23rd March 1967, art 13). At the same time the *greffier* sends a copy of all the documents deposited with him to the national commercial register (*registre nationale du commerce*) in Paris (*ibid*, arts 7 and 14).

2 Shares and bonds

(a) Shares

An SA is a legal person distinct from its shareholders (*actionnaires*), and they are consequently liable to contribute towards payment of its debts only to the extent of the capital unpaid on their shares (art 73). Under the former law, if all the company's shares became vested in one person, the company was automatically dissolved, and he became personally liable for debts incurred with the business thereafter (French Supreme Court, D 1867 1 937). The uniting of all the shares in one hand does not now effect a dissolution, but any interested person may petition the court to wind up the company if there are not at least two members of the company one year after the shares were so acquired (art 9).

Shares paid for in kind (*actions d'apport*) are fully paid when they are issued, but up to three-quarters of the nominal value of shares issued for cash (*actions de numéraire*) may remain to be paid after they are issued, the balance then being payable by one or more instalments fixed by the board of directors or the executive board of the company, but the whole issue price must become payable within a period of five years from the date of registration of the company in the Commercial Register (Law of 1966, arts 75(2) and 84). Shares may not be issued at a discount, nor may the holders be released from their obligation to pay for them in full. If a shareholder fails to pay an instalment of the issue price, the company may sue him, or after giving him one month's final notice, may sell his shares on the stock exchange or by public auction if they are not quoted; the purchaser takes the shares credited as paid up to the extent that they were paid up before the sale to him plus the amount he has paid the company for them, but if that amount exceeds the instalment in arrear, only the amount of the instalment is credited, and the surplus is paid to the former shareholder: if the price paid by the purchaser is insufficient to pay the instalment in full, the former shareholder remains liable for the deficit (art 281). Former holders of partly paid shares are liable not only for instalments falling due while they hold the shares, but also for those becoming payable within two years after the transfer by them was presented to the company for registration (art 282). If an instalment due in respect of a share is unpaid for thirty days after the company serves final notice demanding payment, the holder cannot participate in shareholders' meetings or claim dividends or exercise rights to subscribe for further shares until the call or instalment is paid (art 283).

Shares may be in registered or, if the articles so provide, in bearer form, but bearer certificates may not be issued in respect of shares paid for in cash until they are fully paid (arts 263 and 270), and no certificates at all may be issued in respect of shares paid for by a consideration other than cash until two years after the company comes into existence, but this does not apply where shares are allotted by a public company which has been in existence for two years in consideration for assets transferred to it in connection with a merger (arts 278 and 279(1)). Furthermore shares held by directors or members of the executive or supervisory board of a listed company in the company itself, or in its subsidiary or parent company or in its fellow subsidiary company, must be in registered form. This rule is also applicable to shares held by the unemancipated minor children* of such persons, and their spouses unless they are separated by a judicial decree. As an alternative to having the shares in registered form, bearer certificates in respect of them may be deposited with a bank (art 162(1)).

Transfers of registered shares are effected by the transferor signing an instrument of transfer (*bordereau de transfert*) which must also be signed by the transferee unless the shares are fully paid, and sending it to the company which must register the transfer in its register of share transfers within ten days (Decree in respect of investment securities of 7th December 1955, arts 35(1) and 43). The articles may validly provide that the registration of the transfer of shares which are required to be in registered form by law or the company's articles shall be subject to the approval of the directors (or the executive board) if the transfer is a voluntary disposition

---

* The age of majority in France is eighteen. A minor is emancipated by operation of law upon his marriage, and may be emancipated by the guardianship judge (*juge des tutelles*) on the application of either or both of his parents after he has reached the age of sixteen (Civil Code, arts 476 and 477).

made *inter vivos* to a third party (art 274(1)). If no reply is given to
the request for registration within thirty days if the transfer is
effected through a stockbroker, or within three months in any other
case, the approval is deemed to be given. If approval is refused
within this time, it is nevertheless deemed given unless within thirty
days, if the transfer is effected through a stockbroker, or within
three months in any other case, the directors (or the executive
board) arrange for the shares to be bought either by another
shareholder, an outsider, or the company itself. If the original
transfer was to have been made through a broker, the price offered
by the alternative purchaser found by the directors must be not less
than the price agreed to be paid by the original transferee, or the
quoted price at the date the directors rejected the transfer to him,
whichever is the greater (art 276). If the original transfer was not to
have been made through a broker, the price to be paid to the
transferor is fixed by an expert appointed by the court if the parties
cannot agree (art 275(2)).

The registered holder of registered shares is conclusively taken to
be the holder of the shares (art 255(2) and Decree of 7th December
1955, art 1(1)). This is so not only in respect of matters between the
company and the registered holder (eg liability for calls, exercise of
voting rights), but also as between the registered holder and the
former owner of the shares when the transfer to the registered
holder was forged or unauthorised (French Supreme Court, DP
1901 1 132). But if a company registers a transfer which it should
have realised was forged or unauthorised, it is liable in damages to
the former holder, who cannot recover his shares (Tribunal civil,
Seine, Gaz Pal 1923 2 289). A company is protected against liability
however if the transferor's signature was certified by a stockbroker
or a notary (Decree of 7th December 1955, art 36).

In practice fully paid shares of an SA are always in bearer form,
and transfers are effected by delivery of the transferor's share
certificate to the transferee (art 265(1)). A purchaser in good faith
of bearer shares obtains a good title thereto, even though his vendor
obtained the share certificate from the former owner by fraud (Civil
Code, art 2279), but if they were stolen, the former owner may
reclaim them within three years of the theft on reimbursing the
purchaser (Civil Code, art 2280). Moreover, an owner of bearer
shares who loses his certificate (by theft or otherwise) may protect
himself by giving notice to the Paris Stock Exchange for publication
in its *Bulletin officiel des oppositions*; the notice must be republished
annually until the certificate is recovered or cancelled (Decree in

respect of the procedure for lost bearer securities of 11th January 1956, arts 1, 2, 7 and 8). Any transfer of the certificate after the date when copies of the *Bulletin* reached, or should have reached, the place where the transfer took place is then ineffective against the owner, and the transferee is reduced to suing his transferor for damages (*ibid*, art 9). Two years after the owner has had his first notice published in the *Bulletin*, he may apply to the court for an order that the company shall henceforth pay dividends and repayments of capital to him, if no other person has proved a good title to the shares by a purchase of the certificate before the time mentioned above; if such an order is made, the owner can require the issue of a duplicate certificate and the cancellation of the original by the company when five years have elapsed from the publication of the first notice in the *Bulletin* (*ibid*, arts 20–25). Although these provisions are operated by the Paris Stock Exchange, they apply to unquoted as well as to quoted bearer shares (Court of Appeal, Toulouse S 1938 2 184).

Quoted bearer shares are often deposited with banks and stockbrokers, and unless otherwise instructed, they may redeposit them with an official body, *la Société interprofessionelle pour la compensation des valeurs mobilières* (SICOVAM) (Decree in respect of negotiable securities of 4th August 1949, arts 5 and 10). The shares are then held as a common fund with like shares deposited by other persons, and the depositor is treated as having a claim for their return at any time similar to the claim of the holder of a current account at a bank. Transfers of shares are effected by a written instruction given by the depositor to SICOVAM (*ordre de virement*) requiring his account to be debited in respect of the number of shares transferred, and the transferee's account to be correspondingly credited; the transfer is then carried out without any physical movement of the share certificate (*ibid*, art 24). Dividends are paid by the company to SICOVAM in respect of deposited shares, and are then credited to the respective accounts of the depositors.

The rules contained in art 217 of the Law governing commercial companies governing the purchase by a company of its own shares and certain related matters have been amended by Law No 81–1162 of 30th December 1981. The new rules, which became effective for all companies as from 1st July 1982 (Law No 81–1162, art 33), are explained below.

A company may not subscribe for or purchase its own shares either directly or through an intermediary acting in his own name but on behalf of the company (art 217(1)). However, an extraordinary general meeting which resolves on a reduction of capital for any reason other than a loss of capital may authorise the board of directors (or the executive board) to purchase a specified number of outstanding shares in order to cancel them (art 217(2)).

There are two exceptions to the general principle stated above. The board of directors (or the executive board) of a company may purchase its listed shares, or its shares which appear in a special part of the daily statement concerning shares dealt in on the official market, in order to provide its employees with shares under a profit-sharing scheme (art 217–1). Secondly, subject to compliance with certain required conditions, a company whose shares are listed on a stock exchange or which appear in a special part of the above mentioned daily statement may purchase its shares on the stock exchange in order to regularise the market in them. The company must be authorised to deal in its own shares on the stock exchange by a resolution passed at an ordinary general meeting, which must fix the conditions under which dealings may take place, and in particular the maximum purchase price and the minimum sale price, the number of shares to be acquired, and the period within which such acquisition is to be effected. The duration of the period for which the authorisation is given may not exceed eighteen months (art 217–2(1)). If the shares are admitted to dealings on the future settlements market of the stock exchange, the company may not purchase them at a price greater than the average of the opening prices for its shares on this market during the thirty preceding stock-exchange sessions. If the shares are not admitted to dealings on the future settlements market, the opening prices on the cash settlements market are substituted for those on the future settlements market (art 217–2(2)).

A company may not hold more than 10 per cent of its own shares of any class. For the purposes of this prohibition, shares held by a nominee acting on behalf of the company are treated as belonging to the company. Shares which a company holds in itself must be put into registered form, and must be fully paid at the time of their acquisition. A company may not acquire its own shares if this would have the effect of reducing the net assets of the company below the amount of its capital plus legal reserve and any other reserves which may not be distributed in accordance with the provisions of the articles. The company must have and maintain reserves, other than the legal reserve, at least equal to the value of the shares which it holds in itself. The latter shares carry no voting or dividend rights (arts 164 and 217–3).

The restrictions contained in arts 217 and 217–2 are inapplicable to shares acquired as the result of a universal transfer of assets (eg on a merger). However, such shares must be disposed of within two years of their acquisition to the extent that their nominal value exceeds 10 per cent of the company's capital (art 217–7).

An SA is prohibited from acquiring shares in another company which already holds more than one-tenth of its own share capital (art 358(1)), and a company other than an SA is prohibited from acquiring shares in an SA which already holds more than one-tenth of the first company's capital (art 359(1)).

Despite the general prohibition on an SA purchasing its shares or repaying its share capital except by a duly authorised reduction of capital, it may repay the capital paid up on its shares out of profits or revenue reserves, and the shares, now called reimbursed shares (*actions de jouissance*), then carry the same rights as other shares save that they do not qualify for a first dividend (see p54) or repayment of capital on a reduction of capital or on a winding up (arts 209 and 210). A company's own shares may not be mortgaged to the company (art 217–8). Furthermore, a company may not advance funds, nor make loans, nor provide security with a view to the acquisition of its shares by a third party (art 217–9).

The articles of a company may provide for the issue of different classes of shares, such as preference shares (*actions de priorité*), and when a company increases its capital, it may resolve that the new shares shall be preference shares carrying such rights in respect of dividends and capital as it thinks fit (art 269). The rights attached to a class of shares cannot be modified without the consent of a special meeting (*assemblée spéciale*) of the holders of the shares of that class: the meeting is governed by the same rules as to quorum, majority, etc, as an extraordinary general meeting (see p53) (art 156).

A special class of preference shares, hereafter called 'savings shares' although the French legislation does not employ this term, has been recognised by Law No 78–741 of 13th July 1978, which incorporated arts 269–1 to 269–9 into the Law of 24th July 1966. Unlike other classes of preference shares, the rights and obligations attached to which are largely determined by the company's articles, savings shares are subject to a number of mandatory provisions laid down in arts 269–1 to 269–9. Such shares may be issued only if the company has paid at least two dividends during the last three years (art 177–1). The total amount of savings shares issued may not exceed three-quarters of the company's capital (art 269–1).

The holders of savings shares are entitled to a preferential dividend before any other distribution is made. The net profits of the company must be applied in paying a dividend to the holders of savings shares equal to at least 5 per cent of the paid up value of their shares plus any premium, and the dividend paid must be at least equal to any other preference dividend paid by the company (art 269–2).

In addition to their right to a preferential dividend, the same rights are attached to savings shares as to ordinary shares, except the right to participate in and vote at general meetings (art 269–1). However, if the dividends due on savings shares have not been paid in full for three years, the holders of such shares are entitled to vote at general meetings under the same conditions as the holders of ordinary shares. They continue to be so entitled until the dividends on the savings shares have been paid in full for three years (art 269–3).

Directors, executive directors and members of the supervisory board, and general managers of an SA and certain of their relatives may not hold savings shares (art 269–6). Special rules exist which are designed to safeguard the rights of holders of savings shares in the event of an increase or reduction of capital (arts 269–5 and 269–7). The articles may make provision for the redemption of savings shares. The redemption price may be fixed by agreement between the company and a special meeting of the selling shareholders, or be fixed by an expert appointed by the court (art 269–8, and Civil Code, art 1843–4).

Although the holders of savings shares cannot normally participate in general meetings, they are entitled to attend and vote at special meetings of their class. The class meeting may give its opinion before any decision is taken by the general meeting: this opinion must be brought to the knowledge of the general meeting. One or more common representatives of the holders of savings shares may attend general meetings and, where the occasion arises, explain the opinion of the class meeting thereat. The class meeting is also required to approve any decision of the general meeting affecting the rights of the holders of the savings shares. The requirements of art 156 as to quorum and voting are applicable to the meeting (art 269–4).

Since the Law of 24th July 1966 came into force in May 1967, it has not been possible for companies to issue founders' shares (*parts bénéficiaires* or *parts de fondateur*) (art 264). Such shares previously issued are still valid, but only carry the right to participate in the company's profits while it is a going concern (Law on founders' shares of 23rd January 1929, art 1). Their holders may not vote at shareholders' meetings, but the articles may require their consent to particular transactions undertaken by the company, and for this and other purposes they may hold separate class meetings and appoint persons to represent them in dealings with the company (*ibid*, arts 1 and 2).

(b) Bonds

An SA may issue bonds (*obligations*) only if it has existed at least two years and its accounts for its first two financial years have been approved by general meetings, but this is not necessary if the bonds are guaranteed by the state or a public administrative body (*collectivité publique*), or by another SA which complies with the conditions imposed on the issuer (art 285(1) and (2)). Furthermore, no capital must remain unpaid on the company's issued shares if it is to issue bonds (art 285(3)), and the issue must be authorised by an ordinary general meeting (art 286), or, if the bonds are convertible into shares, by an extraordinary general meeting. Bonds may be offered to the public for subscription, subject in the case of convertible bonds to the waiver of the existing shareholders' preferential rights of subscription by the resolution creating them (arts 186 and 195(1)). If a public offer is made the company must publish a notice in BALO giving short particulars of its constitution and its outstanding issues of bonds, and setting out its most recent balance sheet (art 289 and D arts 211 and 212), and prospectuses in respect of the bonds must contain the same information (D art 213). Bonds may be issued at a discount, but convertible bonds cannot be issued at a price less than the nominal value of the shares into which they can be converted (art 195(4)). Bonds may be in registered or bearer form (art 263), and transactions in respect of them, including the consequences of the loss of bearer certificates and the deposit of bearer bonds with banks, brokers and SICOVAM, are governed by the same rules which govern similar transactions in respect of shares.

Bonds may be secured by mortgages of the company's movable or immovable property, but floating charges over a company's assets for the time being are not recognised by French law (Court of Appeal, Nantes, J Soc 1907, 228). It is, however, possible for a company to mortgage its business (*fonds de commerce*), and this is interpreted as a mortgage of its fixed assets as they exist from time to time, but not of its stock in trade or its trade debts (Law in respect of the sale and mortgage of business of 17th March 1909, arts 8 and 9). In practice, only small businesses use this facility, and most bonds issued by the larger *sociétés anonymes* are unsecured.

The holders of a series of bonds form a class (*masse*) and may hold meetings which are convened either by the company or on the requisition of the holders of one-thirtieth of the outstanding bonds, and are governed by the same rules as extraordinary general meetings of shareholders (arts 293, 305 and 306). A meeting of a class of bondholders may appoint up to three representatives (*mandataires*) to protect their interests (art 294), and the company and the other companies which hold one-tenth or more of the issuing company's capital, or in which the issuing company holds one-tenth or more of their capital, together with all the officers of the companies, are disabled from being appointed bondholders' representatives (art 296). The representatives may perform ordinary acts of conservation (*actes de gestion*) to protect bondholders, but they require authorisation by a meeting of bondholders to sue the company or realise any security (arts 300, 301 and 312). An extraordinary general meeting of bondholders is required by a resolution passed by a two-thirds majority and approved by the court to give its consent to an alteration in the company's objects, a compromise of the bondholders' claims, a modification of their security (if any) or a deferment of the payment of interest or the repayment of capital, but no resolution may treat different bond-holders unequally (arts 313, 314, 316 and 317).

While convertible bonds are outstanding, the company cannot reimburse its shares out of profits, repay share capital on a reduction of capital, or alter the rights of shareholders to the distribution of profits (art 195(5)). The company may, however, issue new shares for cash or on a capitalisation of profits or reserves, or it may issue new convertible bonds or distribute profits or reserves to its existing shareholders notwithstanding the existence of convertible bonds, but only on condition that the rights of bondholders who exercise their conversion rights are preserved (art 196(1)). For this purpose, the company must permit bondholders who opt for conversion to apply for the allotment of new shares, or new convertible bonds, or to claim a cash dividend (as the case may be) in the same way and on the same conditions as if they had been holders of the number of shares they take on conversion at the date of issue of new shares or convertible bonds or the distribution of profits or reserves (art 196(2)).

If the shares of an SA are listed on a stock exchange, it may anticipate the exercise of conversion rights by bondholders by issuing shares to a bank which holds them in registered and non-transferable form as an agent pending conversion (arts 200, 201 and 205). The same rules then apply as if convertible bonds had been issued in the ordinary way (arts 201(2), 203(1) and 206(1)), and the bank is obliged to subscribe for and hold all further shares allotted in right of the original ones as agent for the bondholders who convert (arts 204 and 206(2) and (3)).

Shares and bonds of *sociétés anonymes* may be dealt with on a French stock exchange only if the Stock Exchange Commission (*Commission des Opérations de Bourse*) decides to grant a listing on the proposal of the company or the governing council (*chambre syndicale*) of the Stockbrokers' Association (*Compagnie des Agents de Change*), and once a listing has been granted, sales may be effected only through the agency of brokers who are members of the stock exchange (Commercial Code, art 76).

3 Management and control

(a) Board of directors and president

Unless it adopts the alternative form of management mentioned below, every SA must have a board of directors (*conseil d'administration*) of between three and twelve members (*administrateurs*) who may be natural persons or corporate bodies, but who must be shareholders in the company (arts 89(1), 91 and 95(1)). Apart from the first directors, who may be appointed in the articles for a term of not more than three years, all directors must be appointed by a general meeting of shareholders for terms of not more than six years (arts 88 and 90(1)). Any director may be removed from office for any reason by a resolution of a general meeting (art 90(2)). No one person may be a director of more than eight companies, but this rule does not apply to corporate directors (art 92). An employee of the company may be appointed a director only if his contract of employment relates to a real area of activity or responsibility different from his activities or responsibilities as a director and was entered into at least two years before his appointment; employees may not hold more than one-third of the directorships (art 93). Directors must each hold the number of shares specified in the articles, which must be in registered form, and all such shares form a fund which may be resorted to to compensate the company for breaches of duty by any of them (art 95).

Directors may only be remunerated by fees for attending board meetings (art 108). The board may, however, pay additional fees for exceptional tasks performed by its members (art 109). Loans may not be made by a company to its directors, or their spouses, parents or children (art 106(1) and (3)). Contracts with the company in which a director is interested must be reported to the board and the director's interest approved by it, but this does not apply to transactions on normal terms in the ordinary course of the company's business (art 101). Contracts in which a director is interested must also be notified to the auditors, who report on them to a general meeting of the shareholders; the meeting may disapprove such a contract even though it has been sanctioned by the board, but the contract is not invalidated by shareholder disapproval, the only consequence being that the interested and other directors are liable to compensate the company for any loss it has suffered by the contract being carried out (arts 103 and 104).

The board of directors nominally has 'full power to act within the limits of [the company's] objects and subject to the powers conferred by law on the general meeting of shareholders', and no restriction on its powers in the articles is effective against outsiders (art 98(1)). In fact, the functions of the board are circumscribed by the fact that the directors must elect one of their number to be the president (*président*) of the company (art 111); he 'undertakes on his own responsibility the general direction of the company' and 'subject to the powers of the general meeting conferred by the law and the limits imposed by the company's objects, is invested with full power to act in all circumstances in the name of the company' (art 113(1) and (2)). A general manager (*directeur générale*) may be similarly appointed on the nomination of the president and, if the company's capital is at least 500,000 F, there may be two general managers (art 115), but no other delegation of the board's powers is permissible.

The result of these provisions is that the board's effective functions have been reduced to calling meetings of shareholders and presenting the directors' annual report (art 158(1)), consenting to share transfers where this is necessary (art 274(1)), approving contracts in which directors are interested (art 101), and approving the creation of mortgages over the company's property and the giving of guarantees by it (art 98(2)). The president is therefore the power centre of the company, but he is at least subject to the influence of his fellow directors, who can remove him at any time for any reason (art 110(3)). Because of the important and continuous nature of his functions, a person cannot be president of more than two companies (art 111), and it is not possible to appoint a company to be president of another company. A company is bound in relation to third parties by acts of its president which are outside the company's objects, unless it can prove that the third party knew that the act was unrelated to the company's objects, or that he must have known that this was so from the circumstances (art 113(3)). The mere publication of the company's articles is not evidence of the third party's knowledge or imputed knowledge of the scope of the company's objects (art 113(4)). Restrictions on the powers of the president contained in the company's articles or in resolutions passed by its board are effective as between the company and its president, but cannot be invoked against third parties (art 113(3)).

(b) Executive board and supervisory board

As an alternative to the management structure described above the articles may provide that the company shall have an executive board (*directoire*) and a supervisory board (*conseil de surveillance*) (art 118). This alternative is based on the German management structure of executive and supervisory boards. The members of the executive board are referred to as executive directors in the text below. The members of the supervisory board (three to twelve in number) are elected by the shareholders for the same period as members of an ordinary board of directors, and the rules governing them are exactly the same as those for ordinary directors (arts 129, 130 and 134–140). The supervisory board in turn elects up to five individuals (who need not be shareholders) to be the executive board of the company; the executive board must consist of at least two persons, unless the company's capital is less than 600,000 F when there may be a sole general manager (*directeur générale unique*) (arts 119(1) and (2) and 120). The fundamental distinction between this kind of management structure and the ordinary one lies in the fact that members of the executive board cannot be members of the supervisory board as well (art 133), whereas a president must be a member of the board of directors (art 110(1)). Like a president, however, a member of an executive board cannot hold that office in more than two companies (art 127(1)), and the two offices are treated as equivalent for this purpose, so that no one individual may hold more than two offices as president and memberships of executive boards (art 151(2)). Similarly, no individual may be a member of the boards of directors or the supervisory boards of more than eight companies (art 151(2)). The tenure of

office of a member of an executive board is different from that of a president of a company. A member of an executive board is appointed for four years, and can only be removed by resolution of a general meeting of shareholders at the request of the supervisory board (arts 121(1) and 122).

The powers of an executive board are defined in the same way as those of a president, and restrictions on its powers in the articles are ineffective against outsiders (art 124). Transactions in the company's name are concluded by the chairman of the executive board on its behalf, but the articles may enable the supervisory board to empower any other member of the executive board to represent the company (art 126(1) and (2)). The supervisory board exercises a general control over the management of the company's affairs by the executive board; nevertheless, the articles may require the committee's consent for specified transactions, and its consent is always required for the creation of mortgages over the company's property, or the giving of guarantees in its name (art 128(1) and (2)). The supervisory board may carry out such checks on the work of the executive board as it thinks fit, and the executive board must report to it at least once every four months (art 128(3) and (4)).

The same rules as to interests in contracts with the company and the same prohibition on loans by the company apply to members of the executive and supervisory boards of a company as to ordinary directors (arts 143–147).

Employees in an SA are not entitled to appoint members of the board of directors or the supervisory board as they are in the case of a German AG. But if an SA employs more than fifty persons, it must establish a works council (*comité d'entreprise*) whose members are elected by the employees from among their numbers (Law of 16th May 1946, arts 1, 5 and 6). The council may send two of its members as observers to meetings of the executive board or the supervisory board, but they cannot vote (*ibid*, art 3(9)).

(c) General meetings

There are three kinds of general meetings of shareholders, namely, the annual ordinary general meeting (*assemblée générale ordinaire annuelle*), which must be held within six months after the end of each financial year to receive and approve the annual accounts and the reports of the board of directors or the executive or supervisory board and the auditors, and to declare dividends and to appoint directors, members of the committee of supervision and auditors (arts 90(1), 128(6), 134(1), 157(1)–(3), and 223(1)); other ordinary general meetings (*assemblée générale ordinaire*) which exercise all the other powers of the shareholders, except those for which an extraordinary general meeting is required (art 155(1)); and finally the latter kind of meeting (*assemblée générale extraordinaire*) which is called to resolve on amendments to the articles, increases and reductions of capital and mergers (arts 153(1), 180(1), 215(1) and 376), and to change the company's nationality, which may be done if the country to which the company is to transfer has agreed with France that the company will acquire its nationality, and will preserve its corporate character (art 154).

General meetings may be called by the board of directors, or by the executive or supervisory board of the company, or by its auditors, or by the court on the application of the holders of one-tenth of the company's capital (art 158). General meetings are convened by publishing a notice at least fifteen days before the meeting in a local newspaper carrying legal notices and also in BALO if the company has invited the public to subscribe for its shares or bonds (art 159 and D arts 124–126). If all the company's shares are registered, however, meetings are called by notice sent to all the shareholders at least fifteen days before the meeting is held (arts 159(2) and D arts 125 and 126). The company must send or make available to the shareholders for fifteen days before the meeting is held the detailed agenda of the meeting, including in the case of an annual ordinary general meeting the annual accounts and the auditors' reports, the reports of the directors or the executive and supervisory board, and the list of candidates for election at the meeting, and any shareholder can up to five days before the meeting request copies of these documents to be sent to him (arts 162(1) and 168, and D arts 135, 138 and 139). If the company sends out proxy solicitations, they must be accompanied by the same documents, and must intimate that proxy appointments returned to the company without an indication how they are to be used may be voted in support of the management's proposals (D arts 133 and 134). Any shareholder may appoint another to act as his proxy, but a separate appointment is required for each of several meetings (art 161(1) and D art 132(2)). The holders of one-twentieth of the company's capital (or a smaller fraction if the capital exceeds 5 m F) may require resolutions proposed by them to be placed on the agenda of any general meeting (art 163(2) and D art 128(3)).

The quorum for an ordinary general meeting is the presence in person or by proxy of the holders of one-quarter of the company's capital, but there is no quorum for an adjourned meeting; resolutions are passed by a simple majority vote (art 155(2) and (3)). The quorum of an extraordinary general meeting is the similar representation of the holders of one-half of the company's capital or one-quarter at an adjourned meeting; resolutions are passed by two-thirds of the votes cast (art 153(2) and (3)). Votes are cast at general meetings in proportion to the nominal value of shares, and shares cannot be issued without voting rights or with restricted voting rights (art 174). The articles may, however, prescribe the minimum number of shares, not exceeding ten, which must be held in order to vote at an ordinary general meeting, but small shareholders may aggregate their holdings to make up this minimum (art 165). Furthermore, the articles may depart from the principle of uniformity of voting rights by conferring double voting rights in respect of registered shares which have been held by the same registered holder for at least two years (art 175(1)).

Before the annual ordinary general meeting, the directors or the executive directors must prepare annual accounts comprising an inventory, trading account, profit and loss account, and balance sheet, and submit them to the auditors (who must be professionally qualified) for examination and report (arts 218, 228(1) and 340). The accounts and the auditors' report, together with the reports of the directors or executive directors and the supervisory board, are then laid before the annual general meeting of shareholders for approval (arts 128(6), 157(2) and (3) and 228). One-twentieth of the profits shown by the accounts must be transferred to statutory reserve until it amounts to one-tenth of the company's capital (art 345). The distributable profit consists of the amount of the net profits at the end of the last financial year plus any profits brought forward and sums drawn from reserve available for this purpose, less any losses brought forward and sums placed to reserve in accordance with the law or the articles. The distribution of sums drawn from reserves requires the consent of general meeting (art 346). The shareholders in general meeting determine what dividend is to be paid after approving the annual accounts for the last financial year and determining the existence of distributable profits (art 347).

Dividends may be paid only out of profits (art 348), but the articles may stipulate for the payment of a first dividend in the form of a rate of interest on capital which has not been reimbursed, before a normal dividend is paid rateably on reimbursed and non-reimbursed shares of the same class (art 349). An ordinary general meeting may resolve to capitalise profits and issue fully paid bonus shares, or capitalised profits may be appropriated to pay up unpaid capital on existing shares (arts 178(1) and (3) and 180(2)).

French law contains no detailed rules in respect of associated companies. A company is the subsidiary (*filiale*) of another if the other holds more than one-half its share capital (art 354), and a company has a participation in another if it holds between 10 and 50 per cent of that other's capital (art 355). But the only consequence of these relationships, apart from the prohibition on cross-holdings of shares which has already been mentioned, is that the parent or participating company must list subsidiaries and participations acquired during the year in its directors' report to the annual ordinary general meeting, and the accounts laid before the meeting must have a schedule annexed to them showing the earnings and financial condition of subsidiaries and companies in which a participation is held (arts 356 and 357). This schedule may, but does not have to, take the form of consolidated accounts (D art 248). A Bill at present before the French Parliament would require French listed companies to prepare such accounts.

(d) Employees' share of profits

All companies, whatever the character of their activities or their legal form, which habitually employ more than 100 persons must annually transfer to a special reserve for the benefit of their employees a fraction of half their annual net profits after deducting corporation tax and 5 per cent of the net worth of the company in France and its overseas *départements* (Ordonnance of 17th August 1967 (No 67–693), arts 1 and 2(1) and (2)). The relevant fraction is obtained by dividing the total wages and salaries paid during the year by the company's 'added value', which is defined as the total of the company's trading profit plus wages, salaries and taxes paid (other than turnover tax), plus provisions made for depreciation and by way of provision for contingencies (art 2(4)). Each employee of more than three months' standing is entitled to participate in the special reserve in proportion to the wage or salary received by him, subject to certain maxima (art 3), but benefits are conferred not in cash, but by issuing shares or bonds of the company credited as paid up out of the company's profits and revenue reserves, or by the setting up of an investment fund or savings scheme; the exact arrangement is determined by a participation agreement between the company and its employees (art 4(1)). Shares or bonds so issued cannot be realised by the employee for five years after allotment, and until the expiration of that time they must be in registered and non-transferable form (art 6).

SAs may establish option schemes for the benefit of the employees of the company or of its subsidiaries, whereby such employees are given an option to buy existing shares of the SA, or to subscribe for new shares out of an increase of its capital effected for the purpose (art 208–1(1) and 208–4). The total number of shares available for immediate subscription under the option scheme but not yet subscribed must not at any time exceed the following percentages of the capital of the company: 5 per cent of that part of its capital which does not exceed 10m F; 3 per cent of that part of its capital which exceeds 10m F, but does not exceed 50m F; and 1 per cent of that part of its capital in excess of 50m F (art 208–6(1) and D art 174–17). No options may be granted to any employee who holds shares in the company exceeding a fraction of its capital determined by an extraordinary general meeting, not being more than 5 per cent (art 208–6(4)).

A resolution of an extraordinary general meeting of the company based upon a report by the directors and a special report by the auditors of the company is necessary for the purpose of creating subscription or purchase options (art 208–1(1) and (2)). Options must be exercised by employees within five years from the date when the option is given (art 208–7(1)). The rights vested in an employee under an option granted to him are not transferable until the option has been exercised (art 208–7(2)). However, where an employee dies, his heirs may exercise the option within six months of the date of his death (art 208–7(3)).

Special rules are applicable to companies whose shares are listed on a stock exchange, or are dealt in regularly on the unofficial market, and which have distributed at least two dividends during the last three financial years (art 208–9). The directors or executive directors of such companies may be authorised by an extraordinary general meeting to offer the employees of the company the opportunity of purchasing shares on the stock exchange by means of having a special account opened in their name funded by equal and regular deductions from their pay, and, possibly, by supplementary contributions made by the company. The offer may relate not only to shares in the company, but also to shares of a parent or subsidiary company, provided that the latter company has its seat (*siège*) in France (art 208–10 and 208–18). The shares must be in registered form, and may not be transferred for a period of five years after their subscription (art 208–16).

The Law (No 80–834) of 24th October 1980 makes provision for the issue of shares to employees of certain SAs and companies of any kind in which an SA directly or indirectly holds more than one-half of the company's capital, but the issue of shares must be approved by a resolution passed at an extraordinary general meeting of the SA. Companies are able to issue shares to employees under this provision if they have distributed at least two dividends in respect of two complete financial years during the five calendar years preceding the holding of the relevant extraordinary general meeting (art 1). The directors or executive directors of such companies whose shares were listed on a French stock exchange, or were dealt in on the special section of the unofficial market of a French stock exchange, or which were significantly and regularly dealt in on such a market, were required to call an extraordinary general meeting to decide whether shares shall be issued to the company's employees (art 2(1)). This meeting was required to take place at the latest by the date of the annual general meeting which next followed the enactment of the Law No 80–834 (art 2(2)). Companies which did not fulfil the requirements of art 2(1) were permitted to hold an extraordinary general meeting for this purpose before the end of the second financial year beginning after the entry into force of Law 80–834, but they were not bound to do so (art 3).

The issue of the new shares to the employees takes place by means of an increase of the company's capital. The number of shares issued is initially determined so that the increase in capital is equal to 3 per cent of the company's nominal capital after the increase, but this number is ultimately reduced so that when it is multiplied by the market value of the new shares (which is determined in accordance with rules contained in art 6–I(3) and (4)), it equals the product of 5,000 F and the number of employees benefiting (art 6–I(1)).

If a company increases its capital for the purpose of issuing shares to employees in accordance with art 6–I, it has a claim against the state for 65 per cent of the market value of the shares so issued or their total nominal value, whichever is the greater (art 7–I(1) and (2)). That part of the amount of the claim which equals the nominal value of the share is treated as a contribution in kind, and any excess amount is treated as a share premium (art 7–I(6) and 7–IV). The number of shares or fractions of shares issued to employees who are entitled to them is determined either on the basis of the employee's wages or salary and his length of service, with the proviso that no employee's entitlement may exceed three times that of another

employee, or in accordance with the rules contained in the participation agreement (art 9). The shares cannot generally be realised by
an employee for a period varying between three and five years, the
exact length of which is determined by the extraordinary general
meeting (art 10–I).

Although the effect of the above law will be spent in the near
future, the law may provide a framework for future action on the
part of the French legislature.

4 Provisions for the protection of shareholders and creditors

Apart from the provisions already dealt with, French law protects
the shareholders and creditors of an SA in the following ways:

(1) If a company is ordered to be wound up under the court's
control (*règlement judiciaire*) or is put into compulsory liquidation
(*liquidation des biens*), any person who is or has been responsible for
the management or supervision of the affairs of the company in law
or in fact, whether personally or through intermediaries, and
whether remunerated or not, may have an order made against him
that his assets shall be added to those of the company, and that they
shall be realised so as to satisfy the company's debts rateably as well
as his own private debts. This is done by the court making an order
for the winding up of his affairs under its control, or the compulsory
liquidation of his affairs concurrently with that of the company
(Bankruptcy Law (No 67–563) of 13th July 1967, art 101(1) and
(2)). Such a person who has been guilty of certain wrongful acts may
be adjudicated as a bankrupt. This is a separate proceeding from the
winding up or liquidation of his affairs, involving the loss of rights
and the imposition of prohibitions (Bankruptcy Law, arts 105 and
111). Similarly, without making a winding up or liquidation order
against him, a person who is responsible for the management or
supervision of the affairs of a company or partnership in law or in
fact, whether directly or through intermediaries, and whether remunerated or not, may be ordered by the court to pay the whole or
part of the company's debts personally unless he can show that he
exercised all the necessary care and skill in managing the company's
affairs (art 99(1) and (3)). These provisions were applied to public
companies by the Law on Commercial Companies of 24th July
1966, art 249(2), and they are also applicable to persons responsible for management or supervision of all other kinds of companies
and partnerships.

(2) The holders of at least one-tenth of the company's capital

may apply to the commercial court for the appointment of an expert to investigate and report on any aspect of the management of the company (art 226(1) and D art 195). The expert's report is sent to those demanding it and the directors, and is annexed to the next annual report of the auditors (art 226(3)). If it reveals irregularities in management, however, there is no provision by which proceedings are automatically instituted against the persons responsible. Under a Bill at present before the French Parliament (*Projet de loi* No 249 of 1980) auditors, the Public Prosecutor and, in the case of companies which appeal to the public for funds, the Stock Exchange Commission, would be able to institute proceedings under art 226. This Bill has not yet been enacted.

(3) Directors or members of the executive board of a company who are guilty of breaches of the legislation governing companies, or of the company's articles, or who are at fault in managing the company's affairs (*fautes commises dans leur gestion*) are liable in damages to the company, its shareholders individually and to other persons (eg creditors) for any loss they sustain (Law of 24th July 1966, arts 244(1) and 249(1)). No provision in the company's articles may absolve them from such liability, nor may a resolution passed by a general meeting, and a shareholder's right to sue cannot be made conditional on the approval of a general meeting (art 246). Shareholders holding one-twentieth of the company's capital may enforce the company's claim to damages by suing on its behalf (art 245 and D art 200). Under the above-mentioned Bill, any shareholder or group of shareholders would be entitled to enforce the company's claim, irrespective of the fraction of the company's capital which they held.

5 Take-overs and mergers

(a) Take-overs

For various reasons, the take-over bid is comparatively rarely used for the purpose of obtaining control of a French company. Such bids are now regulated by the Stock Exchange Commission's Code of Practice on Cash and Exchange Offers (*offres publiques d'achat ou d'échange*), which was approved by the Minister of Economic Affairs, and came into force on 25th July 1978, and by Chapter II of Title VI of the General Regulations of the National Association of Stockbrokers, which also received the approval of the Minister of Economic Affairs and was published in the Official

Journal on 13th August 1978. The regulations governing take-over bids require prompt and timely disclosure by the participating companies, and emphasise the duty that directors owe to their companies and all the shareholders equally (General Regulations, art 181 and Code of Practice, Principles, and Rules B1–11). Directors are required to maintain strict secrecy once a bid has been decided on but not made public (Code of Practice, Rule A2). Any kind of artificial dealing for the purpose of manipulating prices is prohibited (Code of Practice, Rule D1). The offeror and offeree company and persons acting in concert with them must make daily declarations to the governing body (*chambre syndicale*) of the National Association of Stockbrokers during the bid period showing all transactions entered into by them in the shares of the offeror and offeree companies. This requirement extends to directors, persons holding more than 5 per cent of the capital of their company, and all other persons acting on their behalf (Code of Practice, Rule D2).

The regulations governing take-over bids are now administered by a supervisory committee presided over by the chairman of the Stock Exchange Commission, together with a representative of the Treasury and the *chambre syndicale.*

Special rules govern the purchase of controlling blocks of securities, which are also applicable where such purchases take place otherwise than on the Stock Exchange (General Regulations, arts 201–206). A person wishing to acquire a holding which will result in his acquisition of control of the company must follow the procedure required for a take-over bid or, alternatively, he must undertake to make a continuous offer to buy all the other shares of the company which are tendered to him at the same price as he will pay to acquire the controlling shareholding during a period of at least fifteen Stock Exchange daily sessions from the date of the publication of his notice of intention to acquire the controlling holding in the Stock Exchange Official Bulletin (General Regulations, art 205(1) and (2)).

(b) Mergers

A merger may take place by an existing company absorbing one or more other companies, the former company acquiring the whole of the assets of the absorbed company or companies (*fusion par absorption*), or by the creation of a new company (*fusion par creation d'une société nouvelle*) to which the assets of each of the existing companies are transferred in return for the issue of the new company's share capital to their shareholders (art 371). Mergers may be carried out between companies of different kinds (eg SA and SARL) (art 372(1)). Subject to certain special rules governing the different kinds of company, the rules for carrying out mergers between them are the same irrespective of their individual characters.

A merger scheme must be drawn up by the management organs of the companies concerned, and copies must be signed by the representatives of each company involved (art 374 and D art 254(1)). The merger scheme must include certain required particulars (D art 254(2)). A copy of the scheme must then be sent to the registrars of the commercial courts of the districts in which each of the companies involved has its registered office (art 374(1). A notice giving particulars of the scheme must be inserted in a newspaper carrying legal announcements which circulates in each of the *départements* in which the companies involved have their registered offices (art 374(2) and D art 255(2)). A similar notice must be published in BALO if any of the participating companies has appealed to the public for funds (art 374(2)).

The management of a transferor company which is an SA or an SARL must send copies of the scheme to the auditors of that company at least forty-five days before the date of the general meeting of the company called to approve the scheme (art 377 and D art 256). The auditors submit a report on the scheme which must be made available for inspection by shareholders at least fifteen days before the general meeting called to approve the terms of the merger; the report must in particular deal with the adequacy of the consideration to be given by the transferee company for the assets to be transferred (art 377 and D art 257). If the transferee company is or will be an SA or an SARL, special auditors must prepare a report containing their valuation of the assets transferred or to be transferred (arts 40, 80 and 193(2)).

All the merging companies must pass resolutions approving the merger by the same majority and with the same quorum as a resolution for the alteration of the company's statutes (arts 372(2) and 376). If there are several classes of shareholders in any of the merging companies, the merger must be approved by separate meetings of each class (art 376). The bondholders and creditors of the transferor companies are entitled under certain conditions to the immediate payment of the amounts owed to them, or alternatively, to the provision of sufficient security (arts 380–389, 197 and 207, and D arts 261–264).

A merger results in the dissolution of the transferor company or companies and the acquisition of all the assets, rights and liabilities of the transferor company or companies by the transferee company; the creditors of the transferor company or companies automatically become creditors of the transferee company (arts 381(1) and 385).

6 Dissolution and liquidation

Most of the rules relating to dissolution and liquidation apply in the same way to SAs and other types of companies and to partnerships. The dissolution of a company precedes its winding up, and is the event which gives rise to the winding up. The personality of the company survives for the purposes of the liquidation, and until the liquidation is concluded (art 391).

(a) Dissolution

Certain of the causes for dissolution are common to all kinds of companies and partnerships. Thus a company or partnership is dissolved automatically on the expiration of the term fixed by its articles for its duration, and upon the cessation of the purpose or the accomplishment of the objects for which it was formed (Civil Code, art 1865(1)). Any member of a company or partnership may apply for its judicial dissolution if he has a legitimate interest to protect (Civil Code, art 1871).

Both an SA and an SARL must be dissolved if the court so orders where accounts laid before the members of the company show that the net assets have fallen to less than one-half of the amount of the company's capital, and the members have neither resolved to dissolve the company by extraordinary resolution, nor within two years reduced the company's capital by the amount of the losses or contributed assets to bring the company's net assets up to at least one-half of its original capital. The court may allow a period of up to six months to regularise the situation (Law of 24th July 1966 governing commercial companies, arts 68 and 241, as amended by Law No 81–1162 of 30th December 1981).

The following causes of dissolution are peculiar to SAs; for causes peculiar to SARLs see p68.

(1) An SA may be dissolved by the court on the application of an interested person when the number of its members has fallen below seven for more than a year. However, the court may allow a period of up to six months in order to regularise the situation (art 240).

(2) If the capital of the company is reduced to less than the legal minimum, the company must within a year increase its capital up to that minimum or convert itself into a company or a partnership of another kind (art 71(2)). If this is not done, any interested party may apply to the court for an order dissolving it, but this application must be dismissed if the company rectifies the situation before the court reaches its decision (art 71(2) and (3)).

The dissolution of an SA, like that of any other company or partnership, must be entered in the Commercial Register (Decree of 23rd March 1967 governing the Commercial Register, art 33(2)), and be publicised in other ways (D art 270(1) and (2)).

(b) Liquidation

The rules explained below are equally applicable to SAs and other companies and partnerships, except where the contrary is stated. The liquidation of a company comprises all the operations necessary to complete its current transactions, to collect and realise its assets, to discharge its liabilities and repay its capital, and to distribute any surplus of assets among its members. A company goes into liquidation as soon as the dissolution is effective, but the dissolution takes effect in relation to third parties only as from the date when it is published in the Commercial Register (art 291(1) and (3)).

The articles of a company or an agreement between its members may provide for the appointment of liquidators and determine their powers. Certain mandatory rules are applicable to voluntary liquidations in order to secure the regularity of the liquidation proceedings and the protection of creditors (arts 391–401 and D arts 266–271).

The liquidation of a company may be ordered by the court if there are no provisions for liquidation in the articles or any agreement made between its members, and even if the articles contain provisions for liquidation, a judicial liquidation may be ordered on the application of the holders of at least one-tenth of the share capital of an SA, or on the application of any creditor of the company (art 402). If the court orders the liquidation of a company's affairs, it may appoint one or more liquidators who have the fullest powers needed to carry out the liquidation, and may at any time distribute surplus assets among the creditors (art 412). Any amount which cannot be distributed must be deposited in a bank account in the company's name (D art 280). Within six months after his appointment, the liquidator must call a special meeting of the members of the company to report on the assets and liabilities, and the progress of the liquidation.

The liquidator's final accounts must be filed with the registrar of the commercial court, accompanied by copies of the resolutions of the final liquidation meeting, or in the absence of such resolutions, the order of the court to the same effect (art 270). The liquidator must publish a notice stating that the liquidation has been concluded in the same newspaper as that in which his appointment was advertised, and if an SA has appealed to the public for funds or has a stock exchange listing, the notice must also be published in BALO (art 399).

(c) Winding up under the court's control and compulsory liquidation

The procedure for winding up a debtor's affairs under the court's control (règlement judiciaire) and for compulsory liquidation (liquidation des biens) applies to SAs and all other companies and partnerships which have ceased to pay their debts as they fall due (Law of 11th July 1967, art 1). A dissolved company may be wound up under the court's control or put into compulsory liquidation at any time before the resolution or order for the conclusion of the liquidation has been published, or within one year after it was consequently removed from the Commercial Register (Law of 11th July 1967, art 4(1)).

An order for the winding up of a company under the court's control or for compulsory liquidation is made by the commercial court on the application of the company itself or of any of its creditors, and the court may make such an order of its own motion (ibid, arts 1, 2 and 5(1)). The court will make an order that the company's affairs shall be wound up under its control if it appears that the company will be able to propose an acceptable arrangement for the discharge of its liabilities, so that it may recommence its undertaking as a solvent business: in any other case, the court must make an order for compulsory liquidation (art 7(1)). Furthermore, it is possible for the court to convert a winding up under the court's control into a compulsory liquidation at any stage in the liquidation proceedings where it appears that the company is unable to propose an arrangement acceptable to its creditors (art 7(2)). The officers who carry out the winding up or liquidation, namely the supervising judge (juge commissaire) and between one and three liquidators (syndics), are appointed by the court (arts 8 and 9).

The winding up of a company under court control and the compulsory liquidation of a company do not bring about its dissolution. Thus the president, directors, members of the executive and supervisory board and general managers of an SA and the managers of other companies and partnerships continue to hold office, unless they are disqualified by a judicial or administrative order or unless they are removed. In the case of a winding up under the court's control, the officers of the company or partnership cannot enter into transactions on behalf of the company or partnership or dispose of any of its assets without the consent of the liquidator (art 15(1)). A company which is in the course of winding up under court control may continue to carry on its business only if so permitted by the supervising judge; such permission may be given only for renewable periods of three months at a time (art 24(1)). The court may authorise a company in compulsory liquidation to carry on business only if this is required for the purpose of the liquidation, or if it is in the interests of the creditors (art 25(1)). Authorisation can only be granted for renewable periods of three months, and can be given for a total period greater than a year in exceptional cases only (art 25(2) and (3)).

Once the order for the winding up or compulsory liquidation of a company has been made, the persons who are or who have been responsible for the management or control of its affairs in law or in fact, whether directly or through intermediaries, and whether remunerated or not, may transfer their shares in the company only if so permitted by the supervising judge. As shown above, officers of the company may be made liable for its debts where its assets are insufficient to cover them (art 99(1)); the scope of a winding up under court control or a compulsory liquidation may be extended to cover them under certain circumstances (art 101(11)), and they may also be adjudged personally bankrupt where they have been guilty of certain wrongful acts (arts 105 and 111).

SOCIÉTÉ À RESPONSABILITÉ LIMITÉE (SARL)

The SARL is a far simpler form of company than the SA, and the fact that it is not governed by the legislation of 1966 in such detail gives far more scope for flexibility in drafting its constitution. However, like an SA, it is subject to the general provisions of the legislation, and to its provisions in respect of accounts, subsidiaries, mergers, dissolution and winding up, which are either the same or substantially the same for both types of companies (arts 340–422). Like an SA, an SARL is a company with limited liability as its name indicates, and its members are only liable for its debts to the extent of the consideration that they give for its shares, and not personally (art 34(1)). The following are the principal differences between an SARL and an SA:

(1) An SARL is formed by the articles of association (*statuts*) being executed by all the members (*associés*), of whom there must be at least two and who may not exceed fifty (arts 36(1) and 37). The articles must set out: (*a*) the form of the company; (*b*) its duration, which may not exceed ninety-nine years; (*c*) the name of the company, which must include the words *société à responsabilité limitée*, or the abbreviation SARL, and may include the names of one or more of its members; (*d*) the intended registered office of the company; (*e*) the nature of the company's business (*objet social*); (*f*) the capital of the company, which must not be less than 20,000F (£1,800 approximately), and must be divided into shares (*parts*) with a nominal value of 100F or a multiple thereof (art 35(1) and D art 21); (*g*) the number of shares allotted to each member and the number and value of any consideration given in cash (arts 38(1) and 40(1)). The whole of the consideration for all the shares, whether payable in cash or kind, must be furnished to the company before it is registered (art 38(1)). For this reason, there is no possibility of the present holder of shares or any person who has held them before him being liable for unpaid capital. If shares are allotted for a consideration other than cash, a report by a professionally qualified examiner (*commissaire aux apports*) appointed by the members unanimously or by the court must be attached to the articles (art 40(1) and D art 25). If the consideration in kind is worth less than the nominal value of the shares, all the members are jointly liable for the deficit if the company is wound up or sued by creditors within five years (art 40(2)).

The company comes into existence as a legal person when the articles and a declaration of compliance with the procedural requirements of the Law of 1966 are deposited at the commercial court for the locality where the company will have its registered office, and the company is registered by the official responsible for the commercial register (arts 5(1) and 6(1)). The registration of the company is then published, and copies of the documents deposited are sent to the national commercial register in the same way as for an SA.

(2) An SARL cannot issue bearer shares or bonds (art 42), and its shares can be transferred only by a written instrument of transfer notified to the company (art 48), a copy of which must be filed at the

commercial court where the company is registered (D arts 14 and 31). Moreover, a member who wishes to transfer his shares to a non-member must first obtain the consent of his fellow members who between them hold three-quarters of the company's shares; if no reply to the member's request for consent is received within three months, the consent is deemed to be refused, and the other members must buy the shares at a price fixed by an expert appointed by the court; if the purchase has not been completed within a further three months, the member who wishes to transfer his shares to the non-member may do so (art 45). These provisions apply to transfers of shares to fellow members only if the articles so provide (art 47). The articles may place other restrictions on share transfers (eg may give preemption rights to other members on a sale of shares).

(3) The rules contained in Law No 81–1162 of 30th December 1981 concerning the acquisition by a company of its own shares do not apply to SARLs. An SARL may not acquire its own shares except in order to cancel them on a reduction of capital.

(4) The business of an SARL is conducted by one or more managers (*gérants*) who must be individuals, but who need not themselves be members of the company: they are appointed by the articles or by the original members or by a subsequent meeting of members for any length of time (art 49(1) and (2)). The holders of more than one-half of the company's capital may remove a manager for any reason, but if they do so without just cause (*sans juste motif*), the company is liable to the manager in damages (art 55(1)). The court may remove a manager on the application of any member (art 55(2)). The powers of the managers may be prescribed by the articles, but if they do not define them, the managers may carry out all transactions for carrying on the company's business in the ordinary way (*actes de gestion*) and they may act separately, though any of them can forbid a transaction proposed by another (arts 13 and 49(3)). The company is, however, bound by a transaction entered into by any manager with an outsider if it is within the company's objects, and restrictions on the powers of the managers in the articles are ineffective against outsiders (arts 14 and 49(3)).

(5) An SARL must hold an annual meeting within six months after the end of each financial year to approve the annual accounts and the managers' annual report (art 56(1)). The meeting is called by at least fifteen days' clear notice being sent to each member, accompanied by a copy of the annual accounts and the managers' and auditors' reports (D arts 36 and 38). The accounts must be audited by one or more professionally qualified auditors chosen

from the same list of qualified accountants as for SAs and appointed by a meeting of members; if the capital of the company does not exceed 300,000 F, a single auditor may be appointed, but if it exceeds that figure there must be at least two auditors (arts 64 and 65 and D art 43). The accounts of an SARL, unlike those of an SA, do not have to be deposited with the register of the commercial court. The position will change when legislation is introduced to conform with the Fourth Directive on Company Accounts.

(6) Other meetings of members may be held at any time, and the articles may also permit decisions to be made on the basis of the written expression of the members' wishes (art 57(1)). The holders of at least a quarter of the company's capital may requisition a meeting, and a meeting may be called on the direction of the court (art 57(3) and (4)). At all meetings, each member has one vote for each share he holds and he may appoint another member to vote for him as his proxy (art 58). Resolutions are passed by the votes of more than one-half of the company's capital, but if this majority cannot be obtained at an adjourned meeting, a resolution may be passed by a simple majority of the votes cast (art 59). Alterations of the articles require the support of the holders of three-quarters of the company's capital (art 60).

(7) Certain causes of dissolution are peculiar to SARLs, which are dissolved (a) if the membership of the company rises above fifty and is not reduced to fifty or less within two years, unless the company is converted into an SA in the meantime (art 36); or (b) if the court so orders because the capital of the company has been reduced to less than 20,000 F, and has not been increased to at least that amount within one year after the reduction, and the company has not been converted into a different form of company or partnership within that time (art 35(2)).

CHAPTER 3

ITALY

The legislation governing Italian companies is contained in Book V of the Italian Civil Code of 1942 (as subsequently amended), which extends to all forms of association intended to carry on any economic activity in common (Civil Code, art 2247). Book V therefore governs all forms of business associations, namely the partnership (*società in nome colletivo*), limited partnership (*società in accommandita semplice*), public company (*società per azioni*), public company whose directors are personally liable for its debts (*società in accommandita per azioni*), and private company (*società a responsabilità limitata*), and it also applies to civil partnerships (*società semplice*) which are formed for carrying on a non-commercial activity for gain, such as farming or a profession. Additionally, it is possible to form joint ventures which are not partnerships (*associazione in participazione*); these are governed by Title VII of Book V of the Civil Code, and are not treated as a type of company. This chapter will deal only with public and private companies, both of which are companies whose assets (including unpaid capital) alone are liable for satisfaction of their debts, so that their members' liability is limited to the amount unpaid on their shares (Civil Code, arts 2325(1) and 2472(1)). The law governing public and private companies was reformed by the Law of 7th June 1974 (No 216). This reform, although somewhat limited in scope, covers a number of important matters. Its most significant feature consists of the creation of an independent agency, called the National Commission for Companies and the Stock Exchange (*Commissione Nazionale per le Società e la Borsa* – CONSOB), entrusted with the task of supervising the activities of public companies whose shares are listed on one or more Italian stock exchanges.

Only the First Directive of the Council of Ministers of the European Communities on the harmonisation of company law has been implemented by legislation in Italy.

Except in the parts which deal with bankruptcy and compulsory administrative liquidation proceedings, the articles referred to by number in this chapter are articles of the Italian Civil Code, unless otherwise stated.

SOCIETÀ PER AZIONI (SpA)

1 Formation

Italian law differs from that of most other European countries in that two documents are, or may be, required to set out the constitution of a public or a private company. In the case of a *società per azioni* (SpA) the first of these documents, the *atto costitutivo*, must be executed by the founders, who must be at least two in number (art 2247), in the presence of a notary, and must set out (Civil Code, art 2329(1)):

1 Particulars of the founders and the number of shares subscribed by each of them.
2 The name of the company, which must include the words *società per azioni* or the abbreviation SpA (art 2326) and the address of its registered office, and, if applicable, of its branch offices.
3 The nature of the company's business (*l'oggetto sociale*).
4 The share capital of the company, which must not be less than 200 m lire, (£85,500 approximately) (art 2327).
5 The nominal value of the shares (*azioni*) into which the company's capital is divided, each share having the same nominal value, and whether the shares will be in registered or bearer form (art 2348(1)).
6 The value of assets contributed in kind for the allotment of shares.
7 Any provisions governing the distribution of profits, including provisions for the benefit of founders and promoters.
8 The number of directors and auditors to be appointed, and the powers of the directors.
9 The duration of the company, in order to establish when it will be considered as dissolved by lapse of time or by reference to the fulfilment of one or more stated conditions or by the occurrence of one or more stated events.

If the company's share capital is to exceed 2,000 m lire, the prior approval of the Italian Treasury must be obtained before proceeding with the formation (Law No 428 of 3rd May 1955 as amended by the Law of 16th December 1977 (No 904) art 14(1)). The remaining provisions of a company's constitution may be set out in the *atto costitutivo* or in a separate document, the *statuto*, but in the latter case, the separate document is treated for all purposes as though it were part of the *atto costitutivo* (art 2328(2)). Both documents are hereafter referred to as the articles of the company.

Like the French *société anonyme*, an SpA may be formed in one of two ways. By the first and most commonly used method, which is known as simultaneous incorporation, the founders subscribe for the whole of the company's share capital in the articles. They must pay at least three-tenths of the issue price of the shares which they subscribe for in cash into an account in the company's name at the *Banca d'Italia* (art 2329(1)) and obtain a report verified on oath by an expert appointed by the president of the local civil court as to the value of the consideration in kind to be given by them for the remainder of the company's shares (art 2343(1)). Since shares cannot be issued at a discount (art 2346), the report must show that the value of that consideration is at least equal to the nominal value of the shares to be allotted for it. The next step is for the notary who attested the articles to send them together with the acknowledgment of payment by the *Banca d'Italia* and the expert's report to the local civil court, which, after ensuring that the documents are formally in order, directs that the company shall be registered in the register of business kept by it (art 2330(1), and (3)), whereupon the company is incorporated (art 2331(1)). The articles of an SpA and certain other particulars relating thereto must be published in the companies gazette (*Bulleteino officiale delle società per azioni e delle società a responsabilità limitata*), which is an annex to the Official Journal of the Italian Republic (arts 2330 *bis* and 2457 *bis*). A summary of the articles of an SpA and certain other matters must also be published in the Bulletin for Legal Notices (*Foglio di Annunzi Legali*).

The second method of incorporation, which is now practically obsolete, is for the promoters to issue a prospectus inviting the public to subscribe for the company's shares (art 2333(1)). In that case, application forms must be signed by subscribers and notarially attested (art 2333(3)), the shares must be allotted, and the subscribers must pay at least three-tenths of the issue price to the *Banca d'Italia* (art 2334); a meeting of subscribers must be held to approve the articles of the company by a resolution passed by a majority of those present (half the subscribers constitute a quorum, and each subscriber has one vote) (art 2335), and all the subscribers present at the meeting must execute the articles (art 2336). The remaining steps leading to incorporation are the same as if the founders subscribed for the whole share capital, and the same steps must be taken with regard to shares allotted for a consideration other than cash. The prospectus need contain only the barest information about the company and its undertaking (art 2333); however, this is increased where the company applies for a stock exchange listing for its shares (Presidential Decree of 31st March 1975 (No 138), art 8). The promoters who issue the prospectus are absolutely liable to the company and its subscribers for the accuracy of its contents and for the existence of the assets for which shares are allotted otherwise than for cash, and the law also obliges them to take up and pay for those shares offered by the prospectus for which the public do not subscribe (art 2339(1)).

2 Shares and bonds

(a) Shares

The company is a legal person, and so it alone is liable to perform its obligations (arts 2325(1) and 2331(1)). Its shareholders (*soci*) are only liable to contribute to the extent of the unpaid part of the nominal value or higher issue price of their shares. If all the shares become vested in one person, the company is not dissolved, but the sole shareholder is liable to contribute without limit to satisfy the company's obligations incurred when he is a sole shareholder (art 2362).

The unpaid part of the issue price of shares may be made payable by instalments or left at call. If a shareholder fails to pay a call or instalment, the directors may sell his shares on his behalf through a stockbroker or a bank, or if they are unsaleable, may forfeit them; the company may then sue the former shareholder for the difference between the issue price of the shares and the amount realised on the sale, or the amount already paid up on the shares as the case may be (art 2344(1) and (2)). Persons who transfer partly paid shares remain liable for calls made thereon within three years after the transfer is registered, if the calls cannot be recovered from the present holder (art 2356). If shares on which calls or instalments are unpaid are not sold by the company during the financial year in which the default occurred, they must be cancelled and the company's capital correspondingly reduced (art 2344(3)). No voting rights may be exercised in respect of shares on which calls are in arrear (art 2344(4)).

The Civil Code provides that the fully paid shares of an SpA may be in registered or bearer form at the choice of the shareholders of the company, unless the articles expressly require them to be in registered form (art 2355(1) and (3)), but subsequent legislation has severely restricted the use of bearer shares. At present the only shares which may be issued in this form are savings shares (*azioni di risparmio*) (Law No 216 of 7th June 1974, art 14(4)). When shares have been issued for a non-cash consideration, certificates may not be issued in respect of them until the directors and auditors have verified that the value of the consideration is not less than the amount stated in the expert's report filed on the company's incorporation: if the directors' and auditors' valuation is less than four-fifths of the expert's, the number of shares allotted to the shareholder in question must be reduced correspondingly (art 2343(2) and (3)), so that the loss falls on him and not on the shareholders generally. The post-incorporation valuation of the non-cash consideration must be carried out within six months after the company is registered (art 2343(2)).

A company may issue shares carrying different rights (art 2348(2)), but the freedom to do so is subject to certain restrictions where the difference in question concerns the right to vote. Shares with plural voting rights are now generally prohibited, but shares carrying limited voting rights are permitted provided that they carry preferential rights in the distribution of profits and the repayment of capital: the total nominal value of such shares may not exceed half of the issued capital of the company (art 2351(2)). Preference shares (*azioni privilegiate* or *azioni di priorità*) are not frequently encountered in Italy. Savings shares (*azioni di risparmio*) are a special class of preference shares which have been recognised by the Law No 216 of 1974. They may only be issued by companies whose ordinary shares are listed on a stock exchange, and their holders have no right to attend and vote at the company's general meetings (Law No 216 of 1974, arts 14(1), 14(5) and (6). The total nominal values of savings shares and preference shares carrying limited voting rights under art 2351(2) of the Civil Code may not exceed half the company's capital (Law No 216, art 14(2)). Savings shares must carry preferential rights in the distribution of profits and on the repayment of capital (Law No 216, arts 14(3) and 15(1)). The preferential dividend will be 5 per cent or the higher percentage fixed by the company's articles and is cumulative for two years following the year in which it should have been paid. Additionally the holders of savings shares are entitled to a further noncumulative participating dividend which ensures that the total paid to them exceeds the dividend paid on the ordinary shares by 2 per cent (Law No 216, art 15(1)–(4)).

A company may reimburse the capital paid up on shares out of profits, and the reimbursed shares (*azioni di godimento*) then carry no voting rights unless the articles otherwise provide, carry the right to an equal dividend with non-reimbursed shares only after interest at the current legal rate has been paid on the latter, and participate in surplus assets on a liquidation only when capital on non-reimbursed shares has been repaid (art 2353). Such shares are rarely encountered in practice. The same is true of employees' shares, which are allotted to the employees of a company on an increase of capital by the reservation to them of a preferential right of subscription (art 2441(7)), or allotted to them on the capitalisation of a fraction of the company's profits (art 2349). Such shares are governed by any special rules set out in the articles of the company relating to their form, the method of transferring them, and the rights vested in their holders (art 2349(1)).

Registered shares are transferred by the transferor requesting the company by a notarised document to enter the name of the transferee in its register of shareholders and surrendering the share certificate for this purpose, or by the transferor executing a notarised instrument of transfer to the transferee and delivering his share certificate to him and the transferee presenting these documents to the company to procure his own registration (art 2022(1) and (2)). Alternatively, the transferor may endorse a note of the transfer on his share certificate (*trasferimento mediante girata*): the endorsement must name the transferee, and be signed by the transferor and attested by a notary or a stockbroker; the transferee, or the ultimate transferee if there is a chain of such endorsements, may present the share certificate to the company and require it to register him as holder of the shares (art 2023). The person shown in the company's register of shareholders and the current share certificate as the holder of the shares is entitled to them even if the title of his transferor was defective (art 2021), unless he acquired the shares in bad faith (art 1994). Bearer shares are transferable by delivery (art 2003) and the transferee obtains a good title to them if he acts in good faith, whether he gives value for them or not (art 1994). An SpA which registers a transfer which is forged or which has been procured by fraud is liable to the former holder in damages only if it was negligent in not discovering the defect (art 2022(4)).

The articles of an SpA may impose restrictions on the transfer of shares (art 2355(3)), and it has been held by the Italian Supreme Court that such a restriction is valid if it gives the board of directors an absolute right to refuse to register a transfer without giving reasons (Giur ital, 1958 15 48), or if it subjects transfers to rights of pre-emption by the shareholders (Dir fall, 1959 2 904).

Where there is an issue of new shares on an increase of capital, the existing shareholders or convertible bondholders have, as a rule, a right of preferential subscription (art 2441 as amended by Law No 216 of 1974). This right is inapplicable to shares to be allotted for a consideration in kind (art 2441(4) as amended). It may be waived with the approval of the holders of not more than half of the issued share capital of the company where the interests of the company so require (art 2441(5) as amended). Furthermore, where the new shares are offered for subscription by the employees of the company pursuant to a resolution of an extraordinary general meeting (see p82), the shareholders' subscription rights may be waived in respect of not more than one-quarter of the new shares: the approval of the holders of not more than one-half of the issued capital of the company is necessary if the waiver extends to more than one-quarter of the new shares (art 2441(7) as amended). The waiver of preferential subscription rights in respect of shares issued on the conversion of convertible bonds is necessary, and the law provides that a conditional increase of capital to satisfy the conversion rights of bondholders must be resolved on when the shareholders in general meeting approve the issue of the bonds (art 2420 *bis* (2)). Normally, a resolution by a general meeting increasing capital must be passed at the time the new shares are issued, for Italian law, like German and French, does not generally accept the possibility of a company's capital comprising unissued shares. It is possible, however, for the articles to reserve a certain number of shares to be issued at the discretion of the directors within one year after the company's incorporation, and such a power may also be conferred for one year at a time afterwards by the shareholders in general meeting appropriately amending the articles (art 2443).

Except on a properly authorised reduction of capital, an SpA may only purchase its own shares out of its profits and with the consent of the shareholders in general meeting: such acquired shares carry no right to vote or to payment of a dividend so long as they are owned by the company (art 2357). An SpA may not make a loan on the security of shares issued by it, nor may it make a loan to facilitate subscriptions or purchases of its own shares. Furthermore, a controlled or subsidiary company may not subscribe for or purchase shares of its controlling or parent company, whether this is an SpA or an SRL, unless the subscription or purchase is made out of the controlled company's reserves other than its statutory reserve. In no case may a controlled company purchase shares of its controlling company which are not fully paid (art 2359 *bis* (1), introduced by the Law of 7th June 1974). A controlled company may not exercise the voting rights attached to shares held by it in its controlling company (art 2359 *bis* (2)). Shares of a controlling company which are subscribed for or purchased or held by a controlled company in violation of the prohibitions contained in art 2359 *bis* (1) must be sold within the prescribed time limits: otherwise the court will order their sale on application being made by the auditors (art 2359 *bis* (3)). A company, whether an SpA or an SRL, is considered as being controlled by another company in three situations, namely:

1 When the other company holds enough of its shares to be able to cast a majority of the votes which may be cast at an ordinary general meeting.

2 When the company is subject to the dominant influence of the other company in consequence either of the number of shares the latter holds, or of particular contractual commitments entered into with the other company.

3 When the other company holds a controlling shareholding in a third company which itself controls the company in question under 1 or 2.

In the case of companies whose shares are listed on a stock exchange, additional and more stringent rules have been introduced by the Law No 216 of 7th June 1974. An SpA or an SRL which holds more than 2 per cent of the issued share capital of a company whose shares are listed on a stock exchange must give written notice to the latter company and to CONSOB. The same duty of disclosure is placed on an SpA whose shares are listed on a stock exchange in respect of any shareholding in an SpA whose shares are not listed or in an SRL if the holding exceeds 10 per cent of the issued share capital of that company. Changes in such notifiable holdings which exceed certain limits must also be notified. A shareholding company may not exercise voting rights in respect of shares for which the prescribed notification has not been given (Law No 216 of 7th June 1974, art 5(1)).

When there are mutual shareholdings between companies which on both sides exceed the percentages calling for notification, the company which first receives notice from the other company is prohibited from exercising voting rights attached to the excess shares which it holds in the other company, and it must sell or otherwise dispose of the shares within twelve months of receiving a notice from the other company of its holding (Law No 216 of 7th June 1974, art 5(2)). If notices of mutual shareholdings are received by both companies on the same date, the suspension of voting rights and the duty to dispose of the holding applies equally to both companies, unless they agree on a different mode of adjustment which is immediately notified to CONSOB (Law No 216 of 7th June 1974, art 5(2)).

Non-voting shares are not taken into account for the purpose of calculating the percentage of a company's shareholding in another company, but shares held through controlled companies, fiduciary companies and nominees must be taken into account for this purpose (Law No 216 of 7th June 1974, art 5(4)).

An SpA may not issue shares to another company in consideration of a reciprocal issue of that company's shares to it (art 2360).

(b) Bonds

An SpA may issue bonds (*obbligazioni*) only if authorised by an extraordinary meeting of its shareholders (art 2365). The nominal value of all its outstanding bonds must not exceed its paid up share capital unless the bonds are secured on land owned by the company or on Government securities, but the Minister of the Treasury may waive this restriction for any particular issue (art 2410). Furthermore, the total amount an SpA raises by issuing bonds must not exceed 500m lire unless the Treasury Minister consents (Law No 428, 3rd May 1955, art 1). Bonds may be in registered or bearer form (art 2410(1)), and the rules set out above in respect of the transfer of registered or bearer shares apply equally to them. Bonds may be secured by a mortgage of the company's movable or immovable property, but it is not possible for a floating charge over the whole of the company's undertaking to be created. Bondholders may hold meetings to resolve on the appointment or dismissal of a bondholders' representative (*rappresentante commune*), to consent to variations in the terms of the bonds, and to resolve on other matters of common interest (art 2451(1)). The directors or the representative may call a bondholders' meeting at any time, and it must be called on the requisition of the holders of one-twentieth of the outstanding bonds (art 2415(2)). The representative of the bondholders is appointed for not more than three years by a meeting of bondholders, or if they fail to appoint one, by the court; he may not be a director, auditor or employee of the company (art 2417). His duties are to give effect to the resolutions passed by the shareholders (eg that he shall realise their security) and generally to protect their interests (art 2418). The appointment of a representative does not prevent individual bondholders from suing the company on their bonds, provided that the action is not inconsistent with a resolution passed by the bondholders' meeting (eg a resolution for a moratorium) (art 2419). If an SpA reduces its capital after issuing bonds, it must redeem a proportionate amount of the bonds at the same time (art 2412).

Companies may issue various categories of bonds having special features. Convertible bonds are the most important of these categories, and are subject to express statutory regulation (art 2450 *bis*, introduced by the Law No 216 of 7th June 1974). An issue of convertible bonds requires the approval of an extraordinary general meeting of the issuing company (art 2420 *bis* (1)), which must also approve an increase of capital of an amount equal to the aggregate nominal value of the shares which would be issued if the bondholders' conversion rights were fully exercised (art 2420 *bis* (2)). The existing shareholders have a preferential right of subscription for an issue of convertible bonds (art 2441 *bis* (1)).

3 Management and control

(a) Directors

The company's affairs are managed by one or more directors (*amministratori*) appointed for periods not exceeding three years by the shareholders in general meeting or, in the case of the first directors, by the articles (arts 2380(2) and 2381(1) and (2)). Directors need not be members of a company. The better view appears to be that companies and other corporations may be directors of another company, although some authors deny this possibility. The shareholders may reappoint a retiring director and may remove a director from office by a resolution in general meeting, but without prejudice to his right to damages if there is no just cause for his dismissal (art 2383(3)). The board must appoint one of its members to be its chairman (*presidente*) unless the shareholders in general meeting have already done so (art 2380(4)). The chairman's function is merely to preside at board meetings: he has no independent executive functions conferred by law, like the president of a French *société anonyme*.

The board of directors (*consiglio di amministrazione*) exercises its powers by the vote of a majority of its members at board meetings, the quorum of which is a majority of the directors personally present (art 2388). If the articles so provide or a general meeting so resolves however, the board may delegate any of its powers to one or more of its members, other than its powers to issue shares and to prepare annual accounts and the directors' annual report (art 2381). In practice, the powers of day-to-day management are usually delegated to a managing director (*direttore* or *direttore generale*) or to several managing directors (*comitato esecutivo*) in the same way as to the managing director of a British company, and often the managing director or one of them is the same person as the chairman of the board. A company is bound to third parties by all the acts of its board of directors or the body to which the appropriate power has been delegated, whether the act falls within the objects of the company and conforms to the restrictions on directors' powers in its articles, or not. Restrictions on powers of representation imposed by the articles have no effect on third parties even if they are published, unless it is proved that the latter acted knowingly to the detriment of the company (art 2384 (2)).

The remuneration of non-executive directors is fixed by the articles or the general meeting. The remuneration of the non-executive directors is fixed by the board of directors after consultation with the auditors: it consists of a salary or a share of the company's profits (arts 2389 and 2431). Directors and auditors of companies whose shares are listed on the stock exchange must declare annually to CONSOB the aggregate amount of remuneration of any kind whatsoever received from the company or its subsidiaries (Law No 216 of 7th June 1974, art 17). Directors must exercise the diligence of commercial agents (*mandatari*) in managing the company's affairs, and, in particular, a director is liable to the company in damages if he fails to supervise the management of its business properly (so that absence from board meetings or failure to check a managing director's report may entail liability), or if he fails to do everything within his power to avert loss or harm which he knows threatens the company; however, a director may avoid liability for an improper transaction resolved on by the board by recording his dissent in the minutes and notifying the company's auditors (art 2392).

A director may not take part in the management of a business which competes with the company's, nor be a partner in a competing firm or a director of a competing *società in accommandita per azioni*; if he does any of these things, he may be dismissed from his directorship and is also liable for damages (art 2390).

A director who has a personal interest in a transaction concerning the company must disclose his interest to his fellow directors and the auditors, and must not speak or vote at the board meeting which resolves on the transaction; failure to do this involves the director in liability for damages, but the transaction cannot be set aside if the other party entered into it in good faith (art 2391). As security for performance of the board's duties, each director must deposit with the company a mortgage or charge on registered shares in it or on registered securities issued or guaranteed by the state amounting to one-fiftieth of the company's share capital or with a nominal value of at least 200,000 lire, whichever is the less (art 2387(1)). The shares (*azioni di garanzia*) are transferable notwithstanding the mortgage, but it is still enforceable by the company against the transferee to recover compensation for the board's defaults, and it can be cancelled only when the annual general meeting which is held immediately following the director ceasing to hold office has approved the accounts covering his last period in office (art 2383(3)). Failure by a director to deposit an appropriate mortgage of registered shares within thirty days after his appointment results in him ceasing to be a director (art 2387(2)).

An action for breach of a director's duties may be brought in the company's name if the shareholders in general meeting so resolve, and if the holders of at least one-fifth of the company's share capital vote for the resolution, the director is also automatically dismissed (art 2393(1) and (3)). Directors may only be released from liability for a breach of duty if a shareholders' meeting so decides by a resolution from which the holders of not more than one-fifth of the company's share capital dissent (art 2393(4)). Also individual shareholders may sue directors for the diminution in the value of their shares caused by the directors' fraud or negligence (arts 2043 and 2395), and individual creditors may sue the directors for the loss caused to them by the directors wrongfully disposing of the company's assets (eg by paying a dividend out of capital) (art 2394(1)), or by any other fraudulent or negligent acts (Supreme Court, Dir fall 2 385).

(b) Committee of auditors

Every SpA must have a committee of three or five auditors (*collegio sindacale*) appointed for periods of three years by shareholders in general meeting, or in the case of the first auditors, by the articles (arts 2397(1) and 2400(1)). If the company's share capital is not less than 500m lire, one of the three auditors, or two of the five auditors, must be public accountants (*revisiori ufficiale dei conti*), and in the case of the smaller companies, one of the auditors (*sindaci*) must be a professionally qualified accountant.

The annual accounts of an unlisted company must be audited by the auditors, for which purpose they may inspect the company's books and require explanations from the directors (arts 2403(1) and (3)). The accounts of a listed company are subject to external control: they must be audited and certified by a duly qualified auditing firm (*società di revisione*) approved by CONSOB whose members are independent of the company and professionally qualified (Decree No 136 of 31st March 1975, arts 1, 4 and 8(2)). The board of auditors is required to report on the accounts to the general meetings of both listed and unlisted companies (art 2432(2)).

In addition, the auditors must attend board meetings, and may also attend meetings of the executive committee of the board of directors (art 2405(1)). They must carry out a quarterly check of the company's cash and investments (art 2403(2)), and may investigate any aspect of the management of the company on their own initiative; they must carry out an investigation if requested to do so by the holders of one-twentieth of the company's share capital (art 2408(2)).

The auditors have in practice adopted the role of a committee of supervision over the directors, although this is not recognised by the Italian legislation as being within their province. The system of internal supervision has been criticised as inadequate on the grounds that the method of appointment of auditors does not secure their independence, and that they sometimes lack professional competence and standing. An attempt was made in the Law No 216 of 7th June 1974 and the Decree No 136 of 31st March 1975 to remedy these and other defects in the case of listed companies by introducing two forms of external control, namely, the approval of the appointment of independent and professionally qualified auditors by CONSOB and the requirement that listed companies should disclose certain relevant information to CONSOB: for example, the submission of draft annual accounts, proposals for the amendment of the articles or the issue of bonds, and draft documents relating to mergers with other companies.

(c) General meetings

General meetings of shareholders are either ordinary meetings (*assemblea ordinaria*), or extraordinary meetings (*assemblea straordinaria*). Ordinary meetings are held annually within four

months after the end of the company's financial year (or within six
months if the articles so provide) to approve the annual accounts
and reports, to declare dividends and to appoint directors and
auditors (art 2364), and are also held at other times to deal with
matters (other than those for which an extraordinary meeting is
required) which are put within the competence of the shareholders
by law or the company's articles (art 2364(1) No 4). Since the
powers of management of the company's business are reserved to
the directors, however (art 2384), a general meeting cannot pass a
valid resolution on a management matter or instruct the directors to
exercise their powers in a particular way unless invited to do so by
the board (art 2364(1) No 4). Extraordinary meetings are called to
resolve on the issue of bonds and the alteration of the articles
(art 2365), including increases and reductions of capital (arts 2445
and 2446), mergers (art 2502), the conversion of the company into
a *società a responsabilità limitata* (art 2498) and the dissolution of
the company (art 2448).

Meetings are called by the directors (art 2366(1)), but the holders of one-fifth of the company's share capital may require the
directors to convene a general meeting and may specify the items to
be included in the agenda, and if the directors fail to call the
meeting, the president of the local civil tribunal may do so
(art 2367). The auditors must call the annual general meeting if the
directors fail to do so (art 2406), and they must call a general
meeting if they have investigated the company's affairs at the
request of the holders of one-twentieth of the company's share
capital (art 2408(2)). All meetings are called by at least fifteen days'
notice in the Official Gazette (*Gazetta Ufficiale*) setting out the
agenda of the meeting, but failure to give this notice does not
invalidate the meeting if all the shareholders attend or are represented (art 2366(2) and (3)). Members who hold at least one-fifth
of the company's capital represented at a general meeting may
declare that they are insufficiently informed as to any matter on the
agenda, and require the adjournment of the meeting for not more
than three days (art 2374). Shareholders may only participate in the
meeting if they are registered in the register of shareholders five
days before the meeting is held, or in the case of bearer shares, if
they deposit their share certificates at the company's office five days
before the meeting (art 2370). Unless the articles otherwise provide, members may appoint proxies to represent them: each appointment must be in writing and is only valid for the specific
meeting in respect of which the appointment is made (art 2372(1)

and 2373(2), as amended by Law of 7th June 1974). The full name of the proxy must appear on the proxy form (art 2372(3), as amended by Law of 7th June 1974). Shareholders may not appoint directors, auditors or employees of the company to be proxies for them, nor may they appoint as proxy a company which is controlled by the company in which they hold shares, or the directors, auditors or employees of such a controlled company. Banks and banking institutions cannot be appointed as proxies (art 2372(4), as amended by Law of 7th June 1974). A proxy cannot represent more than ten shareholders at the same meeting, or in the case of a company whose shares are listed on a stock exchange, more than 50 shareholders if the company's capital does not exceed 10,000 m lire, or more than 100 shareholders if the company's capital exceeds 10,000 m lire but does not exceed 50,000 m lire, or more than 200 shareholders if the company's capital exceeds 50,000 m lire.

A quorum at a general meeting is the holders of one-half of the company's share capital present in person or by proxy. The quorum at an extraordinary general meeting is not specified by law, but it is implied by the rule that resolutions at such a meeting must be passed by a majority representing more than one-half of the total capital of the company (art 2368). If a quorum is not present at a general meeting, the meeting must be called a second time within thirty days from the date of the first meeting, and this is done by publishing an appropriate notice in the Official Gazette at least eight days before the date of the second meeting; however, the original notice of the general meeting can set out the date of the second meeting, and there is then no need to publish separate notice of it (art 2369(1) and (2)). No quorum is required at an adjourned ordinary general meeting, but a resolution is validly passed at an adjourned extraordinary general meeting only if supported by a majority representing more than one-third of the total capital (art 2369(3)). However, a majority representing more than one-half of the total capital is required if an extraordinary general meeting is to resolve on an alteration of the objects of the company, the conversion of the company into a company of another type, the dissolution of the company before the expiration of the period for which it was formed, the transfer of its registered office abroad, the issue of preference shares (art 2369(4)), or the waiver of shareholders' preferential rights of subscription on an increase of capital (art 2441(5)).

In the case of a company whose shares are listed on the stock exchange, an extraordinary general meeting must be called a third time if a quorum for passing resolutions is not present at the first two meetings (art 2369 *bis* (1)), introduced by the Law No 216 of 7th June 1974). At the third meeting resolutions are passed by the votes of shareholders representing one-fifth of the share capital, except where the resolutions fall within art 2369(4) of the Civil Code, in which case the majority must represent more than one-third of the total capital of the company (art 2369 *bis* (2)).

As a rule each share confers on its holder the right to one vote. However, preference shares can be issued which entitle their holders to vote only at extraordinary general meetings, but such shares may not exceed one-half of the company's total share capital (art 2351(2)). Holders of savings shares may not attend or vote at any general meetings (Law No 216 of 7th June 1974, art 14(5)). Whilst shares of a company are in the ownership of the company itself, it cannot cast votes in respect of them (art 2357(2)). It is not clear whether a shareholder may exercise his voting rights as he wishes, or whether he is under a duty to vote only in conformity with the interests of the company. A shareholder is prohibited from voting at all if he has an interest in the matter under discussion which conflicts with the interests of the company, or, if he is a director, on questions concerning his duties and responsibilities: shareholders who are thus disabled from voting do not count towards a quorum (art 2373(1), (3) and (4)). If a shareholder votes in defiance of the prohibition, and the required majority for the resolution would not have been obtained without his vote, the court may set the resolution aside (art 2373(2)).

Resolutions which are not passed in accordance with the law and the articles are invalid, and may be annulled on application being made to the court where the company is registered (art 2277(2)). The prevalent opinion of the courts is that resolutions cannot be annulled under art 2277 simply because they resulted from an abuse of the power of the majority. If a resolution passed by an extraordinary general meeting alters the company's objects, or converts it into a company of a different type, or transfers its principal registered office outside Italy, any dissenting shareholder may require the company to buy out his shares at the current market price, or, if the shares are not listed on a stock exchange, at a price calculated on the basis of the company's latest balance sheet; the dissenting shareholder must exercise his right of withdrawal by giving written notice to the company within three days after the meeting, or within fifteen days if he did not attend it, but his right cannot be in any way further abridged by the articles (art 2437).

If a resolution prejudices the rights of a particular class of shareholders, it is valid only if approved by an extraordinary meeting of the shareholders of that class (art 2376(1)). This provision applies only if the rights of the class of shareholders are affected without similar rights of all shareholders being modified or abrogated equally. Thus, the Italian Supreme Court has held that the cancellation of pre-emption rights conferred on all shareholders by the original articles does not require the approval of separate class meetings (Foro ital, 1961 1 19), but, on the other hand, the alteration of the articles to permit the company to issue preference shares does necessitate the approval of the classes of shareholders whose rights in respect of dividend and capital will be subordinated to those of the preference shareholders (Foro ital, 1961 1 948).

The company's annual accounts, comprising a balance sheet and a profit and loss account and the directors' and auditors' reports, and, where the company has a stock exchange listing, the audit certificate of the external audit firm, must be made available for inspection at the company's principal office for fifteen days before the annual ordinary general meeting and must be submitted to the meeting for approval (arts 2364 No 1 and 2432 (2) and (3) and Decree of 31st March 1975, art 5(1)). Participations in controlled companies and associated companies must be listed in an annex to the balance sheet. Copies of the complete balance sheets of controlled companies and a summary of the essential parts of the balance sheets of associated companies must be attached to the balance sheet (art 2424). An associated company is a company not listed on a stock exchange in which another company has a participation of more than 10 per cent of the issued share capital, or a company listed on a stock exchange in which another company has a participation of more than 5 per cent of the issued share capital (art 2539). After approving the accounts, the meeting may declare a dividend out of the net profits shown therein (art 2434(1)), or may resolve to transfer the whole or part of the profits to reserves or carry it forward, but before a dividend is declared, at least one-twentieth of the year's profits must be transferred to statutory reserve unless it already amounts to one-fifth of the company's share capital (art 2430). An extraordinary meeting may resolve to capitalise undistributed profits or reserves and to issue new fully paid bonus shares, or alternatively, to increase the nominal value of the existing shares by the amount of the capitalisation (art 2442).

4 Provisions for the protection of shareholders

If members holding at least one-tenth of the capital of the

company, or in particularly serious cases, the Public Attorney (*Ministero Pubblico*) complain to the court that the directors or the auditors are guilty of serious breaches of duty, the court may order an investigation of the management of the company (art 2409(1), (2) and (6)). When this investigation has ended the court may, if it finds that the reported irregularities exist, order the appropriate protective measures to be taken, and require the holding of a general meeting for the purpose of passing the appropriate resolutions; in more serious cases, it may remove the directors and auditors from office, and appoint a judicial administrator to manage the company's business temporarily (art 2409(3)). Article 2409 is regarded by many Italian text-writers as providing an effective means of protecting minority shareholders.

5 Take-overs and mergers

(a) Take-overs

Law No 216 of 7th June 1974, art 18, provides a statutory basis for the legal regulation of take-over bids. Before the passing of this law, the Council of the Milan Stock Exchange had made an attempt to fill the gap in the regulation of take-over bids by issuing a Code of Conduct covering general bids for shares and bonds. The Code contains rules governing the minimum period (twenty-five days) and the maximum period (forty-five days) during which a bid must be open for acceptance; the minimum amount of the issued shares or bonds for which the bid must be made, namely 10 per cent in nominal value of the securities in question, other than those held by the offeror; control over the conduct of the bid by the Stock Exchange Committee; the possibility of competing bids; and the conduct of the directors of the offeree company. The Code is not legally sanctioned, and it only applies when the offeror makes a bid for shares of a company listed on the Milan Stock Exchange.

The Law No 216 of 7th June 1974, art 18, now provides a statutory basis for the legal regulation of take-over bids and general bids. Under this Law, any person who makes a public offer to purchase or sell shares or convertible bonds of a company must notify CONSOB by a notice containing the terms, conditions and time limit for the acceptance of the öffer. Within twenty days after receiving the offer, CONSOB may determine the manner in which it is to be made public and the information which must be included in the offer document. CONSOB may thus protect investors by requiring that all the matters affecting the price offered for shares be made public, and that information be given as to the economic and financial situation of the offeree company and as to market conditions in the field in which that company operates. Infringements of the requirements governing notification and disclosure are criminal offences punishable by fines from 2m to 20m lire.

(b) Mergers

Mergers between companies (including SpAs) of the same or different kinds are governed by arts 2501 *et seq* of the Civil Code. A merger may take place either by the formation of a new company into which the existing companies are absorbed, or by means of absorption of the existing companies by one of their number (art 2501). Merger resolutions must be passed by the general meetings of all the participating companies (art 2502). If the merger involves an increase in the capital of a participating company or the alteration in its objects, that company's merger resolution must be an extraordinary resolution. The merger resolutions must be entered in the appropriate Companies Registers and published in the Official Bulletin for SpAs and SRLs (art 2502).

A creditor who believes himself to be adversely affected by a merger may oppose the merger resolutions taking effect by bringing an action against the debtor company within three months from the registration of the merger resolutions and applying to the court to prevent the merger being carried out. The merger may only be carried out after the period of three months has elapsed if no creditor has sought to prevent it, or where any creditor has done so, if the court has rejected all the creditors' applications. However, where an application to prevent the merger has been made, the court may order that the merger may nevertheless be carried out subject to adequate security for the creditors' claims being provided by the company concerned. Furthermore, a merger may be effected before the expiry of the initial period of three months if all the creditors of the participating companies give their consent, or if those creditors who have not consented have been paid off or if the amount of their claims has been deposited with a bank.

The resolutions for a merger may be carried out if the period during which creditors may apply to the court has expired, or if all applications by creditors have been rejected by the courts, or if the court has ordered that the merger may proceed (art 2503(1)). The representatives of the participating companies execute a notarised deed, copies of which must be registered in each of the registers where the companies themselves are registered, and if the merger is to be carried out by forming a new company, in the register in which it is to be registered (art 2504). The registration of the merger resolutions has the effect of dissolving the participating companies, other than the acquiring company or the new company, and so terminating their legal personalities.

6 Dissolution and liquidation

(a) Dissolution

The grounds for the dissolution of an SpA are set out in art 2448(1) of the Civil Code, which is also applicable to SRLs and public companies with personally liable directors (arts 2497(1) and art 2464). The grounds are: (a) the expiration of the period fixed for the duration of the company by its articles; (b) the attainment of the objects of the company set out in its articles; (c) the supervening impossibility of achieving the objects of the company; (d) the continued inactivity of the general meeting; (e) the reduction of the company's capital below the statutory minimum, unless provision has been made for its restoration to the legal minimum, or the conversion of the company into a company of another type has been resolved on; (f) the passing of a resolution for dissolution by an extraordinary general meeting; (g) the occurrence of other causes of dissolution for which provision is made in the articles; and (h) the bankruptcy or the compulsory administrative liquidation of the company (arts 2443(1), 2464 and 2497).

The occurrence of a ground for dissolution results in the immediate dissolution of the company, and it is not postponed until the dissolution is registered. Within thirty days after the dissolution occurs, the directors must call a general meeting to pass the resolution required for the liquidation of the company's affairs. They must abstain from entering into new transactions, and they incur unlimited personal liability if they enter into them. The directors are also responsible for the preservation of the company's assets until they hand them over to the liquidators (art 2449).

(b) Liquidation

Unless the articles provide otherwise, the liquidators are appointed by a resolution of a general meeting passed by the majority required for a resolution passed by an extraordinary general meeting (art 2450(1) and (2)). The liquidators may do all acts necessary for the purposes of the liquidation; however, a general meeting may give them instructions as to the performance of their functions by resolutions passed by the majority required for an extraordinary general meeting (art 2252(2)). If the liquidators undertake new transactions as distinct from completing unfinished transactions, they incur unlimited personal liability (art 2279). The liquidators are entrusted with the task of realising the company's assets and satisfying its liabilities before distributing its residual assets to its members. A copy of the final balance sheet, signed by the liquidators, and accompanied by the auditors' report and a scheme for distributing the company's remaining assets, must be filed at the Companies Registry (art 2453(2)). Within three months thereafter, any member may make a claim against the liquidators for losses resulting from breaches of their duties (art 2453(3)); if several claims are made they must be consolidated and be disposed of in a single judgment which is binding on all members of the company, including those who did not intervene in the proceedings (art 2453(4)). If three months elapse without any claims being made in connection with the final balance sheet or the distribution scheme, or when any claims have been disposed of by the court, the balance sheet and the distribution scheme are deemed to be approved, and the liquidators are released from liability to the members except for their duty to distribute the company's remaining assets in conformity with the distribution scheme (art 2456(1)).

The liquidation proceedings end with the approval of the final balance sheet and the distribution scheme, and the entries in respect of the company in the Companies Register are then cancelled on the request of the liquidators. The company thereupon ceases to exist (art 2456(1)). After the date of the cancellation, any creditors whose claims have not been satisfied may recover the sums due to them only by claiming those sums from the members of the company to the extent of the payments made to them by the liquidators on the basis of the final balance sheet, or by suing the liquidators themselves if they were at fault in not paying the creditors' claims out of the company's assets (art 2456(2)).

(c) Bankruptcy and compulsory administrative liquidation proceedings

Although bankruptcy or a compulsory administrative liquidation of a company results in the dissolution of the company and the liquidation of its affairs, a liquidation in such proceedings is distinguished from the ordinary process of liquidation regulated by arts 2448 *et seq* of the Civil Code both in respect of the persons who carry it out, and the substantive rules governing it, which are contained in the Royal Decree No 267 of 16th March 1942 (hereafter referred to as the Bankruptcy Law). Bankruptcy does not entail the dissolution of the company, which remains in existence until the completion of the liquidation of its affairs.

A commercial company or a company carrying on a commercial activity which is unable to meet its liabilities as they fall due may be adjudged bankrupt (*fallimento*). The initiative for adjudication in bankruptcy may be taken by the company itself, or by one or more of its creditors, or by the Public Attorney (Bankruptcy Law, art 6). An application for adjudication in bankruptcy made by creditors of the company takes the form of a petition to the civil court with jurisdiction in the area in which the company carries on business. The directors, acting on a resolution of the general meeting of an insolvent company, are generally empowered to apply for adjudication on the company's behalf. After the court has verified that the conditions for adjudication are fulfilled and that the company is insolvent, it makes an order declaring the company to be bankrupt (Bankruptcy Law, art 16). Such an order may be appealed against, and an opposition may also be entered against it by a third party (Bankruptcy Law, art 18).

Control over the entire bankruptcy proceeding is vested in the court which made the bankruptcy order. This court has the power to appoint and replace the judge delegated to supervise the bankruptcy (*giudice delegato*) and the trustee in bankruptcy (*curatore*), who administers the assets of the bankrupt under the supervision of the judge (art 31). The ordinary organs of a bankrupt company remain in existence during the bankruptcy proceedings, and continue to perform their functions subject to the pre-eminence of the powers of the bankruptcy organs.

The Bankruptcy Law contains special provisions permitting transactions by the bankrupt to be rescinded in the interests of the creditors. All transactions entered into by a bankrupt during the two years before his adjudication are subject to rescission (arts 64, 65 and 67). A number of detailed rules exist governing incomplete legal transactions which have been entered into before bankruptcy: these rules are of considerable importance to companies (arts 72–81). The bankruptcy organs are required to take various steps and proceedings in connection with the administration of a bankrupt's assets in order to secure equality between his creditors. Bankruptcy proceedings conclude with an order of the court for the final distribution of the bankrupt's assets and the extinction of all the bankrupt's existing debts (art 117). If there is at any time an insufficiency of assets to cover the prospective costs of the bankruptcy proceedings, the court may terminate them for that reason (art 118).

Bankruptcy terminates if a scheme of arrangement becomes effective. A scheme of arrangement must be consented to by the creditors and the bankrupt, and becomes effective when approved by the court (arts 124 *et seq*). The scheme is proposed by the bankrupt, and in the case of companies it must also be approved by an extraordinary general meeting of shareholders, unless the directors are granted the necessary powers by the articles (art 152). The scheme must indicate the proportion of the bankrupt's debts which will be paid under it, and the means by which the scheme will be carried out, and it must also set out any guarantees or securities offered for this purpose. The scheme must then be approved by a majority in number of the bankrupt's creditors, who between them are entitled to at least two-thirds of the total amount of the bankrupt's indebtedness. The approval of creditors is assumed if they do not dissent within a certain period after the scheme is published. The court then verifies that all these conditions have been fulfilled, and it may approve the scheme if it considers it fair and reasonable (art 130).

A compulsory administrative liquidation (*liquidazione coatta amministrativa*) is a procedure instituted by the competent authority to wind up the affairs of certain kinds of companies carrying on civil or commercial activities when it is in the public interest to do so because of their insolvency, or because of serious irregularities in the conduct of their affairs, or because the appropriate authority considers it opportune that they should be wound up. Undertakings which are subject to a compulsory administrative liquidation are not subject to bankruptcy proceedings, unless the special law governing them otherwise provides (art 196). Although the rules relating to compulsory administrative liquidation contained in the Bankruptcy Law do not override any conflicting rules contained in the special laws governing the undertakings in question, certain of the bankruptcy rules are always applicable in a compulsory administrative liquidation, for example the rule that in the event of concurrent proceedings for a compulsory administrative liquidation and for bankruptcy, the proceedings first instituted exclude the commencement of the other proceedings (art 196).

(d) Extraordinary administration

Companies which are indebted to banks or social security institutions for a sum equal to more than five times the amount of their paid-up share capital, the amount of such debts being in excess of 20,000m lire (at least 1,000m lire of which must consist of financial aid (*finanziamenti agevolati*)) are subject to a special type of insolvency procedure, called extraordinary administration (*amministrazione straordinaria*) (Law No 95 of 3rd April 1979, art 1). If the court determines, on the application of a person entitled to apply for the company's adjudication in bankruptcy, that the company is insolvent, or that it owes wages and salaries in respect of at least three months' services to its staff, and if it finds that the requirements mentioned in the last sentence are met, the court must declare the company insolvent and refer the matter to the Minister of Industry, who will make an order determining the date of commencement of the company's extraordinary administration. Extraordinary administration may be regarded as a substitute for bankruptcy proceedings applicable to large companies in serious financial difficulties.

The order will normally provide for the continuance of the company's business by one or three receivers appointed by the Minister, for a period not exceeding two years, which may be extended by a further year. The receivers must submit a scheme for the reorganisation of the company under their management to the Minister for his approval. The opinion of the Interdepartmental Committee for Savings and Credit (*Comitato Interministeriale per il Credito ed il Risparmio*) must be sought on this scheme. If the receivers find it impossible to formulate an acceptable reorganisation scheme, the company will be placed in liquidation (Law of 3rd April 1979, art 2).

The rules governing extraordinary administration are in general the same as those governing compulsory administrative liquidation. If the company cannot be reorganised within the maximum period of three years, it must be placed in liquidation. Insolvent companies which belong to the same group as the company undergoing extraordinary administration must themselves be placed under extraordinary administration under the same receivers as the original company. The receivers have an enhanced power of securing the revocation of transactions between the company placed under extraordinary administration and other companies in the same group. Furthermore, where a company undergoing extraordinary administration is placed under the unified management (*direzione unitaria*) of another company, the liability of the directors of the former company to compensate it for damage caused to it as a result of their defective management extends as well to the directors of the company exercising unified powers of management over it. A company is treated as belonging to the same group as a company undergoing extraordinary administration: (a) where it directly or indirectly controls that company; (b) where it is directly or indirectly controlled by that company, or its parent company; (c) where by reason of the composition of its board of directors, and that of the company undergoing extraordinary administration, it is under the same unified management as that company; and (d) where it has granted loans or given guarantees to that company, or to another company within the categories (a)–(c), which amount to at least one-third of its total assets as shown on its last balance sheet (Law of 3rd April 1979, art 3(1)(a)–(d)).

SOCIETÀ A RESPONSABILITÀ LIMITATA (SRL)

The differences between an SpA and a *società à responsabilità limitata* (SRL) are not so great as the differences between public and private companies in German and French law, and consequently the SpA is employed for carrying on small and medium concerns which are never likely to make a public issue of shares or bonds to a far greater extent than the AG or the SA is used by similar concerns in Germany and France. Briefly the differences between an SpA and an SRL are as follows:

(1) The articles of an SRL must be executed by all its members (*soci*) and attested by a notary; the contents of the articles are the same as for an SpA, except that the nominal value of the share taken by each member and the consideration given by him for it must be specified, as also must the way in which the company's profits will be divided between members (art 2475(1)). The company's name must include the words '*società a responsabilità limitata*' or an abbreviation thereof (SaRL and SRL are both acceptable and are widely used) (art 2473). Its capital must be at least 20m lire (£8,800 approximately), and must be divided into shares (*quote*) of not less than 1,000 lire, and if this results in the nominal value of a share exceeding the value of any consideration in kind given for it, the difference must be paid to the company in cash (art 2474, as amended by the Law No 904 of 16th December 1977). Each member has only one share, but the nominal value of the different shares may vary. If shares are allotted for a consideration other than cash, the consideration must be valued by an expert appointed by

the court in the same way as in the case of an SpA (art 2476). At least three-tenths of the nominal value of shares allotted for cash must be paid up before the company is incorporated (art 2475(2)), and the remaining part of the issue price must be paid at the times specified in the articles, or when called up by the directors. If any such call or instalment is unpaid for thirty days after the directors serve a final demand, the directors may sell the defaulter's share to the other members or to an outsider if they will not buy it, and if no such sale can be effected, the share is cancelled, but without affecting the company's right to sue the defaulter for the instalment or call (art 2477). Shares in an SRL cannot be represented by negotiable share certificates (art 2472(2)), and cannot be transferred by endorsement and delivery of the share certificate. The shares of an SRL are transferable to other members or outsiders by a notarised deed or a privately signed document, but the articles may restrict or exclude their transferability; transfers are often made subject by the articles to the consent of the directors of the general meeting (art 2479(1)). A transfer is effective against the company only when it has been registered (art 2479(2)). A share may be divided on a transfer of part of it, but the resulting derivative shares must still have a nominal value of 1,000 lire or a multiple thereof (art 2482(2)). An SRL cannot issue bonds (art 2486(3)).

(2) The managers (*amministratori*) of an SRL are subject to the same rules as the directors of an SpA except that they may be appointed for longer periods than three years (art 2487). An SRL must have a board of auditors if its share capital is not less than 100m lire, or if the articles so provide, and the rules which govern the auditors of an SpA then apply (art 2488). If there is no board of auditors, each member is entitled to inspect the company's books and records and to require information from the managers (art 2489). Meetings of members are called by notices setting out the agenda being sent to each member at least eight days beforehand (art 2484). All members are entitled to one vote for each 1,000 lire nominal value of their shares (art 2485). A resolution is passed at ordinary meetings if the holders of more than one-half of the company's capital vote for it and at extraordinary meetings if the holders of at least two-thirds of the capital vote for it (art 2486(1) and (2)). There are no provisions for reduced majorities at adjourned meetings as in the case of an SpA. An SRL must hold annual general meetings for the approval of the annual accounts and directors' and auditors' reports in the same way as an SpA (art 2486(2)), but there is no need for the meeting to declare

dividends, for unless the articles provide otherwise the whole of the profit shown by the annual accounts is divisible rateably among the members in proportion to the nominal value of their shares (art 2492).

CHAPTER 4

THE NETHERLANDS

The account of Dutch company law which follows below is restricted to the public company (*naamloze vennootschap*) (NV) and the private company (*besloten vennootschap met beperkte aansprakelijkheid*) (BV). Dutch law also recognises the partnership (*vennootschap onder firma*) and the limited partnership (*commanditaire vennootschap*). In addition to these forms, it also recognises the company governed by civil law (*maatschap*), which is generally employed as a vehicle for cooperation between members of the independent professions, such as lawyers, accountants and tax consultants. All these three forms of association have a contractual basis. The public and the private company have a more institutional basis, and are regulated by Book 2 of the new Dutch Civil Code, which came into force on 1st July 1976, and which has been subsequently amended.

The First and Second Directives of the Council of Ministers of the European Communities on the harmonisation of company law have been implemented in the Netherlands. The requirements of the Third and Fourth Directives have not yet been implemented.

Except in the parts which deal with the Works Councils Law 1971, as amended, and with the Rules of Conduct for take-overs and mergers concerning the protection of shareholders and employees, the articles (arts) referred to by number in this chapter are articles of the Dutch Civil Code, as amended, unless otherwise stated.

NAAMLOZE VENNOOTSCHAP (NV)

1 Formation

Certain of the legal requirements governing the formation of a *naamloze vennootschap* are new, and are contained in the Law of 15th May 1981 (*Staatsblad* No 332) implementing the requirements of the Second Directive of the Council of Ministers of the European Communities on the harmonisation of company law (OJL 26/1 of 1977) in the Netherlands.

An NV may be formed by two or more persons executing the instrument of incorporation (*akte van oprichting*) in the presence of a notary (Civil Code, art 64(2)). The principal part of the *akte van oprichting* consists of the articles (*statuten*), which must set out:

1 The name of the company, which must commence or end with the words '*naamloze vennootschap*', or the abbreviation NV (art 66(1) and (2)).
2 The address of the registered office, which need not be where the main centre of the company's activities is situated, but which must be in the Netherlands (art 66(1) and (3)).
3 The objects of the company (art 66(1)).
4 The amount of the company's nominal or authorised capital; in the case of companies formed on or after 1st September 1981, the date when the Law of 1981 came into force, this must be at least Dfl 100,000 (£21,300 approximately); companies in existence before that date are given three years from that date to comply with the new requirement; the nominal capital may not be more than five times the capital issued on the company's formation (arts 67(1) and 68(2)).
5 The number and nominal values of the shares (*aandelen*), and if these are divided into different classes, such particulars in relation to each of these classes: particulars of the nominal and paid up capital must be included in the instrument of incorporation (art 67(1)).
6 Whether the shares are in registered or bearer form (art 82(1)).
7 Provisions concerning the provisional management of the company in the event of the absence of a managing director or his inability to act (art 134(4)).

The names of the first managing directors of the company must be set out in the instrument of incorporation: subsequent managing directors are appointed by the general meeting, or in the case of a large company, by the supervisory board (art 132(1)).

Full particulars of legal transactions (*a*) in connection with the subscription for shares whereby special obligations are imposed on the company; (*b*) relating to the issue of shares or other securities on terms different from those on which the public are invited to subscribe for the company's shares; (*c*) relating to any special advantages granted to a promoter or person connected with the

formation of the company, must appear in the instrument of
incorporation, or an original or authentic copy of the instrument
setting out the transaction, making reference to the instrument of
incorporation, must be attached thereto (art 94).

When shares are issued for a non-cash consideration, the founders must make a report describing the assets contributed in payment
for the shares, and stating their value and the methods used to
determine it, which must conform to normal commercial practice.
The report must relate to the condition of the property at a date not
more than five months before the formation of the company
(art 94a(1)). It must be signed by all the founders and be attached to
the notarial instrument. A registered and qualified accountant is
also required to make a report stating that the value of the consideration given is at least equal to the nominal value plus any issue
premium for the shares (art 94a(2)). The valuation and report may
be dispensed with if 90 per cent in nominal value of the shares are
issued to one or more companies to whose accounts the special rules
governing large companies are applicable. The companies in question must have non-distributable reserves equal to the nominal
value of the shares issued to them, and they must guarantee the
debts of the issuing company which are incurred between the time
when the shares are issued and one year after the publication of the
annual accounts for the year during which the non-cash consideration was furnished (art 94a(3)).

The incorporation of the company is subject to a declaration of no
objection from the Ministry of Justice (art 68(1)). In practice, this is
obtained before the execution of the notarial instrument. Such a
declaration may only be refused on the ground that, in view of the
intentions or the past conduct of those who will determine or help
determine the company's policy, a serious danger exists that the
company will be used for an unlawful purpose, or that its activities
will be carried out in a manner prejudicial to creditors, or that its
notarial instrument contains provisions which are contrary to law,
morals or public order, or that it is not shown that those who form
the company will hold at least one-fifth of the authorised capital. A
company comes into existence and obtains its legal personality
when the declaration of no objection by the Ministry of Justice has
been issued, and the notarial instrument constituting the company
has been signed by the founders.

When the declaration of no objection has been given, the company must be registered in the Commercial Register which is kept
by the local Chamber of Commerce under the Commercial Register

Law of 1918. The managing directors are responsible for registering the company (art 69(1)). After registration the Chamber of Commerce advertises the incorporation of the company in the official gazette (*Nederlandse Staatscourant*) (Law of 1918, art 30a(1)). Until registration has occurred, and the paid up capital amounts to at least Dfl 100,000, and at least 25 per cent of the nominal value of each share subscribed by the founders has been paid up, each managing director is jointly and severally liable together with the company for debts and obligations incurred in its name. The new requirement will not affect managing directors of existing companies until a transitional period of three years has elapsed (art 69(2)).

2 Shares, other securities and bonds

(a) Shares and bearer certificates

The company is a legal person distinct from its shareholders, and they are only liable to contribute to its debts to the extent of the amount unpaid on their shares (art 64(1)). Shares may not be issued at a discount, except where they are allocated to underwriters, in which case a discount of up to 6 per cent may be allowed as underwriting commission (art 80(1) and (2)). The amount of the capital subscribed on formation must be at least one-fifth of the authorised capital, being not less than Dfl 100,000 (art 68(2) and 69(2)). One-quarter of the nominal value of each share subscribed for on formation, being not less than Dfl 100,000, must be paid up (art 69(2)). Companies in existence on 1st September 1981 are given three years to comply with the latter requirement. Shares paid for in kind must be fully paid as soon as possible after they are issued (art 80b). Each former holder of partly paid shares remains jointly and severally liable to the company for the amount of the issue price which remains unpaid, unless the board of management and the supervisory board have explicitly released the previous holder from further liability. Where this is done, a previous holder remains liable only in respect of unpaid capital falling due or paid up within one year after the date of the transfer (art 90(1)).

The special rules applicable when shares are issued for a non-cash consideration on the incorporation of the company have been described above. Similar rules are applicable when shares are issued for a non-cash consideration after incorporation (art 94b). Furthermore, the acquisition of assets within two years after the incorporation of the company from one of the promoters or from a participation in the foundation of the company for a consideration amounting to not less than one-tenth of the subscribed capital requires the approval of the general meeting. The company must make a report on the arrangements, which must contain a valuation of the assets. A report and valuation of the assets is also required from a registered and qualified accountant (art 94d).

Shares may be in registered or bearer form, but bearer certificates may be issued only when the shares are fully paid (art 82(3)). Registered shares are transferred by the transferor or transferee delivering an instrument of transfer to the company, or by a written acknowledgment of the transfer being issued by the company after an instrument of transfer has been submitted to it (art 89(1)). Where partly paid registered shares are transferred, the company's acknowledgment of the transfer may be given only if the instrument of transfer bears a fixed date (art 86(1)). The names and addresses of the holders of registered shares are recorded in a register which must be kept by the company (art 85(1)). Only the contents of the register concerning partly paid shares are open to the public inspection (art 83(4)). The company is estopped from claiming against a subsequent *bona fide* holder of a bearer share certificate which has been issued without full payment of the issue price that the shares in question have not been fully paid up. It is also estopped from claiming against a *bona fide* holder of registered shares that the shares have not been paid up to the extent appearing on the certificate representing them (art 83).

In addition to shares in registered or bearer form, shares in Dutch companies are often represented by bearer certificates (*certificaten*) for whole shares or fractions of shares issued by an *administratiekantoor*, which is usually a subsidiary of a bank or an associated company of the NV in which the original shares are held. An *administratiekantoor* is the legal owner of the shares which it holds, and it acts as a trustee for the certificate holders to whom it pays the dividends received on the shares. The terms of issue of the *certificaten* determine whether or not a certificate holder may exchange his *certificaten* for a share in the company. A certificate holder is not a shareholder and has no voting rights at general meetings. However, the holders of *certificaten* issued by an *administratiekantoor* with the consent of the company concerned are allowed to attend general meetings of the company and speak thereat, and, like the same fraction of shareholders, the holders of such *certificaten* representing 10 per cent of the company's capital have the right to convene a general meeting (arts 110(2) and 117(2)). In addition, the holders of *certificaten* issued with the consent of the company are entitled to receive without charge a copy of the annual accounts when the annual general meeting to receive those accounts has been called (art 103(3)).

No distribution may be made out of the company's profits if, on the closing date of the last financial year, the net assets as set out in the company's accounts are, or following such a distribution, would become of a lesser value than the amount of the subscribed capital plus those reserves which may not be distributed under the law or the articles (art 105(2) and (3)). The appropriation of the profits as shown by the accounts after they have been confirmed and approved by the general meeting (art 101), or in the case of a company fully subject to the rules governing large companies, by the supervisory board (art 163), is effected by a resolution of the annual general meeting. The articles usually give the directors power to transfer profits to reserve with the approval of the supervisory board.

The Law of 15th May 1981 implemented the provisions of the Second Directive relating to preferential subscription rights and the purchase by a company of its own shares. Article 96a of the Civil Code, which was incorporated into the Code by the Law of 1981 provides that, if an NV increases its capital by consideration in cash, its existing shareholders have the right to subscribe for the newly created shares before they are offered to outsiders. Unless the articles provide otherwise, this preferential subscription right is not applicable to shares which carry only a limited right to participate in profits, or in the company's assets in the event of a liquidation. The other shareholders have no preferential subscription rights in respect of the latter types of shares, unless the articles determine otherwise. The offer of the preferential subscription rights and the period within which they must be exercised must be published in the *Staatscourant* and in a newspaper having a national circulation unless all the company's shares are in registered form. In the latter case, all the company's shareholders must be informed in writing of the offer. The preferential subscription rights may be limited or excluded by a resolution passed in general meeting by a majority of not less than two-thirds of the votes attaching to the shares; a simple majority is sufficient when at least half the subscribed capital is represented at the meeting. The articles or the general meeting may give power to limit or exclude the preferential subscription rights to the organ of the company which is empowered to decide on an increase of the subscribed capital within the limits of the authorised capital for a period not exceeding five years (art 96(1)).

The above rules are applicable to the issue of securities which are convertible into shares or which carry the right to subscribe for shares, but not to the conversion of such securities or to the exercise of the right to subscribe for them (art 96a). In the case of companies existing on 1st September 1981, the above rules only become applicable eighteen months after that date (Law No 332 of 1981, art 9(1)). If, both on 1st September 1981 and eighteen months thereafter, the articles of the company stipulate that an organ of the company other than the general meeting is authorised to issue shares, that organ retains its authority until 1st September 1986, unless the articles are amended before that date (Law No 332 of 1981, art 9(2)).

The company is not permitted to subscribe for its own shares (art 95). An acquisition by the company of its own fully paid shares is void, unless it takes place as the result of a universal transfer of assets (art 98(1)). However, a company may acquire its fully paid shares where it is permitted to do so by its articles, and the general meeting, which is required to discuss the terms and conditions of such acquisitions, authorises the managing directors to acquire them on the company's behalf. The maximum period for which the authorisation can be given is eighteen months. The total amount of the shares so acquired may not exceed one-tenth of the company's subscribed capital. The acquisition is only permissible if the net assets of the company less the sum paid for the shares is at least equal to the amount of the subscribed capital plus those reserves which may not be distributed under the law or the articles (art 98(2) and (3)). None of the restrictions on the acquisition of shares apply where a company accepts a gratuitous transfer of its own shares, or acquires them as the result of a universal transfer of assets (art 98(2) and (5)). They are also inapplicable to the acquistion of its own shares by an investment company with a variable capital. The issued capital of such a company reduced by the value of the shares which it holds in itself must amount to at least one-tenth of its authorised capital (art 98(7)). In addition, an authorisation by the general meeting is not necessary when the company's articles permit the company to acquire its own shares for distribution to its employees, or to the employees of an associated company, and the shares in question must be listed on the stock exchange (art 98(4)). The provisions relating to the acquisition by a company of its own shares are also applicable to *certificaten.*

The acquisition by a company of its own registered shares in contravention of the provisions of art 98(2) and (3) is void. The managing directors are jointly and severally liable to a vendor who sells registered shares in good faith, and suffers a loss owing to this invalidity (art 98a(1)). If a company acquires bearer shares or *certificaten* in contravention of art 98(2) and (3), they are transferred automatically to the managing directors at the time of such acquisition. The managing directors are then jointly and severally liable to pay the company the purchase price of the shares together with legal interest from the date of acquisition (art 98a(2)). If a company, after having been converted into a public company or after it has accepted a gratuitous transfer of its own shares or has acquired them as the result of a universal transfer of assets, holds fully paid up shares in itself having a total value of more than one-tenth of the issued capital for a period of three years, any of the shares still held by the company at the end of the three years is transferred to the managing directors. Each managing director is jointly and severally liable to the company for the value of the shares on that date, together with legal interest therefrom. The same rule is applicable to *certificaten* (art 98a(3)).

The requirement of the consent of the general meeting to the acquisition by a company of its own fully paid shares (except in the case of gratuitous acquisitions of shares and acquisitions as the result of a gratuitous transfer of assets) contained in art 98(3), will not be applicable for a period of eighteen months to acquisitions of their own shares by companies in existence on 1st September 1981 (Law No 332 of 1981, art XI).

If a company acquires shares in itself, or has a usufruct over or a lien on its own shares, the voting rights in respect of those shares are suspended (art 118(7)).

Unless the articles provide otherwise, all shares carry equal rights in respect of dividends and the repayment of capital in a winding up (arts 105(1) and 168). In practice, the articles often provide for the issue of different classes of shares. Preference shares (*preferente aandelen*) are in common use. They may, in addition to their preferential dividend carry the right to share in the annual profits after the ordinary shares have received the same rate of dividend as has been paid on the preference shares. They are then called participating (*winstdelende*) preference shares. The dividend on preference shares is not treated as being cumulative unless the articles expressly so provide. Preference shares must be distinguished from priority shares (*prioriteitsaandelen*), which are used by their holders, who are usually members of the board of management or the supervisory board, to retain control over the company. The priority shares are often vested in a foundation (*stichting*), whose board is composed of the members of the management and supervisory boards of the company. Their powers may include making 'binding' proposals for the nomination, suspension and dismissal of the members of the management and supervisory boards. Such proposals can nevertheless always be overruled by a two-thirds vote of the shareholders' meeting (arts 133, 134, 144). In large companies which are not fully exempt, these oligarchic powers of making binding proposals are fully or partly excluded (arts 161 and 162).

(b) Profit-sharing certificates

Profit-sharing certificates are not shares, and confer no voting rights at the general meeting, but only the right to share in the profits of the company after the shareholders have been paid a dividend of a certain amount. They may be created when the company is established and if they are, they are called *oprichtings-bewijzen* or founders' certificates, which must not be confused with founders' shares (*oprichtingsaandelen*), which are real shares issued to the founders as remuneration for their services in connection with the formation of the company; they are seldom met with in practice. The rights of the holders of founders' certificates or profit-sharing certificates, once entrenched in the articles of the company, cannot be altered to their disadvantage without their agreement, unless the power to make alterations was explicitly reserved by the articles from the outset (art 122).

(c) Bonds

A company may issue bonds (*obligaties*) which may be in registered or bearer form, and which may be secured by a charge on any specific item of the company's assets. In the Netherlands, a floating charge on the assets of the company is unknown. Different types of bonds exist, the most important of which are convertible bonds. Issues of bonds must be registered in the Commercial Register in which the company itself is registered (Commercial Register Law of 1918, art 15).

3 Management and control of small and exempt large companies

The rules governing the management and control of small and exempt large companies differ from those which govern the management and control of large companies and partially exempt large companies. The rules governing large companies are sometimes called the 'special rules' by Dutch writers, and are principally concerned with the appointment, composition and functions of the supervisory board of such companies (arts 158–164). These functions include the confirmation of annual accounts, the appointment of managing directors, and the approval of certain important decisions of directors (arts 162–164). The rules governing the appointment and composition of the supervisory board of a partially exempt large company are the same as those applicable to the supervisory board of a large company fully subject to the special rules, but the powers of the board are limited to the approval of important decisions of the managing directors listed in art 164. However, the articles of a partially exempt large company may provide that the supervisory board shall be responsible for the appointment of the managing directors and the confirmation of the accounts (art 157(2)).

By art 153(2) of the Civil Code, an NV is deemed to be a large company if:

(a) according to its balance sheet the issued capital of the company and its reserves amount to at least Dfl 10 m or the higher amount to which the Dfl is adjusted by Royal Decree every two years on the basis of a price index; and

(b) the company, or any other company in which it holds at least half of the issued share capital directly or indirectly for its own benefit, has been compelled by law to establish a works council (*ondernemingsraad*); and

(c) the company or any such other company usually employs at least 100 workers.

Exempt large companies comprise companies at least 50 per cent of whose shares are directly or indirectly held by a company whose supervisory board is subject to the rules governing large companies or by a group of such companies bound by a cooperation agreement; also exempt are companies exclusively or almost exclusively managing or financing their subsidiaries within the same group, provided that the majority of the employees of the group work outside the Netherlands (art 153). Partially exempt companies are companies in which at least half of the shares are held by the company or group of companies bound by a cooperation agreement, if the greater part of the employees of the group are working outside the Netherlands (art 155).

Where small and exempt large companies have established a works council, they may adopt the special rules as a whole, or adopt the special rules other than those contained in art 162 (appointment of managing directors) and art 163 (confirmation of annual accounts) or adopt the special rules other than those contained in one of these sections but not the other. If they fail to take one of these courses of action, the rules governing their management and control are those set out below. As in the case of large companies, a petition for the investigation of the company's affairs may be filed with the Chamber of Enterprises of the Court of Appeal of Amsterdam (art 345). The articles of a small or an exempt large company generally provide that it will have a supervisory board, but they are not bound to do so (art 140).

(a) Board of management

Small and exempt large companies are managed by one or more managing directors, who are appointed by the members in general meeting or, in the case of the first directors, by the articles (art 132). The articles frequently contain an oligarchic clause by which the proposal of candidates for appointment as managing directors is made by persons who are members of the supervisory board or who are holders of priority shares. Such binding proposals must name at least two candidates for each vacancy. The members may appoint persons not on the list of candidates by a resolution passed by a two-thirds majority, provided that shareholders holding more than half of the company's issued share capital vote for the resolution (art 133). A general meeting may suspend or dismiss a managing director for any reason (art 134). Unless the articles otherwise provide, the managing directors' remuneration is fixed by the general meeting (art 135).

The board of management is charged with the conduct of the affairs of the company, subject to the restrictions contained in the articles (art 119). Except where the articles provide otherwise, the board of management and its members individually have power to bind the company in dealings with third persons. The articles may provide instead that this power shall be vested exclusively in two or more managing directors acting jointly, or in one designated managing director together with another person who is not a member of the board of management, or exclusively in one managing director (art 130(1) and (2)). Such provisions may be relied upon by the company against third parties only if they have been entered in the Commercial Register and published in the official gazette; no other restrictions on the powers of managing directors imposed by the articles may be relied on by the company to invalidate transactions with third parties (Commercial Register Law, arts 8(1) and 30a(1)). Moreover, limitations imposed by law, for example in connection with the division of powers between the board of management and the general meeting, do have an external effect. If the managing directors enter into a transaction which is beyond the objects of the company, they are liable to it for any resulting damage. However, the company is bound by such a transaction, unless it can show that the other party knew or could not have been unaware that the transaction was beyond the company's objects. Mere publication of the articles will not afford sufficient proof of knowledge by the third party (Civil Code, art 6). A board resolution may be annulled if the board has exceeded its powers, or if it violates the articles or if it is contrary to good faith (Civil Code, art 13).

(b) Supervisory board

The articles of a small or exempt large company may provide for the establishment of a supervisory board (*raad van commissarissen*) consisting of one or more persons appointed for any desired length of time by the members in general meeting, or in the case of the first members of the board, by the articles (arts 140 and 142(1)). The articles may provide that up to one-third of the members of the supervisory board shall be appointed by persons other than the shareholders in general meeting (art 143). A person who has attained the age of seventy-two cannot be appointed to membership of a supervisory board (art 143(4)). When the appointment of members of the supervisory board is made by the general meeting, its choice is frequently restricted by an oligarchic clause. A member of the supervisory board may be dismissed or suspended at any time by the persons who are entitled to appoint him (art 144).

The supervisory board is entrusted with the task of supervising the policy of the management board and the general course of the affairs of the company and its business, and of rendering advice to its management (art 140(2)). Unless the articles otherwise provide, it exercises the managing directors' powers in transacting business in which any of them are interested (art 146), and it may suspend a managing director at any time subject to the setting aside of the suspension by the general meeting (art 147). The supervisory board may be entrusted with additional powers by the articles (art 140(3)).

(c) Works council

Although the law will be changed in the near future when the amending Law of 22nd May 1981 comes into effect, at the time of writing a company is only bound to set up a works council in every enterprise carried on by it which has at least 100 employees, although it may do so voluntarily if an enterprise has less than that number of employees. However, until the entry into force of the amending Law of 22nd May 1981 (*Staatsblad* No 416), the Social and Economic Council, which is a tripartite body made up of representatives of the government and both sides of industry, is empowered to make an order requiring companies to establish works councils in enterprises in which they have less than 100 employees (Works Councils Law 1971, art 3(1)). An enterprise is defined as an organisation operating as an independent unit where work is performed under a contract of employment (art 1(1) (*c*)).

The Law of 22nd May 1981 amended the Works Councils Law 1971 (which was earlier amended by the Law of 1979). It will require a company having less than 100 employees in an enterprise carried on by it to set up a works council for the enterprise, provided that at least thirty-five employees work in the enterprise for at least one-third of the normal weekly working-hours (ie thirteen hours). For enterprises with less than thirty-five employees in which a works council has been introduced by virtue of an order made by the Social and Economic Council, the latter order will continue to apply (Law of 22nd May 1981, art 1). As is shown below, the facilities and functions of a works council set up under the new Law will be somewhat less than those of a works council set up under the earlier legislation. The new Law has not yet come into operation. It is likely to be made applicable first of all in the construction and metal trades.

The members of a works council are directly elected by secret ballot (Works Councils Law 1971, art 9). In the case of enterprises with 100 or more employees, all persons employed in the enterprise for at least six months will be entitled to vote in the election (Works Councils Law 1971, art 6(2)). In the case of enterprises employing not less than thirty-five but fewer than 100 employees, only employees who have worked in the enterprise for more than a year and for at least one-third of the normal working hours will be entitled to vote and stand for office (Works Councils Law 1971, art 35a(*c*)). The council will be presided over by a chairman chosen from among its members (art 7).

A works council has important functions both in a small company and in an exempt large company, and can properly be regarded as an organ of such companies, as well as of large and partially exempt large companies, where it has additional tasks. The works council must meet at least six times a year, and at at least two of these meetings it must discuss the general conduct of the business of the enterprise (art 24). The company must place its annual accounts at the disposal of the works council as soon as they have been drawn up (art 31a(2)). In enterprises with more than 100 employees, the opinion of the works council must be sought on the matters enumerated in art 25(1) (*a*) (i) of the Works Councils Law of 1971, which include the transfer of control over the enterprise or any part of it; the making, alteration or termination of arrangements for continuous cooperation with another enterprise; the acquisition or disposal of a substantial financial participation in another enterprise; the cessation of the business of the enterprise or any part of it; any substantial expansion, contraction or other change in the business activities of the enterprise; and a change in the place where the business activities are carried on. If the management decision in connection with any of these matters does not conform to the opinion expressed by the works council, the company must delay the implementation of that decision for one month, during which time the works council may appeal to the Chamber of Enterprises of the Court of Appeal of Amsterdam against the decision (art 26).

In enterprises employing not less than thirty-five but fewer than 100 employees, the opinion of the works council will only have to be sought where the management decision is capable of leading to dismissal or a major change in the working conditions or conditions of employment affecting at least one-quarter of the work force (art 25a(*g*)). The company will only be required to delay the implementation of decisions relating to the closure of the enterprise or a major part thereof, or to any substantial expansion, contraction or other change in the business activities of the enterprise, or to the relocation of the enterprise. The required period of delay is one month.

The management must request the opinion of the works council on any decision it intends to take in connection with one of the social matters enumerated in arts 27(1) (*a*)–(*j*). These matters include the prescription of rules governing working conditions; pension insurance; profit-sharing or saving schemes; work evaluation schemes; the establishment of principles for the appointment, dismissal or promotion of employees; occupational safety, health or welfare measures; principles for the appointment, dismissal or promotion of employees; and complaints procedure. If the works council fails to give its consent, the management may apply to the appropriate industry committee (*bedrijfscommissie*) of the Social and Economic Council, from which an appeal lies to the Minister (art 27(4) and (5)). If the management takes a decision in connection with one of the listed matters without the consent of the works council or the approval of the court, the industry committee, it may be annulled on application being made to the district court (*Kantonrechter*) by the works council within one month of the works council becoming aware that the management had implemented the decision (art 27(5)). These rules will also apply to works councils set up in accordance with the new rules contained in the Law of 15th May 1981.

Article 35b of the Works Councils Law 1971, which was incorporated therein by the Law of 15th May 1981, provides for a simplified form of employee participation in enterprises employing not less than ten but fewer than thirty-five persons. This article, which will not extend to enterprises which have already established a works council in accordance with an order of the Social and Economic Council at the time when it comes into effect, provides for the direct participation of all employees who have worked in the enterprise for at least six months for at least one-third of the normal weekly working hours. The company will be obliged to hold a meeting with these qualifying employees at least twice a year, and to convene a meeting if so requested by at least one-quarter of the qualifying employees, giving their reasons. It will be possible to discuss all matters concerning the enterprise on which the management or the employees consider consultation to be desirable at these meetings. Each employee will be entitled to make proposals, and to make his attitude known. The company will be required to discuss the general state of the affairs of the enterprise with its employees at least once a year, and to provide them with written or oral information on the activities and results of the enterprise during the last financial year, together with its prospects for the current financial year. Furthermore, the company will be required to give its employees an opportunity of expressing their opinion on any proposed decision which may result in dismissals or a major change in the work, conditions of employment or employment conditions affecting at least one-quarter of the employees. The company will not be required to comply with this obligation to the extent that the matter in question has already been settled in a collective agreement, or in a regulation made by a body governed by public law.

Employees may have recourse to the district court to secure compliance with the requirements of art 35b.

(d) General meetings

A general meeting of shareholders (*algemeene vergadering*) may be called at any time by the directors or the supervisory board (Civil Code, art 109), or at the request of shareholders who hold at least 10 per cent of the issued capital of a company, or holders of *certificaten* issued with the consent of the company and representing at least 10 per cent of its issued capital (art 110). In addition, an annual general meeting must be held within six months after the end of each financial year of the company (art 108). This meeting approves and confirms the company's annual accounts (art 101(1)). The annual general meeting also receives the directors' report (art 137), and the auditors' report on the annual accounts (arts 103(1) and 148). Where possible, the annual general meeting is also used to pass other resolutions, for example for the appointment of managing directors and members of the supervisory board. If an annual general meeting is not held within six months after the end of the company's financial year, any shareholder or holder of a *certificaat* issued with the company's consent may be authorised by the court to call a general meeting (art 112). The general meeting is not entitled to give the board of management instructions as to the use of its powers. Certain of the powers of the general meeting may be limited by an oligarchic clause or other provisions in the articles. Thus, for example, the power of the general meeting to amend the articles may be restricted by requiring the prior consent of the holders of priority shares or of the supervisory board.

The notice of a general meeting must be addressed to all shareholders and holders of *certificaten* issued with the consent of the company (art 113(1)). The meeting is called by a notice published in the official gazette (*Staatscourant*) and in a newspaper circulating in the locality of the company's registered office (art 113(2)). If the company's shares are all in registered form, the articles may make provision for other ways of calling general meetings, for example by sending registered letters to the shareholders or holders of *certificaten* issued with the consent of the company (art 113(3)). The notice calling a general meeting should be published or dispatched at least fifteen days before the date of the meeting (art 113). The notice must include an agenda, or at least state that the shareholders and holders of *certificaten* may inspect a copy of the agenda at the company's registered office (art 114). If the meeting is an annual general meeting, the annual accounts prepared by the directors and the auditors' report on them must be available for inspection by shareholders and the holders of *certificaten* at the company's registered office from the time when the notice calling the meeting is published until the meeting is held (art 103(1)).

Each shareholder may attend and vote at a general meeting, or may appoint a proxy in writing to represent him, and holders of fractional certificates in respect of shares may combine and appoint one of their number or a proxy to attend and vote in respect of the number of complete shares represented by the certificates (art 117(1)). The holder of a *certificaat* may appoint a proxy to attend the meeting and speak on his behalf; the proxy, like the certificate holder, cannot vote (art 117(2)). The articles may require shareholders and holders of *certificaten* to deposit their securities with the company or its agent in order to be entitled to attend a general meeting (art 117(3)).

Votes are cast at general meetings in proportion to the nominal values of shares, but the articles may restrict the number of votes which may be cast by the same shareholder to six if the company's capital is divided into 100 or more shares, and to three if the capital is divided into less than 100 shares (art 118(1) and (5)). There are no quorum requirements unless the articles so provide. Voting takes place by a show of hands or by a poll. Agreements between shareholders on voting are permissible provided that they are not contrary to good faith. Resolutions are passed by a simple majority vote, unless the articles otherwise provide (art 120(1)). If all the shares of a company are in registered form and no *certificaten* have been issued with its consent, resolutions may be passed unanimously in writing (art 121). The articles quite frequently require a majority of two-thirds or three-quarters of the votes cast and a quorum of one-half of the share capital for the amendment of the articles. An amendment of the articles requires a declaration of no objection from the Ministry of Justice (art 125).

Minutes of general meetings must be kept. An amendment of the articles must be recorded in notarial minutes of the general meeting at which the amendment took place, or in a notarial instrument executed afterwards (art 124). The court may annul resolutions which are contrary to law or the articles, or contrary to good faith.

(e) Public inspection of accounts

All NVs, including small and exempt large ones, must file copies of their balance sheet and profit and loss account and of the explanatory notes attached to both of them, and the auditors' report on them, with the Chamber of Commerce with which the company is registered within eight days after they have been approved. These documents are open to public inspection (art 104).

4 Management and control of large and partially exempt large companies

For the meaning of the term 'large company' see p105. The special rules examined below are equally applicable to large and partially exempt large NVs.

(a) Board of management

The managing directors of a large company which is fully subject to the special rules governing such companies are appointed and removed by the supervisory board. The general meeting must be informed of a proposed appointment, and be given an opportunity of commenting on an intended dismissal (art 162). The works council must be consulted about the proposed appointment or intended dismissal of a managing director (Works Councils Law of 1971, art 30). These rules do not apply to partially exempt large companies, whose managing directors are appointed and removed by the general meeting (art 155(1)). In large companies which are fully subject to the special rules, the power to suspend managing directors is vested in the supervisory board; in other such companies, the general meeting has this power (art 134).

The powers and functions of the board of management of a large or partially exempt large company are the same as those of any other company, but it may not take certain important decisions without the approval of the supervisory board (art 164(1) and (2)). The absence of the approval of the supervisory board cannot be relied on by or against third parties (art 164(3)).

(b) Supervisory board

A large or a partially exempt large company must have a supervisory board consisting of at least three natural persons (art 158(1) and (3)). The first members of the board are appointed by the articles, except when a company having a voluntary supervisory board first comes within the definition of a large or partially exempt large company, in which case the existing supervisory board will constitute the first supervisory board under the special rules (art 158(2)). When a subsequent vacancy occurs, the existing supervisory board co-opts a new member. Before the new member is appointed, the general meeting, the works council and the board of management are given the opportunity to make recommendations (art 158(4)). The supervisory board is required to notify the name of the person whom it intends to appoint to the general meeting and the works council (art 158(5)). These bodies may oppose the proposed appointment on one of two grounds, namely either that it may not be expected that the proposed person will be capable of performing the duties of a member of the supervisory board properly, or that if the appointment is allowed, the supervisory board will not be properly constituted (art 158(6)). The Social and Economic Council, which is a body consisting of representatives of the government and both sides of industry, is empowered to consider such objections and to uphold or reject them (art 158(9)).

The members of the supervisory board of a large or partially exempt large company may be suspended only by the board itself (art 161(3)), and can only be removed from office by the Chamber of Enterprises of the Court of Appeal of Amsterdam at the request of the board of management, the general meeting or the works council (art 161(2)).

The supervisory board of a large company which is fully subject to the special rules appoints, suspends and dismisses the managing directors of that company (art 162). It also confirms the annual accounts of a large company, but not those of a partially exempt large company (art 163). The significance of the confirmation of the accounts by the supervisory board is that the general meeting cannot make changes in them, and is only entitled to approve or reject them (art 101(3)). The supervisory board of a large company or a partially exempt large company is also required to approve certain important decisions of the board of management (art 164(1)). The failure of the supervisory board to approve such decisions cannot be relied on by or against third parties (art 164(3)). Approval is required for decisions regarding: (a) the issue, acquisition or cancellation of shares or bonds; (b) the cooperation of the company in the issue of *certificaten* by an independent *administratiekantoor*; (c) applications for stock exchange listings for securities of the company; (d) long term cooperation agreements with other companies or legal entities; (e) substantial participations in other companies; (f) substantial investments; (g) proposals to alter the articles; (h) proposals to dissolve the company; (i) the presentation of petitions for bankruptcy or receivership of the company; (j) termination of the employment of a considerable number of employees simultaneously or within a short period of time; and (k) radical changes in the working conditions of a considerable number of employees. The supervisory board is also required to appoint the auditors if the general meeting fails to do so (art 148(1)).

(c) Works council

The works council of a large company has the same tasks as that of a small or partially exempt large company, and in addition, it plays an important role in the nomination of members of the supervisory board (Civil Code, art 138), and the annual accounts must be submitted to it for discussion (art 163). The annual accounts do not need to be submitted to the works council of a partially exempt large company, unless the articles so provide.

(d) General meetings

The rules governing the convening and procedure of the general meeting of a large company and the annulment of resolutions passed thereat are the same for large and partially exempt large companies as for other companies. However, as has already been explained above, certain of the powers vested in the general meeting of small and exempt large companies are vested instead in the supervisory boards of large companies, and, to a lesser extent, of partially exempt large companies.

(e) Public inspection of accounts

The rules contained in art 104 of the Civil Code, which have been explained above in relation to small and exempt large companies, are applicable to all NVs.

5 Provisions for the protection of shareholders

Shareholders who between them hold 10 per cent or more of a company's issued capital or shares with a total nominal value of not less than Dfl 500,000, and the holders of *certificaten* who are entitled beneficially to 10 per cent of a company's issued capital or to shares with a total nominal value not less than Dfl 500,000 (art 346), may request the Chamber of Enterprises of the Court of Appeal of Amsterdam to appoint one or more persons to investigate the business policy and the conduct of affairs of the company either as a whole or in part, or in respect of a particular period (art 345). The articles of a company may prescribe a lower qualifying fraction of the company's capital or may confer the right to present a petition on other persons (art 346(c)). A petition may also be presented by an organisation of employees whose members include persons employed by the company (art 346(h)). The public prosecutor of the Court of Appeal of Amsterdam may require an investigation in the public interest (art 345).

The applicants cannot be heard if they have not given previous notice in writing to the board of management and the supervisory board of their objections to the conduct of the affairs of the company, or if the two boards have not been given enough time to investigate the objectives and to take appropriate remedial steps (art 349(1)). A claim by an organisation of employees will not be entertained if it has not previously afforded the works council an opportunity of expressing its opinion in writing (art 349(2)). The Chamber of Enterprises will only order an investigation where there are good grounds for doubting whether the company's affairs have been properly conducted (art 350(1)). If the report of the investigators shows that there has been serious mismanagement, the court may order one or more of a number of remedies listed in art 356(a)–(e), which range from the temporary suspension of any resolution passed by a general meeting to the dissolution of the company and include the court permitting a temporary departure from the provisions of the company's articles.

6 Take-overs and mergers

Dutch law lacks a statutory regulation of take-overs and mergers, although rules of conduct in respect of them have been issued by the Social and Economic Council. The position will be different when legislation is enacted implementing the Third Directive of the Council of Ministers of the European Communities. No such legislation has yet been introduced. A merger is treated as occurring if two companies of more or less the same size unite, whilst a take-over is treated as occurring when a small company is taken over by a larger one.

Where a company wishes to acquire the assets and liabilities of another company, all the assets have to be transferred separately, the liabilities can only be transferred with the approval of the creditors concerned, and employment contracts can only be assigned with the individual agreement of the employees. For this reason, mergers and take-overs by the acquisition of the whole of the assets and liabilities of a company (*bedrijfsfusie*) are not so common in the Netherlands as mergers and take-overs by a purchase or exchange of shares (*aandelenfusie*).

(a) Decisions as to take-overs and mergers

When a merger or take-over is to take place by a purchase or exchange of shares, the board of management and the supervisory board of the acquiring company are usually empowered to decide that the appropriate offer shall be made, since the power to issue new shares is nearly always conferred on them by the articles of the acquiring company. However, where the nominal capital of that company has to be increased to make the issue of new shares possible, a resolution of the general meeting of that company will be necessary.

The offering company's shareholders have to decide whether they will accept the offer. Dutch law does not provide for the acquisition of the shares belonging to a small dissenting minority where the vast majority of the shareholders accept the offer.

The power to decide on an assets merger or take-over is vested in the management of the acquiring company, but if new shares are to be issued, similar remarks are applicable as to the organ which is competent to issue the shares to those made above in connection with mergers by the purchase or exchange of shares. More difficult problems arise in determining which organ of the acquired company is competent to make the necessary decision on behalf of that company. It would seem that where the transfer of the whole of the company's undertaking is involved, a resolution of the general meeting is necessary.

When a merger or take-over is effected by an acquisition of assets and liabilities, the works council must be consulted if the company proposes to transfer its whole undertaking or a substantial part thereof, and a social plan must be submitted to it (Works Councils Law of 1971, art 25(1) and (3)). The works council has the right of appeal to the Chamber of Enterprises of the Court of Appeal if the decision on the merger or take-over is contrary to its advice (Works Councils Law of 1971, art 26(1)). The works council of the acquired company need not be consulted in the case of a merger or take-over by the purchase or exchange of shares, but such consultation usually takes place in practice.

(b) Rules of conduct protecting shareholders

The Rules of Conduct relating to take-overs and mergers are based on a decision of the Social and Economic Council. The Rules of Conduct lack any legal sanction, but for practical purposes they have the force of law. In cases of infringements of the Rules, the Committee on Merger Affairs, a committee of the Social and Economic Council, may administer the sanctions of an admonition (*openbare berisping*) or a public announcement (*openbare mededeling*). The Stock Exchange Association may enjoin all its members to cease to act for or collaborate with a person who infringes the Rules of Conduct, but this sanction has not been frequently used, and is only effective in the case of public offers. It is not yet clear whether an infringement of the Rules may give rise to an action in damages for loss suffered by any of the participating companies or their shareholders.

Chapter 1 of the Rules is concerned with the protection of shareholders, and is applicable to the public offers made by an NV or BV to acquire shares in an NV or BV which are listed on the Stock Exchange or, if unlisted, are regularly dealt in in the Netherlands (Rules of Conduct, art 2(1)). A public offer is defined as an offer which is published either by an announcement in the daily list of dealings of the Stock Exchange Association (*Vereniging voor de Effectenhandel*) to the effect that an offer document is generally available, or by a press notice which must contain the price or share exchange ratio offered (art 1(1)). It is also applicable to offers which are not public offers, and which are made by an NV or a BV in respect of more than half the issued shares of another NV or BV which are in registered form, provided that the shares are listed on the Stock Exchange, or, if unlisted, are regularly dealt in in the Netherlands (art 2(2)).

The board of a company which intends to make a public offer or an offer for registered shares must inform the board of management in writing of its intention, and must invite that board to consult with the offeror about the terms of the offer (art 4(2)). Public announcements have to be made under certain circumstances during a bid. These circumstances include the situation where the board of the offeree company has been notified of an intended public offer (art 3(2)(*b*)); where the negotiations have reached a stage where agreement may be justifiably anticipated (art 3(2)(*a*)); and where developments in the prices of either the offeror or offeree company's shares or other developments indicate that the intention to make a public offer is known to third parties who may make use of this knowledge (art 3(2)(*c*)). Within thirty days after the offeror company makes a public announcement that negotiations with the board of the offeree company have reached such a stage that agreement may be justifiably anticipated, or that the board of the offeree company has been notified in writing by the offeror company of its intention to make an offer, the board of management of the offeror company must either make a public offer by publishing its offer document, or it must announce that it has decided not to make an offer, or announce the time within which a decision to make the public offer may be expected.

The offer document must contain the particulars listed in art 6 of the Rules, which include the names and other information concerning the companies involved; the terms of the offer; whether consultations have taken place with the management board of the offeree company and the outcome of these discussions; a statement that the offer is made for the outstanding shares of the same class; the minimum number of shares in respect of which acceptances of the offer must be given for the offer to become binding on the offeror; any other conditions which the offeror requires to be fulfilled in order for the offer to become binding on it; the date when the offer expires; and details of any direct or indirect mutual shareholdings between the companies involved. The offer document must also state whether the offeror company or any company in the same group as the offeror company has during the last three years acquired shares in the offeree company from the members of its management or supervisory boards, or from their relatives, or whether such acquisitions will take place in the future under existing agreements. If an offer relates to an exchange of shares, further information about the offeror company must be included in the offer document (art 7).

The offeree company must hold a general meeting to consider the offer at least eight days before the expiration of the period for acceptance (art 9(1)). At this meeting, the board of management and the supervisory board of the offeree company must express their views on the offer, provide the shareholders with all the information in their possession which is relevant for making a judgment on the offer and answer shareholders' questions (art 9(4)). Resolutions passed at this meeting are not binding on the shareholders. At least four days before the meeting, the board of management of the offeree company must provide the shareholders with a report giving its views as to the offer and containing recent financial information about the offeree company (art 9(2)). If the bid offers to acquire shares in the offeree company wholly or partly in exchange for shares in the offeror company amounting to more than 25 per cent of its issued capital, the offeror company is also required to hold a general meeting no later than eight days before the expiration of the period for acceptance of the bid (art 10(1)).

(c) Rules of conduct protecting employees

Chapter II of the Rules of Conduct for take-overs and mergers contains provisions for the protection of employees which are sometimes referred to by Dutch lawyers as the 'additional rules'. These rules are applicable whenever direct or indirect control over the activities of an enterprise or part of an enterprise is acquired by a company or by any other legal person or by an individual, unless none of the enterprises which are established in the Netherlands and are involved in the transaction regularly employ 100 or more employees (Rules, arts 14 and 15(1)(a)). If any of the enterprises involved in the transaction as transferor or transferee, or in a take-over as offeror or offeree company, forms part of a group of enterprises under the control of a single individual or company, the relevant figure is the total number of employees of the group in the Netherlands (art 15(1)(b)). An enterprise is defined as any organisation operating as an independent entity in which work is performed under contracts of employment entered into for the purpose of carrying on a commercial undertaking (art 14). The additional rules are not applicable where all the enterprises involved belong to the same group, or the transaction is outside the jurisdiction of Dutch law, or arises from succession on death or from the application of community property rules on marriage (art 15(3)). The additional rules may be extended to enterprises not covered by it under the terms of a collective agreement (art 15(2)).

The acquisition of a minority participation by an acquiring company may be treated as resulting in a transfer of control if it includes priority shares having a veto power, or if the new participation, when added together with an existing participation, results in the acquisition of the majority interest in the company. It should be noted that the additional rules are only applicable if a public offer is made or negotiations for an assets merger are initiated, and they do not apply where control results, for example, from voting agreements.

The most important of the additional rules governing the protection of employees are found in arts 17 and 18, which require the parties to a merger to inform the trade unions to which employees of the enterprises involved belong, and to consult those unions on matters affecting the employees. These unions are defined in art 14(1) as organisations (a) from whose list of candidates at least one member has been elected to the works council of any of the enterprises involved at the most recent election; or (b) which are concerned in the negotiation of wages and other conditions of employment in any of the enterprises involved; or (c) which appear during the two preceding calendar years to have been regularly active on behalf of their members employed in any of the enterprises involved.

Where a public announcement is made in connection with the negotiations for a merger or take-over, each of the trade unions as

defined above must be informed of the contents of the announcement before it is made public (art 17). Article 18 of the Rules, which
is of crucial importance, distinguishes between the different phases
of obligatory consultation with the trade unions. When merger
negotiations reach a stage which justify an expectation that an
agreement will be reached, the trade unions must be notified of this
fact at once (art 18(1)). Shortly after this notification and before
agreement on the terms of the merger or acquisition is reached, the
unions must be given a statement of the reasons for the merger or
acquisition, as well as the anticipated social, economic and legal
consequences of the merger or acquisition to the extent that they
can be foreseen, and the measures which are planned in connection
with these consequences (art 18(3)).

Before a final agreement on the merger or acquisition is reached,
the trade unions must be given the opportunity of expressing their
opinion on the operation from the viewpoint of the employees'
interests, and of discussing it with the boards of management of the
companies involved (art 18(4)). The trade unions are entitled to call
for more detailed information from the companies involved and it
must be supplied if possible (art 18(5)). The Committee on Merger
Affairs is empowered to decide whether the unions have been given
enough information. If a public offer is made for shares without
preliminary discussions between the boards of management of the
offeror and offeree companies, the offeror is required to inform the
relevant trade unions of its intention to make an offer before
deciding on the price or share exchange ratio to be offered, and the
offeror is also required to hold the same consultations with those
unions as though an agreement on the terms of the offer had been
reached with the management of the offeree company (art 20(1)).
In addition, the offeror company must inform the board of management of the offeree company of its intention to make the offer at
least seven days before doing so (art 20(2)). The board of the
offeree company then also has to hold consultations with the
relevant unions before making its opinion on the offer known to the
general meeting (art 20).

The first notification of the merger negotiations to the trade
unions under art 18(1) is confidential, unless the unions are notified
by the offeror or offeree company in writing that they need not
observe secrecy (art 18(2)). On the other hand, information received by the unions under arts 18(3)–(5) is confidential only to the
extent that the communicating company requests them by registered letter to preserve secrecy. The trade unions may reject this

requirement within four days after the receipt of the registered letter, and if they do so, the companies involved may end the consultation and refuse to enter into further consultations with any of the unions involved (art 18(2)). The requirement of secrecy may be waived by mutual agreement, but if the parties fail to agree, the Committee on Merger Affairs decides the matter (art 19(1)). The obligation of secrecy in respect of technical and economic information expressly given in confidence can only be waived by the party providing it, but in the event of a refusal to waive, the Committee can terminate the obligation of secrecy if the refusal is unreasonable (art 19(2)).

7 Dissolution and liquidation

(a) Dissolution

Article 166 of Book 2 of the Civil Code enumerates the cases in which an NV may be dissolved, namely:
   (a) in any case provided for in the articles;
   (b) by a resolution of the general meeting of shareholders to that effect;
   (c) by the adjudication of the company as a bankrupt, or by the termination of bankruptcy proceedings because of the insufficiency of the company's assets to meet the costs of the proceedings;
   (d) by the court in the cases provided for by law.
In practice the dissolution of a company is almost always a consequence of its bankruptcy or the passing of a resolution for dissolution at a general meeting. The articles of the company generally treat such a resolution as if it involved an amendment of the articles, and so the same special majority and quorum are required as for an amendment.

If all the shares of the company are held by one shareholder, this is not a cause for dissolution (art 9). Nor does the fact that the NV has ceased to carry on any of its business activities, or that it has no assets, or practically no assets, necessarily bring about its dissolution. The grounds for the dissolution of a company are confined to those expressly stated in art 166 (Minister of Finance, HR 31st December 1958, N J 1959, No 92). The court is empowered to dissolve a company on the petition of the public prosecutor if the objects of the company can no longer be attained because of its lack of means (art 74).

A dissolved company continues to exist as a legal person in so far as this is necessary for the realisation of its assets and the winding up of its affairs, and its legal personality is extinguished only when its liquidation is completed.

(b) Liquidation

The dissolution of an NV entails its liquidation. If the NV is dissolved by resolution of a general meeting, the managing directors act as liquidators unless the articles of association provide otherwise (art 23(2)). If the company is declared bankrupt, the trustee in bankruptcy appointed by the bankruptcy court (*curator*) acts as liquidator (art 23(3)). If the company is dissolved by the judgment of the court, the court appoints the liquidators (art 23(4)).

Unless the articles provide otherwise, the provisions they contain relating to the appointment, suspension and dismissal of managing directors and their powers, duties and liabilities, and all their provisions governing the supervision of the members of the board of management apply also to the liquidators (art 23(2)). The liquidators are therefore treated as though they were the managing directors entrusted with the special function of winding up the company's affairs instead of continuing its business.

The dissolution of the company must be entered in the Commercial Register by the liquidators; if the dissolution is ordered by judgment of the court, the clerk of the court deals with the necessary registration (art 167).

The liquidators have the task of realising the company's assets and of paying its debts. Dutch law contains no specific provisions governing these matters, and so the liquidators have considerable freedom in determining how the liquidation will be conducted. The law merely provides that the balance of the assets of a dissolved NV shall be distributed to the shareholders and other rightful claimants in accordance with their respective rights (art 168). It is found advisable in practice for the articles to contain express provisions regulating the shareholders' and other persons' rights to the balance of assets remaining after satisfying the company's liabilities, because otherwise uncertainties may well arise as to who is entitled to participate in the proceeds of the liquidation, and questions of priority may also arise. These and other questions may also arise when the liquidators have fulfilled their obligation to file a distribution plan showing how they intend to apply the company's surplus assets. The distribution plan must be filed with the Chamber of Commerce in whose Commercial Register the company is registered and must also be advertised in the official gazette and in appropriate newspapers (art 169(1)). Any interested person may object to the scheme of distribution proposed by the plan within two months after the publication of the advertisements (art 169(2)). The objection is effected by serving a summons on the liquidators calling on them to appear before the district court for the purpose of obtaining a declaratory judgment as to whether the payments proposed by the plan shall be made, or whether they should be varied, or whether they should be made on a different basis determined by the court. Such proceedings prevent any payment being made under the plan until all objections are withdrawn, or a final order has been made by the court (art 169(3)). The court may authorise a provisional payment to the holders of undisputed claims whilst the opposition proceedings are pending (art 170(1)). A liquidation may take a considerable time to complete, and for this reason, the liquidators may decide on their own authority to make advance payments if the amount and condition of the company's assets permit (art 168).

All amounts payable under a distribution plan which have not been collected from the liquidators within six months after the final version of the distribution plan becomes available must be paid into a separate account by the liquidators (art 172). Such amounts will become the property of the state after the expiration of the limitation period of ten years if they are not claimed beforehand by the persons entitled to them.

The liquidators must file accounts covering the whole of the liquidation at the office of the Commercial Register within one month from the expiration of the period of six months mentioned in art 172, and a copy of the accounts must be deposited at an address in the district designated by the liquidators (art 173(1)). The accounts must be open for inspection for a period of three months. If no proceedings are instituted against the liquidator within those three months, the final accounts are deemed to be approved, and cannot subsequently be challenged (art 173(3)). The functions of the liquidators then come to an end, and the company ceases to exist. However, in certain circumstances the liquidation may be reopened by a court order (art 23(7)).

BESLOTEN VENNOOTSCHAP (BV)

The *Besloten Vennootschap* (the private or closed company with limited liability) was introduced into Dutch company law only in

1971, and since then it has proved very popular in the Netherlands. The law governing the BV is largely based on the rules governing the NV, and the majority of arts 195–284 of Book 2 of the new Civil Code, which relate to the BV, are largely copies of the corresponding articles governing the NV. Thus, for example, the same criteria are applicable for large BVs as for large NVs (art 263(2)), and the rules governing the appointment, composition and functions of the supervisory board of a large BV are the same as in the case of a large NV (arts 268–274), as also are the criteria for total and partial exemption from the rules governing large companies (arts 263 and 265). A BV must necessarily be a closely held company resembling a closely held NV. However, some divergence between the rules governing these companies has taken place as a result of the implementation of the Second Directive in the Netherlands, and it is expected that in the future, the BV will acquire further distinctive features of its own. The following are the principal differences between an NV and a BV:

(1) The requirements governing the formation of a BV are considerably less onerous than those governing the formation of an NV. This is true to some extent of those relating to the contents of the articles. The articles must set out: (*a*) the name of the company, which must begin or end with the words '*Besloten Vennootschap met beperkte aansprakelijkheid*' or BV (art 177(1) and (2)); (*b*) the address of the company's registered office, which must be in the Netherlands (art 177(3)); (*c*) the objects of the company (art 177(1)); (*d*) the amount of the company's nominal or authorised capital, which must be at least Dfl 35,000 (£7,460 approximately) (art 178(2)); and (*e*) the number and nominal values of the shares (art 178(1)). The instrument of incorporation must set out the number of shares subscribed by each incorporator (art 178(1)), and the first directors must be appointed therein (art 242). The instrument of incorporation must also contain particulars of certain special types of legal transactions (art 205).

None of the requirements of Law No 332 of 15th May 1981 (*Staatsblad* No 332) are applicable to BVs. Thus, for example, there is no requirement that when shares are issued for cash, a particular part of the nominal value shall be paid up. No founders' report has to be made on contributions in kind made on formation or subsequently, and such contributions do not have to be valued by a registered and qualified accountant, or put at the disposal of the company as soon as possible after the issue of the relevant shares.

(2) The special rules contained in arts 96a, 98 and 98a of the Civil Code relating to preferential subscription rights and the acquisition by a company of its own shares, which have been discussed above, are not applicable to BVs. A BV may acquire up to 50 per cent of its issued shares, provided that the amount of its authorised capital has not fallen below Dfl 35,000, or that such acquisition will not result in the company's authorised capital being reduced below this amount (art 206).

(3) The shares in a BV must be in registered form, and the BV may not issue share certificates for shares (art 175(1)). Consequently, the title of a shareholder is evidenced only by an entry in the register of shareholders which must be kept by the company. However, a shareholder is entitled to have an authenticated copy of the entry in the register concerning his shares, but this copy is not a share certificate, although it may be used as evidence that the shareholder was the holder of the shares mentioned on the date when the copy was issued (art 194(1) and (3)). The issue of *certificaten* to bearers in respect of shares in a BV, with or without the consent of the BV, is prohibited (art 202). As long as *certificaten* to bearers are outstanding in respect of shares in a BV, no rights can be exercised in respect of the shares in question (art 202). It seems to be generally agreed that the issue of *certificaten* which are registered in the name of the holder is permissible, although the closed character of a BV may be destroyed by the issue of such *certificaten*.

(4) A share in a BV is transferred in the same way as a registered share in an NV. The articles must, except for a few complex exceptions made in favour of relatives, provide for a restriction on the transfer of shares, the so-called blocking clause (*blokkeringsklausule*). Article 195 of the Civil Code gives a choice between two forms of obligatory restriction, namely (*a*) the requirement that transfers shall be approved by an organ of the BV; and (*b*) the imposition of pre-emption rights in favour of the other shareholders. It is possible to combine the two restrictions by a provision in the articles. One of the restrictions mentioned in art 195 must be contained in the articles in any event, but the articles may combine it with further restrictions of a kind not mentioned in art 195, provided that they are not such that the transfer of the shares is made impossible or extremely difficult (art 195(7)).

(5) The rules governing the appointment, removal, powers and liabilities of the board of management and the supervisory board of a BV are the same as those applicable to the NV. The only matters

peculiar to the organs of a BV relate to certain aspects of the general meeting. The only persons entitled to take part in a general meeting of a BV are the holders of registered shares and registered *certificaten* issued with the consent of the company. A general meeting is called by sending individual notices to the registered addresses of shareholders, and by notifying the holders of *certificaten* by means of an announcement in the appropriate newspapers, unless the articles provide otherwise (art 224(1) and (3)). The accounts of a BV, like those of an NV, must be submitted for approval by the general meeting (art 263(1)); and in a large BV they are confirmed by the supervisory board, but still need the approval of the general meeting (art 272).

(6) Normally, a BV is not required to publish its accounts. However, if the total assets of a BV shown in the balance sheet is at least Dfl 8 m and the company has at least 100 employees on the date at which the balance sheet is made out, it must file a copy of its balance sheet together with the explanatory notes and the auditors' report at the office where the Commercial Register is kept in which the company is registered (art 214(1)). A BV which is engaged in the business of banking or insurance, or which has issued bearer bonds or bonds for which bearer *certificaten* are in circulation, is required to publish its accounts in full in the same way as an NV. An audit is compulsory for a BV if it has an issued capital of at least Dfl 500,000, or if it is obliged either to publish its annual accounts in full or to publish its balance sheet. In that case, the audit must be undertaken by a registered and qualified accountant. In all other situations, an auditor may be appointed voluntarily, but he need not be professionally qualified.

CHAPTER 5

BELGIUM AND LUXEMBOURG

Belgian company law is contained in Title IX of the Belgian Commercial Code, as amended, and Luxembourg company law in the Law concerning commercial companies of 10th August 1915, as supplemented by the Law of 18th September 1933 in respect of private companies and subsequently amended by other legislation. The Belgian legislation is now generally known as the Co-ordinated Laws on commercial companies (*Lois coordonnées sur les sociétés commerciales*), although amendments of the original Commercial Code of 1873 have been effected by adding to and modifying its articles. The provisions of Belgian and Luxembourg law as to public companies (*sociétés anonymes*) are identical except in a few particulars, and so will be dealt with together in this chapter. In this connection reference to an article of a Law by number is a reference to the Belgian Co-ordinated Law on commercial companies if it is prefixed by the abbreviation 'Bel', or to the Luxembourg law of 1915 if prefixed by the abbreviation 'Lux'. The law relating to private companies differs somewhat between the two countries, and so will be dealt with separately. Private companies in Belgium are known as *sociétés de personnes à responsabilité limitée* (Bel art 2) whereas in Luxembourg they are known by the French title of *Sociétés à responsabilité limitée* (Lux art 2). Under both systems of law the shareholders of public and private companies alike enjoy limited liability in that they are liable to contribute towards satisfaction of the company's debts and obligations only to the extent of the capital they have agreed to contribute, and when that contribution has been made their liability is at an end (Bel arts 26 and 116(1); Lux arts 23 and 179).

Only the First Directive of the Council of Ministers of the European Communities on the harmonisation of company law has so far been implemented in Belgium and Luxembourg.

128

SOCIÉTÉ ANONYME (SA)

1 Formation

The articles (*acte constitutif*) of a *société anonyme* (SA) must be executed by at least seven persons and must be notarised (Bel arts 4(2) and 29; Lux arts 4(2) and 20). The articles must, of necessity, set out:

1 The company's name, which should indicate the nature of its business and must not include the personal names of any of its members nor be the same as that of any other company, but the name need not include the words '*société anonyme*' although these words must be added to its name in all acts, invoices, notices, publications, letters, orders and other documents (Bel arts 27, 28 and 81; Lux arts 24, 25 and 76).

2 The place where the company's registered office (*siège social*) will be, which must appear in all its acts, invoices, notices, publications, letters, orders and other documents.

3 The nature of the company's business (Bel art 30(1)).

4 The amount of the company's share capital, which must be entirely subscribed, and in Belgium must be not less than BF 1,250,000 (£15,400 approximately) (Bel art 29(2)).

5 The number of shares (*actions*) into which the company's capital is divided.

6 The number of directors and auditors and any provisions as to the powers of the directors.

7 The duration of the company, which may not exceed thirty years, although it may be extended for successive periods of thirty years by an alteration of the articles (Bel art 102; Lux art 99).

Additionally, the law requires the articles to set out the nature of the consideration given for shares in the company which are allotted otherwise than for cash together with particulars of the allottees; details of any incumbrances on property which is transferred to the company for allotments of shares and details of dealings during the last five years in land which is so transferred; particulars of special advantages conferred on the founders; and an estimate of the cost of forming the company (Bel art 30; Lux art 27).

Like a French *société anonyme*, a Belgian or a Luxembourg SA may be formed in several ways. The first is for the founders to subscribe the whole of the share capital themselves, in which case

they must pay or contribute one-fifth of the cash or other consideration to be given for their shares (in the case of a Luxembourg
company the payment or contribution must not be less than 50 Fr
(66p approximately)), and the company comes into being when
they have done so (Bel art 29; Lux art 26). The other method is for
the founders to invite subscriptions for that part of the share capital
which they do not subscribe themselves; in that case, the subscribers
must pay at least one-fifth of the issue price of their shares, and a
meeting of subscribers must be held to approve the draft of the
company's articles; the articles are deemed to be approved unless a
majority of the subscribers vote against approving them, and the
company comes into being when the articles have been approved
(Bel arts 32, 33; Lux arts 29, 30). If the company is formed by
subscription, the founders have to take the shares for which subscriptions are not obtained and, furthermore, they are sureties for
the payment of one-fifth of the issue price of the shares which have
been subscribed (Bel art 35; Lux art 32). Whether the company is
formed by subscription or not, in Belgium the founders must apply
to the local commercial court for the appointment of an expert
(*reviseur d'entreprise*) if any of the company's shares are issued for a
consideration other than cash, and he reports to the founders, or in
the case of a company formed by subscription, to the meeting of
subscribers, on the value of the consideration given (Bel art 29 *bis*
(1)). The expert's valuation must be incorporated in the articles of
the company (Bel art 30(2)), and so must be accepted by the
founders or subscribers before the company is formed. Whichever
method of formation is employed, contributions in cash required to
be paid up at the time of incorporation must be deposited before
incorporation in a special bank account opened in the name of the
company, and the account must be at the company's sole disposal
(Bel art 29 *bis* (2)–(4)). In addition, whichever method of formation is employed, the founders must make a report to the officiating
notary in which they justify the need for and the adequacy of the
amount of capital with which the company is to be formed (Bel art
31). The founders are jointly and severally liable for the commitments of the company to the extent determined by the court if the
company is declared bankrupt within three years of formation and
the court finds that its capital was manifestly insufficient to ensure
the normal exercise of its intended activities for a period of at least
two years (Bel art 35(6)).

Within fifteen days after its formation, the company must deliver
a copy of its articles to the commercial court (*tribunal de commerce*)

for the district in which the company has its registered office, and the court officials see to the publication of the articles in full in the official gazette (*Moniteur belge*; *Mémorial luxembourgeois*) (Bel art 10; Lux art 9).

2 Shares and bonds

(a) Shares

Shares may be issued with or without a nominal value (Bel art 41(1); Lux art 37(1)). Belgian law does not prescribe a minimum nominal value for shares, but those of a Luxembourg company must have a nominal value of not less than 50 Fr (Lux art 37(6)). If the shares have a nominal value, they are fully paid, and the shareholder's liability to contribute towards the company's obligations is discharged when that nominal value has been paid to the company, unless the shares are issued at a premium, when the shares are not fully paid until the premium has been paid as well (Bel art 26; Lux art 23). If the company's shares have no nominal value, the company's capital is an aggregate of their issue price (like the stated capital of an American company), and the shares are only fully paid up when the issue price has been paid in full. If paid up capital is returned to shareholders (eg by a dividend being paid when the company has not earned sufficient profits to cover it), shares are treated as unpaid to that extent, and the shareholder can be called on to repay the amount of the improper dividend to the company as though their shares had all along been only partly paid (Belgian Supreme Court, *Pasicrisie* 1955 1 1046).

Apart from the initial one-fifth of the issue price which must be paid on allotment, the issue price of shares may be made payable by instalments or left at call. If a shareholder fails to pay a call or instalment the company may sue him or exercise the power invariably given by its articles to sell his shares as fully paid shares and recover from him the difference (if any) between the amount unpaid on the share and the lesser amount realised on the sale. The original subscriber and possibly all intermediate holders are liable to contribute the amount remaining unpaid on the present holder's default so far as is necessary to discharge debts of the company incurred before the transfer was published in the list of its shareholders which the company is required to insert annually in the official gazette (Bel arts 51, 52; Lux arts 48, 41).

Shares may be divided into sub-shares (*coupures d'action*) representing fractions of a share, and sub-shares may be joined together even though owned by different persons so as to enable their holders to exercise the rights attached to a complete share (eg voting rights) (Bel art 41(2); Lux art 37(4)). In practice, sub-shares are created when shares with a high nominal value have been vested in a bank or depositary company, and the certificates for the sub-shares are then issued by it in the same way as *certificaten* of a Dutch company.

A company may issue different classes of shares. Preference shares (*actions privilégiées; actions de priorité*) are common, and reimbursed shares (*actions de jouissance*) and founders' shares (*parts bénéficiaires*) are met with. The latter are similar to corresponding shares in French companies, but unlike their French equivalents, the holders of founders' shares may be empowered by the articles to vote at general meetings (Bel arts 41(1) and 75; Lux art 37(2)).

A Belgian or a Luxembourg company may not under penalty of criminal sanctions purchase its own shares if this would reduce its net assets below the sum of the share capital and the legally required reserve. Such a company is also not permitted to grant loans or advances for the purchase of its shares (Bel art 206; Lux art 168). However, neither Belgian nor Luxembourg law prevents a company from purchasing its own shares out of its profits.

Shares may be in registered or bearer form, but bearer certificates may not be issued until the shares are fully paid (Bel art 46(2); Lux art 43(2)). Founders' shares are transferable only by a notarised instrument of transfer or by a written transfer notified to the company until ten days after the company publishes its second set of annual accounts after the shares are issued (Bel art 47; Lux art 46). In Luxembourg the same rule is applicable to the transfer of shares paid for by a consideration other than cash (Lux art 44). Registered shares may be transferred by an entry in the register of shareholders signed by the transferor and the transferee, or by the more usual method of the transferor executing an instrument of transfer and the transferee presenting it and the transferor's share certificate to the company for registration (Bel art 43; Lux art 40). The register of shareholders is conclusive evidence of the ownership of shares (Bel art 43(1); Lux art 40(1)). If a forged or fraudulent transfer has been registered, therefore, the former owner of the share cannot impeach the transferee's title if he acquired the shares in good faith. Bearer shares are transferable by delivery (Bel art 45; Lux art 42), and a valid title to the share passes to a *bona fide* transferee despite the defectiveness of the transferor's title (Civil Code, art 2279).

Dividends on shares are declared by the shareholders in general meeting, but may only be paid out of profits earned by the company. Before dividends are paid it is obligatory for the company to transfer at least one-twentieth of the net profit of the year to legal reserve until the reserve amounts to one-tenth of the share capital (Bel art 77(4); Lux art 72(4)).

(b) Bonds

A company may issue bonds (*obligations*) which may be in registered or bearer form and may be secured on any of the company's movable or immovable property, but not by a floating charge on its whole undertaking. The bonds of Belgian companies must have a nominal value of at least BF 1,000 (£13 approximately) (Bel art 89 *ter*). Bonds may be in registered or bearer form and may be transferred in the same way and with the same legal consequence as shares (Bel art 89; Lux art 84). A general meeting of bondholders may be called by the directors or auditors, and must be called on the requisition of the holders of one-fifth of the outstanding bonds (Bel art 91; Lux art 86). The meeting may consent to a variation in the terms of the bonds or to the conversion of the bonds into shares or to release the bondholders' security, and may appoint a representative to act on the bondholders' behalf in dealing with the company (Bel art 98; Lux art 88). Votes are cast at bondholders' meetings in proportion to the nominal value of the bonds, and resolutions are passed by a three-quarters majority of the votes cast (two-thirds in Luxembourg), but in Belgium, unless the resolution is supported by the holders of at least one-third of the bonds outstanding, it is effective only if approved by the Court of Appeal for the district in which the company is domiciled (Bel art 94(4) and (5); Lux art 89(1)). Bondholders' resolutions for the realisation of their security or the appointment of a representative to deal with the company on their behalf require only a simple majority vote (Bel art 94(10) and (11); Lux art 89(1)). If a resolution alters the rights attached to a particular series of bonds, it is effective only if approved by the appropriate majority of holders of that series at a separate meeting (Bel art 95; Lux art 90).

A Belgian SA whose capital is fully paid may issue convertible bonds or bonds carrying the right to subscribe for shares in the company, but the conversion or subscription options must be exercisable not later than ten years after the bonds are issued and the issue must be approved in advance by a general meeting of the company by three-quarters majority vote (Bel arts 101 *bis* and *ter*). The existing shareholders have a preferential right to subscribe for such bonds, but their right may be waived or restricted by the resolution which authorises the issue (Bel art 101 *quater*). While convertible bonds or bonds carrying subscription rights are outstanding, the company may not do any act which reduces the advantages attributed to the bonds by their terms of issue (Bel art 101 *quinquies*), but it can increase its capital provided that a proportionate number of new shares are reserved for the bondholders to acquire as though they had already exercised the option to convert or subscribe conferred by their bonds (Bel art 101 *sexies*).

(c) Issue of shares and bonds

Before a company may issue a prospectus offering its shares or bonds to the public it must publish a notice giving certain information about itself in the Official Gazette, and the prospectus and application form for the shares or bonds must also contain this information (Bel arts 36, 37, 84 and 85; Lux arts 33, 34, 80 and 81). A similar notice must be published by a Belgian company before any of its shares or bonds may be quoted on a stock exchange, unless a notice has been published in connection with the issue of the shares and bonds not more than three months previously (Bel arts 40 and 87).

Both Belgian and Luxembourg companies are subjected to the more stringent requirements that offers of shares or bonds of public companies (*sociétés anonymes*) to the public for subscription or purchase (including offers to exchange existing shares for shares to be issued under a take-over or general bid) must be preceded fifteen days beforehand by the submission of details of the proposed operation to the *Commission Bancaire* or, in Luxembourg, to the *Commissionaire au contrôle des banques* (Belgian Royal Decree No 85 of 9th July 1935, arts 26–27; Luxembourg *Arrêté grand-ducal* of 19th June 1965, arts 14–15). The Banking Commission or Bank Control Commissioner may require the operation to be deferred for three months if he or it considers that the issue will disturb the market, or if the publicity material intended to be used in connection with the operation may lead the public into error as to its nature (Royal Decree, arts 27–29; *Arrêté grand-ducal*, arts 16–17). This delay will effectively kill the issue.

The Belgian Banking Commission also has power to defer the proposed issue of convertible bonds or bonds carrying the right to subscribe for shares for three months because of the insufficiency of the report which the directors of the issuing company are required to circulate to its shareholders in advance of the general meeting which resolves to authorise the issue (Bel art 101 *ter* (2)–(4)).

3 Management and control

(a) Board of directors

The affairs of an SA are managed by a board of directors (*conseil d'administration*) whose members (*administrateurs*) must be at least three in number, and are appointed for periods not exceeding six years by the shareholders in general meeting, except the first directors, who may be appointed by the articles (Bel arts 53, 55; Lux arts 50, 51). In Luxembourg, companies subject to art 21 of the Co-determination Law of 6th May 1974 must increase the number of their directors fixed by the articles to nine so as to facilitate employee representation on the board (art 23). The Law of 1974 is applicable to all undertakings, whatever their form, employing an average of at least 1,000 persons during the preceding three years, and to all undertakings in which there is a state participation of at least 25 per cent, or which exploit a state concession (art 21). One-third of the nine directors must represent the employees of the undertaking (art 24(1)), and they are normally designated by a committee or delegation representing employees by secret ballot according to the rules of proportional representation (art 25(1)). The directors representing employees must be chosen from among the company's employees. In the coal and steel sector trade unions representing the greatest number of employees of the undertaking in Luxembourg are permitted to designate the three directors to represent employees, and they need not be employees of the undertaking in question (art 26).

Except in the case of Luxembourg companies subject to the Co-determination Law of 1974, a director may be removed from office by a general meeting for any reason (Bel art 55(2); Lux art 51(3)). In the case of Luxembourg companies subject to the Law of 1974 directors representing employees may be removed from office by the body or organisation which appointed them (art 28(2) No 2). They may also be removed from office by a general meeting if the court which has jurisdiction in matters connected with employment gives its consent (art 30(1)). Directors may be remunerated in any way desired, usually by a salary or by a share of the company's profits (*tantièmes*). If a director has an interest conflicting with the company's in connection with any transaction which has to be approved by the board, he must disclose his interest at the board meeting and withdraw from discussion of it; furthermore, such disclosures of interest must be reported to the next general meeting of shareholders (Bel art 60; Lux art 57).

The power of the board of directors may be defined in the articles (Bel art 13; Lux art 12), but in the absence of any provision to the contrary, they may do anything required for carrying on the company's business in the ordinary way. Restrictions on the directors' usual powers, even if duly published, can never be relied on against third parties who act in good faith (Bel art 54(1)–(3); Lux art 53(1)–(3)). If the articles permit, one or more directors may be given the power to bind the company in relation to all acts, either by the articles or by the board exercising a power of delegation. Such a delegation of authority affects only the power of external representation of the company and not the making of business decisions at board meetings. However, if a delegation of authority to one or more directors is made, the company will be bound by the signature of those directors, even if the directors were not in fact empowered to enter into the transactions under the arrangements governing the internal management of the company (Bel art 56(4) and (5); Lux art 53(4)).

The day-to-day management of the company and the external representation of the company in respect of day-to-day management matters may be delegated to one or more persons, whether members of the board or not, and whether acting individually or jointly (Bel art 63(1); Lux art 60(1)). The appointment, dismissal and powers of such persons are regulated by the articles (Bel art 63(2); Lux art 60(2)), or in Luxembourg by a decision of the competent organ of the company (Lux art 60(2)), but any restriction placed on their powers of representation in dealings with third persons cannot be invoked against those persons, even if published (Bel art 63(2); Lux art 60(2)). The company is bound by acts performed by the board of directors or by directors empowered to bind the company or by the delegates appointed to carry on the daily management of the company's affairs even where such acts go beyond the company's objects, unless the company proves that the third person concerned knew or ought to have known that the act in question exceeded the company's objects (Bel art 63 *bis*; Lux art 60 *bis*).

Directors are liable to the company for loss caused by their fault (*faute*) in managing the company's affairs (Bel art 62(1); Lux art 59(1) and Co-determination Law, art 29(1)); this imposes on them a duty to act honestly and conscientiously, and also a duty to exercise proper skill and care. They are also jointly and severally liable to the company and to third parties for damages resulting from breaches of the legislation governing companies and the provisions of the company's articles; if they are aware of breaches of the law or articles by other directors but do not take part in them personally, directors can escape liability by reporting the breaches to a general meeting as soon as possible after they become aware of them (Bel art 62(2); Lux art 59(2) and Co-determination Law, art 29(2)).

If a director is guilty of a breach of his duty of care or his duty to conform to the provisions of the legislation or the articles, he can be sued by individual shareholders who have suffered personal damage distinct from that suffered by the company (Trib comm, Ghent, *Pasicrisie* 1944 3 48). As security for the proper performance of his duties each director must have the number of shares specified in the articles registered in his name and denominated as subject to a charge in favour of the company to compensate it for his defaults (Bel art 57; Lux arts 54–56). An exception is made for directors of Luxembourg companies subject to the Co-determination Law of 1974 who represent employees (Co-determination Law, art 31).

(b) Supervisors

The supervisors (*commissaires*) of the management of a company are elected for periods not exceeding six years by the shareholders in general meeting, and they may be removed by a general meeting for any reason (Bel art 64; Lux art 61). In the case of Belgian companies, at least one supervisor must be a certified public accountant (*commissaire reviseur*) if the company has made a public offer of its shares or bonds, or if they are listed on a stock exchange, or if the company is formed or its capital increased by public subscription (Bel art 64 *bis* No 2). In the case of Luxembourg companies which are subject to the Co-determination Law, one of the supervisors must be a certified public accountant appointed unanimously by all the directors, including those who represent the employees (Co-determination Law, art 34). The supervisors' function is to oversee the management of the company's affairs generally, and for this purpose they may inspect the company's records, and they receive half-yearly reports from the directors on the state of its affairs; the supervisors report periodically and as occasion requires to general meetings of shareholders (Bel art 65; Lux art 62). Supervisors cannot undertake the management of the company (Bel art 64 *quater* (1)), and they normally meet separately from the board of directors (Bel art 67; Lux art 64); however, the articles of the company may provide that they shall sit together as a general board (*conseil général*), but even then they still preserve their distinct functions (Bel art 68; Lux art 65).

The directors must submit the company's annual accounts (balance sheet and profit and loss account) together with their report on the company's affairs to the supervisors at least a month before the annual general meeting, and the supervisors must report to the meeting thereon (Bel art 77(5); Lux art 72(5)). The accounts together with the directors' and supervisors' reports are then laid before the annual general meeting for approval (Bel art 79(1); Lux art 74(1)). In this respect the role of the supervisors resembles that of auditors, but their functions are wider than those of auditors and more closely approximate to those of the supervisory board of a German company. Within thirty days after the annual accounts of a Belgian SA have been approved by the annual general meeting they must be published in the official gazette together with a list of the directors and supervisors and a note of the way the profits shown by the accounts have been applied (Bel art 80).

(c) General meetings

A general meeting of shareholders (*assemblée générale*) must be held each year on a date fixed by the articles to approve the annual accounts, receive the directors' and auditors' reports, declare dividends and deal with any other matters (Bel art 73(1); Lux art 70(1)). A general meeting may be called on the requisition of the holders of one-fifth of the company's share capital (Bel art 73(2); Lux art 70(2)).

Notice of the meeting must be given to registered shareholders individually by a letter containing the agenda and sent out eight days before the meeting, and if all the company's shares are in registered form, this is the only notice which need be given (Bel art 73(4) and (5); Lux art 70(4) and (5)). If the company has issued bearer shares, Belgian law requires a notice containing the agenda to be published in the official gazette at least eight days before the date of the meeting and also twice in a national and local newspaper with an interval of at least eight days between the publications. Luxembourg law also requires newspaper notices to be published if there are bearer shareholders; these must be published twice with an interval of at least eight days between the publications in the official gazette and in a Luxembourg newspaper (Bel art 73(3); Lux art 70(3)).

Every shareholder may attend a general meeting in person or by proxy and may vote on resolutions in proportion to the nominal value of his shares, or, in the case of shares without a nominal value, in proportion to the capital he has contributed (Bel art 74(2)–(4); Lux art 71(2)). Shares without voting rights or with multiple voting rights are not permitted, but on the other hand no one shareholder, however large his holding, may vote in respect of more than one-fifth of the company's share capital, or cast more than two-fifths of the total votes cast on a resolution (Bel art 76; Lux art 71(2)).

Resolutions are passed by a simple majority vote, unless the articles otherwise provide, but resolutions to alter the articles, including resolutions to increase or reduce share capital (Bel art 72(1); Lux art 69(1)) and to extend the life of the company (Bel art 102(3); Lux art 99(3)), must in the case of a Belgian company be passed by a three-quarters majority (Bel art 70(5)), and in the case of a Luxembourg company by a two-thirds majority (Lux art 63(8)). The shareholders or their proxies attending the meeting must represent at least one-half of the company's capital (Bel art 70(3); Lux art 67(5)), and if this requirement is not fulfilled, a second meeting must be held whose deliberations will be valid regardless of the capital represented by the shareholders present at the meeting (Bel art 70(4); Lux art 67(5)).

The position is different if a resolution is proposed to alter the nature of the company's business set out in its articles, in which case a four-fifths majority is required for a Belgian company (Bel art 70 *bis* (5)) and a three-quarters majority for a Luxembourg company (Lux art 67(4)). In this case the shareholders or their proxies present at the meeting must represent at least half the company's capital, and in Belgium at least one-half of any outstanding founders' shares as well (Bel art 70 *bis* (5); Lux art 67(4)). If this requirement is not fulfilled, a second meeting must be held whose deliberations will be valid in the case of a Belgian company if those present at the meeting represent at least one-quarter of the company's capital and at least one-quarter of the total number of any outstanding founders' shares (art 70 *bis* (5)), and in the case of a Luxembourg company if those present at the meeting represent at least one-third of the company's capital (art 67(4)).

If an amendment to the articles involves a modification of the rights of shareholders, the resolution passed by the general meeting must be approved by the same fraction of the shareholders of the class concerned at a separate class meeting as is required of the shareholders in order to pass the resolution (Bel art 71A (1); Lux art 69).

4 Take-overs and mergers

(a) Take-overs

The rules governing take-over and other bids in Belgium are an extension of the provisions of arts 26–29 of Royal Decree No 185 of 9th July 1935, which have been considered above. In 1964 legislation was passed by which offers to the public to buy or exchange shares or bonds must be preceded fifteen days beforehand by the submission of details of the proposed operation to the *Commission Bancaire*, which may require the operation to be delayed for three months if it thinks it will disturb the market, or if the publicity material intended to be used in connection with the operation might lead the public into error as to its nature (Law of 10th June 1964, art 22(2)).

The Luxembourg legislation is in precisely the same form as the Belgian legislation of 1935, and is contained in the *Arrêté grand-ducal* of 19th June 1965, arts 14–20. Because the two systems of law are very similar, only Belgian law is dealt with below. It should be emphasised however that the Luxembourg legislation is only applicable to bids for securities where the consideration offered consists of newly issued shares.

Belgian law confers an almost unfettered discretion on the Banking Commission to prohibit the making of bids or to permit them only if the offeror complies with the Commission's requirements as to the terms of the bid, the disclosure of information or the conduct of the offeror while the bid is current. Although the Commission is only empowered to delay the launching or continuance of the bid, its intervention is sufficient in practice to defeat any bid. In addition, if an offeror seeks a stock exchange quotation for shares or bonds offered in exchange for the shares sought to be acquired under a bid, the Ministry of Finance may prohibit the grant of the quotation at the request of the Banking Commission if the latter's requirements in respect of the bid are not respected (Royal Decree No 185 of 9th July 1935, art 32).

The Commission's Annual Reports set out the rulings it has given in dealing with take-over and other bids. Although these rulings do not embody statements of law and can be departed from when occasion demands, they are sufficiently general to be regarded as representing the existing ground-rules for Belgian practice in respect of bids.

The Commission has stated that it does not take a view of the merits of bids (Annual Report 1964, p96). Where competing bids are made it is merely concerned to ensure that they are fairly presented so that the shareholders of the offeree company can effectively decide whether a bid shall succeed or fail (Annual Report 1977–78, p115). Shareholders, including those of different classes, must always be treated on a footing of strict equality (Annual Report 1978–79, pp112–13). The same price must be paid to all of the holders of the same class of shares when a bid is current, whether the shares are acquired under the bid or outside it. If an offeror purchases shares on the stock exchange or by private negotiation when a bid is current, shareholders who accept the bid must be paid the same price as that paid for shares acquired outside the bid if it is higher than the price at which they agreed to sell their shares (Annual Report 1971–72, pp163–4). When a controlling block of shares is acquired by private negotiation, any extra sum paid for the acquisition of control must be divided among all the shareholders. Where a person or group of persons make extensive purchases of shares on the stock exchange and the Commission conclude that they are seeking control of the company in question, it will require them to provide the same information as if they had made a general offer to accept shares tendered to them (Annual Report 1971–72, pp165–7). Where a controlling block of shares is obtained by means of private negotiations with the controlling shareholders, the Commission may require the controllers to make a public offer for the remaining shares. It has, however, permitted holders of a controlling block who acquired their shares at a price below that at which they were listed on the stock exchange to make an offer to purchase all the shares belonging to the remaining shareholders at the price ruling on the stock exchange (Annual Report 1976–77, p103).

The offeror must submit an offer document which contains information on the company to be acquired, the purpose of the bid, the future policy to be followed by the offeror company in respect of the offeree company's undertaking, the basis for calculating the price or other consideration offered under the bid, and confirmation of the availability of the funds needed for the operation

(Annual Report 1964, pp100–3). A bid may only be made subject
to conditions which are objective in character (eg acceptance being
given in respect of a stated minimum number of shares); an offeror
is not allowed to insert conditions enabling him to cancel the bid if
he does not think that he has acquired sufficient influence over the
company's board, or sufficient shares to ensure representation on
the board (Annual Report 1964, p100).

Normally the Commission will allow a bid to be made only if its
acceptance in full will result in the offeror acquiring control of the
offeree company, or if the offeror already has such control (Annual
Report 1971–72, pp158–9). However, bids which cannot result in
the offeror acquiring control and any other kinds of partial bids may
be permitted, but not if their purpose is to defeat a bid for control
made by another person (Annual Report 1971–72, pp158–9).
When a partial bid is made, the same proportion of shares must be
acquired from all the accepting shareholders. The directors of the
offeree company must have the chance to comment on the terms of
a bid before the offer document is published, but they are not bound
to make a recommendation for acceptance or rejection of the bid to
the offeree company's shareholders (Annual Report 1964, p102;
Annual Report 1974–75, p166–7), unless there are competing
bids, when they must at least publish a comparison of the bids for
the shareholders' benefit (Annual Report 1971–72, p162).

The Commission has no direct legal power to prohibit stock
exchange transactions, but it may do so indirectly in connection with
general bids by imposing requirements on the parties to the bid. The
Commission may persuade the stock exchange authorities to suspend the listing of shares subject to a bid whilst it is current (Annual
Report 1976–77, pp107–9) or in order to prevent speculative price
movements when a bid is made (Annual Report 1972–73,
pp141–2). The Commission stated in the latter report that persons
who hold privileged information must not only refrain from any
kind of dealings themselves, but must also display the utmost
discretion and take appropriate steps to ensure the confidentiality
of the information. The Commission may prohibit the offeror and
offeree companies and their directors from entering into stock
exchange transactions in the shares of either company between the
launching of a bid and its expiration (Annual Report 1971–72,
p159). As yet, however, the Commission has laid down no general
principle that an intending offeror may not acquire shares of the
offeree company between the time when it decides to make a bid
and the publication of the bid.

(b) Mergers

Belgian law, unlike the Luxembourg Law (art 148 *bis*), does not contain any specific provisions governing company mergers (*fusions*). However, in practice, two kinds of mergers are distinguished. These are mergers by formation of a new company, which take place when two or more existing companies form a new company to which they transfer all their assets and liabilities in return for shares, and mergers by acquisition, which occur when one company transfers all its assets and liabilities to another already existing company in return for an issue of shares by the latter. The second type of merger is commoner. Mergers by acquisition are subject to special rules which have been developed by a special body of case law and certain of these rules are also applicable to mergers by formation of a new company. There are a number of unresolved controversial issues concerning mergers; these have related in particular to their effects on creditors and employees of the transferee company. Although the reform of the law governing mergers has been under consideration for several years and has been rendered necessary by the enactment of the Third Council Directive on Mergers (OJL 293/36 of 20th October 1978), no new legislation concerning mergers has yet been enacted or is in prospect.

Mergers by acquisition usually require resolutions of the general meetings of the merging companies passed by a three-quarters majority in accordance with the provisions of the articles. The objects clauses of the companies to be merged must be similar, or the objects of one of them must be complementary to or compatible with those of the other company. If this is not so, a prior amendment of the objects clause of one of the companies must take place, for which a four-fifths majority vote at a general meeting is required, and in addition special reports by the directors and by the auditors setting out the reasons for the alteration and stating the financial position of the company must be included in the agenda (Bel art 70 *bis*). The merging companies must be of the same type (ie both SAs or SPRLs) and if they are not, one of the companies must be converted into the other type of company. The merger must be approved by each class of shareholders of the two companies by a three-quarters majority. All the merging companies must have Belgian nationality.

If the above requirements are fulfilled, the operation will be treated as a merger by acquisition, provided that certain other conditions are also fulfilled:

1 All the assets of the transferor company must be transferred to

the transferee company, but sufficient assets may be retained by the transferor company to satisfy debts and claims for which it will continue to be liable after the merger has been completed.

2 The assets of the transferor company must be transferred wholly in exchange for shares in the transferee company, but the assumption of the debts and liabilities of the transferor company by the transferee company is not treated as conflicting with this requirement.

3 The merger is subject to the requirement that the transferor company be dissolved. If a company were to transfer its assets and liabilities but not be dissolved, it would remain liable for all its outstanding debts and on its outstanding contracts, and this would militate against the operation being a merger.

Article 148 *bis* of the Luxembourg Law of 1915 provides that when a public company transfers all its assets and liabilities to another public company, the liquidators of the transferor company may be allotted the shares issued by the transferee company as consideration for transfer of the transferor company's assets and liabilities, and may then distribute those shares to the shareholders of the transferor company after satisfying the transferor company's debts and liabilities not assumed by the transferee company, but without satisfying the claims of bondholders of the transferor company or depositing the amount necessary for that purpose. The transferee company is required to fulfil all the obligations owed by the transferor company to its bondholders, and is also bound by any securities over the transferor company's assets which were created for their benefit. A Luxembourg SA may merge with an SA formed under the laws of another country whose own legislation contains reciprocal provisions.

5 Dissolution and liquidation

(a) Dissolution

An SA is dissolved on the expiration of the period for which it was formed, not exceeding thirty years, but its existence may be prolonged for successive further periods of thirty years by an amendment of its articles (Bel art 102; Lux art 99). An SA may also be dissolved by a resolution of the general meeting that it shall be dissolved before the period fixed for its duration has expired; the resolution must be passed by a three-quarters majority in the case of a Belgian company, and by a two-thirds majority in the case of a Luxembourg company. An SA may furthermore be dissolved by the court on the application of any interested person six months after the number of shareholders in the company has been reduced below seven (Bel art 104; Lux art 101). In this connection a frequently used method for dissolving a company is to obtain the transfer of all the shares to one shareholder; the sole shareholder then appears before a notary who declares the dissolution of the company in a notarial act which must be published in the official gazette.

If an SA has lost one-half of its capital the board of directors must call a meeting to decide whether the company shall be dissolved. In the case of a Belgian company the resolution for dissolution must be passed by a three-quarters majority and in the case of a Luxembourg company by a two-thirds majority (Bel art 103; Lux art 100).

If the loss amounts to three-quarters of the company's capital and shareholders representing one-quarter of the company's capital vote in favour of the company's dissolution, the company is dissolved (Bel art 103; Lux art 100).

A commercial company or partnership of any kind continues to exist during the winding up of its affairs (Bel art 178(1); Lux art 141(1)). The company may complete transactions which have been commenced, but in principle it may not enter into new ones. Its assets continue to belong to it, and it continues to be bound by its obligations during the liquidation. The functions of the directors cease on the dissolution of the company. All documents issued by a dissolved company must mention the fact that it is in liquidation (Bel art 178(2); Lux art 141(2)).

(b) Liquidation

In principle the same rules are applicable to the winding up of all commercial companies and partnerships. Liquidators are appointed in accordance with the provisions of the company's articles. If no provision is made in the articles, the liquidators of an SA are appointed by a resolution of a general meeting passed by a simple majority. If the appointment of liquidators cannot be otherwise effected, the court must appoint them (Bel art 179; Lux art 142). When liquidators have not been appointed, the directors are deemed to be liquidators as far as third parties are concerned (Bel art 180; Lux art 143). The liquidators may make calls on the shareholders to the extent necessary to pay the company's debts and the costs of the liquidation (Bel art 183; Lux art 146). They also have the further powers granted them under arts 181 and 182 of the

Belgian Law and arts 144 and 145 of the Luxembourg Law of 1915, except where the articles or the resolution by which they are appointed otherwise provide. The relevant legislation empowers the liquidators to do all necessary acts for the purpose of realising the company's assets, but after its debts and liabilities have been discharged, its residual assets may be distributed *in specie* between its shareholders (Bel art 185; Lux art 148). Certain acts done for the purpose of realising the company's assets, for example, the continuation of its business or the transfer of its assets as a whole, require the approval of the general meeting (Bel art 182; Lux art 185).

The liquidators may, without prejudice to the rights of preferential creditors, pay the debts of the company on a *pro rata* basis, without distinguishing between debts which are immediately payable and those which are not yet due, but debts which will fall due in the future or which are conditional must be appropriately discounted. However, liquidators may instead pay only debts which are immediately due if it is evident that the company's assets substantially exceed its liabilities, or if debts which are not yet due are adequately secured (Bel art 184; Lux art 147). The Belgian Supreme Court has decided (1939 *Pasicrisie* 1 486) that the principle of equality between unsecured creditors prevents any such creditor from setting off any debt owed by him to the company against his claim against the company. In a further judgment (1964 *Pasicrisie* 1 573) the Supreme Court held that a winding up involves an equality of entitlement on the part of unsecured creditors, so that their rights must be irrevocably determined at the time when the company goes into liquidation. Thus an unsecured creditor of a company in liquidation has a right to be paid the same percentage of the value of his claim and no more as any other unsecured creditor. The Supreme Court has also held (1968 *Pasicrisie* 1 1126) that debts incurred by a company subsequent to its dissolution must be paid fully out of its assets before its existing debts and liabilities.

The liquidators are required to deposit sufficient sums to ensure the payment of an equal percentage of the debts owed to creditors who have not been traced as has been paid on other debts. They may do the same in respect of conditional or disputed debts. After this has been done, they must distribute the residual assets of the company to its shareholders, who become co-owners of those assets as from the completion of the liquidation. The general meeting may authorise the liquidators to repay the shareholders' capital by means of the repurchase of their shares on the stock exchange or by calling on shareholders to tender their shares for cancellation, and all the shareholders are entitled to be treated equally in this respect (Bel art 185; Lux art 148).

The liquidators must call a general meeting each year during the liquidation in order to report on its progress (Bel art 187; Lux art 150). When the liquidation has been completed, the liquidators must call a general meeting to which they must present their accounts. This meeting appoints one or more auditors to review the accounts and report on them. A second meeting must then be called to consider the auditors' report and to approve the liquidators' accounts and discharge the liquidators from further liability. Notice of the conclusion of the liquidation must be published in the official gazette (Bel art 188; Lux art 151). Unpaid creditors may bring an action against the liquidators for the wrongful administration of the company's assets within five years after the date when notice of the conclusion of the liquidation was published.

THE BELGIAN SOCIÉTÉ DE PERSONNES À RESPONSABILITÉ LIMITÉE (SPRL)

The provisions of the Belgian Commercial Code in respect of the *société de personnes à responsabilité limitée* (SPRL) are based on the corresponding French Law, but differ from French law in a number of important respects. The principal differences between a Belgian SPRL and an SA are as follows:

(1) An SPRL may be formed by two or more persons, but corporations may not be members of it and its total membership cannot exceed fifty, except where the members in excess of that number are the spouse, parents or children of a deceased member to whom he has bequeathed his shares, or a spouse to whom shares have been transferred on the division of matrimonial property held in community by spouses (art 119). The articles of the company are executed by all the members and notarised (art 4(2)), and must contain the same information as the articles of an SA (art 121). The company's share capital must be at least BF 250,000 (£3,080 approximately) and must be divided into shares (*parts*) of an equal nominal value of at least BF 1,000 each (arts 120 and 124). The company comes into being when the members have subscribed for the whole of the share capital and have paid to the company at least BF 250,000 for the shares which they subscribe in cash plus one-fifth of the excess of the company's share capital over BF 250,000, and the consideration for the shares allotted otherwise than for cash

has been furnished in full (art 110). If any shares are allotted for a non-cash consideration an expert appointed by the court must verify the value of the consideration as in the case of an SA (art 110 *bis*).

(2) A member (*associé*) of an SPRL may only transfer his shares with the consent of at least half of his fellow members who between them hold three-quarters of the remaining shares; such consent is not necessary for transfer to another member, or to the transferor's spouse, or to any of his lineal ascendants or descendants, or to other persons to whom the articles permit shares to be transferred (art 126). An appeal lies to the court against the refusal of consent, and if the court considers it to have been arbitrarily withheld, the shareholders who have opposed the transfer have three months from the date of the decision in which to find purchasers of the shares at the price and according to the conditions stipulated in the articles. Where the articles contain no applicable provisions, the price and the conditions are fixed by the court, unless the parties agree on them. If the shareholders who oppose the transfer fail to find purchasers at the appropriate price within three months, the intending transferor may within forty days following the expiration of the three months require the company to be dissolved (art 127). An SPRL may not issue bonds.

(3) The affairs of a company are managed by one or more managers (*gérants*) appointed for any desired length of time by the members or by the articles (art 129(1)). Unless the articles otherwise provide, a manager appointed by the articles is assumed to have been appointed for the duration of the company, and in that case the shareholders may only remove him for serious cause (art 129(3)). Each manager may perform all the acts necessary for the achievement of the company's objects, except those which are reserved by law to the general meeting (art 130(1)), and each manager has authority to represent the company in transactions with third persons (art 130(2)).

The articles may empower one or more specified managers alone to act in the name of the company in transactions with third persons, whether alone or jointly, and this provision may be invoked against a third person if it is published in the official gazette (art 130(4)). Otherwise restrictions imposed on the powers of the managers by the articles or by the general meeting are ineffective against third persons, even if published (art 130(3)). The company is bound by acts done by the managers which fall outside the objects of the company, unless the company proves that the third party knew, or must have known, that this was so, and mere publication of the articles is not sufficient proof of such knowledge (art 130(5)).

The members must appoint supervisors (*commissaires*), whose functions are the same as those of the supervisors of an SA; if the membership does not exceed five, however, the members may exercise the supervisors' functions themselves (art 134).

(4) The rules governing meetings of shareholders are the same as for an SA, except that a shareholder may vote by sending a written notice to the meeting instead of attending in person or by proxy (arts 3 and 136). The rules for the presentation of annual accounts are also the same as for an SA, and within thirty days after approval by the shareholders, a copy of the annual accounts must be filed at the office of the commercial court where the company is registered (art 137).

(5) The grounds for the dissolution of an SPRL are substantially the same as those for the dissolution of an SA. However, the reduction of the membership of an SPRL below seven is not a ground for its dissolution, and an SPRL, unlike an SA, may be dissolved by the court if there is just cause for it to be dissolved, for example where a member fails to fulfil his obligations or where prolonged infirmity renders him incapable of attending to the company's affairs (Civil Code, art 1871; Court of Appeal, Brussels, 2nd June 1944, Rev prat soc 1948 59). A serious conflict between members of an SPRL relating to the dismissal of a director may be a just cause for dissolution (Rev prat soc 1956 277).

In addition an SPRL may be dissolved in the circumstances which have been considered above where a shareholder is refused the consent of the other shareholders for a transfer of his shares and those other shareholders fail to find a purchaser of the shares within the appropriate period (art 127). The rules relating to the liquidation of an SPRL are, with certain minor differences, the same as those which govern the liquidation of an SA.

THE LUXEMBOURG SOCIÉTÉ À RESPONSABILITÉ LIMITÉE (SRL)

The Luxembourg Law of 18th September 1933 governing *sociétés à responsabilité limitée* (SRL) follows the French model more closely than does Belgian law. The principal differences between a Belgian SPRL and a Luxembourg SRL are as follows:

(1) Corporations may be members of a Luxembourg SRL.

(2) An SRL may be formed by two persons, but its membership cannot exceed forty, unless the members in excess of that number are legatees of a deceased member's shares, or unless the excess membership results from the division of matrimonial property held in community by spouses (art 181(1)). The capital of an SRL must be at least 100,000 Fr (£1,230 approximately), and must be divided into equal shares whose nominal value is 500 Fr or a multiple thereof (art 182). The whole of the share capital must be paid up before the company comes into being (art 183).

(3) Shares in an SRL may only be transferred to a non-member *inter vivos* with the approval of a general meeting by a resolution passed by a three-quarters majority (art 189). There is no appeal to the court against the refusal of consent. An SRL may issue bonds, but may not offer any of its shares or bonds for public subscription (art 188(1)).

(4) The management and control of an SRL are governed by similar rules to those which apply to an SPRL. However, the Co-determination Law of 1974 may apply to certain SRLs, in which case the number of directors must be nine, one-third of whom must be representatives of the employees. Supervisors (*commissaires*) need only be appointed if the membership exceeds twenty-five (art 200(1)), and an annual general meeting, too, need only be held if the membership exceeds this number (art 196(1)).

(5) The Luxembourg Law of 1933 only contains one specific provision governing the dissolution of an SRL, by which it may be dissolved by the court at the request of the Public Attorney (*Procureur de l'État*) if it carries on activities which infringe the criminal law or which constitute serious breaches of the companies legislation (art 203). However, it would appear that an SRL may also be dissolved when there is just cause (Civil Code, art 1871), or when all the shares become vested in one shareholder. The rules governing the liquidation are substantially the same as those which govern the liquidation of Belgian SAs and SPRLs.

CHAPTER 6

GREECE

The principal types of business association which may be formed
under Greek law are the commercial partnership (*homorrythmos
etairia*), the limited partnership (*heterorrythmos etairia*), the incorporated public company (*anonymos etairia*), and the incorporated
private company (*etairia periosmenis efthynis*). All these kinds of
business associations are commercial by reason of their form.
Certain less common forms of business association exist; these
include the silent partnership (*afanis etairia*), the co-operative
society (*synetairismos*), and the joint ownership of ships (*symp-
loioktissia*). A new type of business association, the maritime company (*naftiki etairia*), was introduced by Law 959 of 1979. The
purpose of this Law was to provide a simple and flexible type of
company for Greek ship owners, and so to induce them to employ
this form rather than to make use of Panamanian or Liberian
companies, or of other flags of convenience, for the purpose of
registering their vessels.*

The present chapter will be limited to a discussion of the
anonymos etairia and the *etairia periosmenis efthynis*. The former
type of company is principally governed by the provisions of Law
2190 of 1920, as modified by Royal Decree 174 of 1963, and
subsequently amended. The latter type of company is principally
governed by the provisions of Law 3190 of 1955. None of the
harmonising directives of the Council of Ministers of the European
Communities in the field of company law has so far been implemented in Greece, and such implementation appears unlikely in
the near future.

Except where otherwise stated, references to articles by number

---

* This law has been translated into English by the Greek Maritime Law Association.
The articles of the company must be in writing and must be registered with the
Registry of Maritime Companies. The company acquires legal personality from the
time of such registration (Law 959 of 1979, art 2). (The authors would like to thank
Mr Zacharias of the National Bank of Greece, 50 St Mary Axe, London EC4 for
the information he has given them concerning this type of company.)

in the first part of this chapter are references to articles of Law 2190 of 1920, as modified by Royal Decree 174 of 1963, and subsequently amended. References to articles by number in the second part of this chapter are references to articles of Law 3190 of 1955.

ANONYMOS ETAIRIA (AE)

1 Formation

There must be at least two founders of an AE, but the subsequent concentration of all the company's shares in the hands of a single shareholder does not entail the dissolution of the company. The articles (*katastaticon*) of the company must be contained in a notarised deed, which must be approved by the Minister of Commerce, who must also consent to the establishment of the company. The Minister must approve the articles and give his consent to the establishment of the company if he is satisfied that the articles have been drawn up in accordance with the laws in force, including the law governing AEs. The articles, together with the decision of the Minister granting permission to establish the company and sanctioning its articles, must be published in the official gazette (*Demosiero Epistemos*). The company is incorporated and acquires legal personality as from the date of such publication (Commercial Code, art 37; Law 2190 of 1920 concerning AEs, art 4).

The articles of an AE must provide for (Law 2190 of 1920, art 2):

1 The name of the company, which must indicate the nature of the company's business, and contain the words '*Anonymos Etairia*'.

2 The nature of the company's business.

3 The registered office of the company, which must be in Greece.

4 The duration of the company.

5 The amount of the company's capital, which must not be less than 5 m drachmae (£44,700 approximately) paid in full at the date of incorporation (art 8(2)), except where the company appeals to the public to subscribe for the whole or part of the company's capital, when this amount is increased to 10 m drachmae (£89,400 approximately) paid in full at the date of incorporation (art 8a).

6 The method of payment for the share capital.

7 The number and method of issue of the shares (*meridia*), the

nominal value of which may not be fixed at an amount less than 100 drachmae, nor an amount more than 10,000 drachmae (arts 14(1) and 10(2)).

8 The method of convening, the composition, the operation and the powers of the board of directors.

9 The method of convening, the composition, the operation, and the powers of the general meetings.

10 The auditors.

11 The rights of the shareholders.

12 The balance sheet and the appropriation of profits.

13 The dissolution of the company, and the winding up of its assets.

They may also contain any other lawful provision that the founders wish to include.

The capital must be fully subscribed by the shareholders at the date of incorporation of the company, and the minimum capital must be paid up at that date (arts 8 and 12). The shares of the company must each have the same nominal value (Commercial Code, art 35), and they may be paid for in cash or in kind, but contributions in kind must consist of assets whose value is capable of assessment, and not of undertakings to perform work or supply services.

The articles of the company may provide that the amount of the company's capital which exceeds the minimum capital need only be partly paid at the date of the formation of the company. At least one-quarter of the company's capital in excess of the minimum must be paid up at the date of incorporation, and the balance together with any premiums must be paid up within ten years of that date. Shares which are not fully paid up must be in registered form (art 12(2)(c)). The board of directors is required to hold a special meeting within two months after the incorporation of the company in order to determine whether the amount of capital required to be paid up at the time of incorporation has actually been paid (art 11). If it has not actually been paid up, the Minister of Commerce may revoke his approval of the articles of the company (art 48(1)(a)).

Contributions in kind made at the time of incorporation of the company, or subsequently on an increase of capital, must be valued by a committee consisting of one or more senior civil servants, a representative of the Chamber of Commerce, and a private individual (art 9). The acquisition of real or other property for the purpose of permanent exploitation within two years after the company comes into existence or within two years following an increase of the company's capital is null and void, if the company gives in return consideration greater than one-tenth of the company's capital, and the sellers of the property are directors or their relations, or have acquired the property from a director or his relation within the twelve months prior to signature of the articles, or the increase of capital (art 10(1)). Such transactions are valid if they have been permitted by a decision of the Minister of Commerce following a valuation of the property by a special committee constituted in accordance with art 9.

A person who transacts business as the representative of a company which has not obtained permission to operate as such, or which does not exist at the time when such transaction is carried out, is liable to imprisonment and to a fine not exceeding 80,000 drachmae (art 54). A founder of a company may not exercise his rights in a manner which clearly offends good faith or morality, or which exceeds or conflicts with the corporate and economic objects which the rights are intended to further (Civil Code, art 281). A founder who causes damage to another by his fault in a manner contrary to law is bound to compensate that other for the damage (Civil Code, art 914). If a founder intentionally causes damage to another in a manner *contra bonos mores*, he is bound to compensate that other for the damage (Civil Code, art 919). A founder, director or manager who knowingly makes false declarations before any authority relating to the subscription and payment of the share capital or the issue price of shares is liable to imprisonment and a fine not exceeding 80,000 drachmae, or to either of these penalties.

2 Shares and bonds

(a) Shares

Shares may not be issued at a discount, but they may be issued at a premium (Law 2190 of 1920, art 14(2) and (3)). If a shareholder fails to pay an instalment of the issue price of shares belonging to him within three months after the expiration of any period fixed by a notice published in at least two daily newspapers, the shares are cancelled and new shares are issued equal in number to the forfeited shares within one month after the expiration of the prescribed period of three months. The issue takes place on the Athens Stock Exchange, and the balance of the issue price of the new shares remaining after the deduction of the sum due and all relevant charges is paid to the former holder. If the shares or some of them remain unsubscribed a further issue takes place within fifteen days, and if the remaining shares are not disposed of on this occasion, the company must reduce its capital by an amount corresponding to the total nominal value of the shares remaining unissued. If such a reduction takes place, the former shareholder remains liable to the company for the unpaid capital on his cancelled shares which have not been replaced by new shares (art 12(2)(e)). Moreover, the former shareholder is jointly and severally liable with the holder of the replacement shares for the payment of the whole of the issue price of these shares for two years after the registration of those shares in the name of the new shareholder (art 12(2)(d)).

Shares may be in registered or bearer form, provided in the latter case that the whole issue price is fully paid up. However, the shares of banking, insurance, railway and airline companies, or companies engaged in the production of gas, the generation and distribution of electric power, the installation and operation of town water supply or sewage systems, telecommunication, broadcasting or production of war material must always be in registered form (art 11a). Bearer shares are in very common use in practice, and the transfer of such shares can be effected by the delivery of the share certificate (Commercial Code, art 35(2); Civil Code, art 1034). A transferee who takes delivery in good faith of bearer shares from a transferor who has no title to them acquires a title to the shares, even though the owner of the shares has lost his share certificate or has had it stolen from him (Civil Code, art 1039).

The articles may require transfers of registered shares to be approved by the company; they may provide that such approval be given by the board of directors or the general meeting, and may also specify the reasons for which approval may be refused (art 3(8)). The transfer of registered shares takes place by means of an entry in a special register kept by the company; such an entry must be dated and signed by the transferor and the transferee or their representatives in the same way as inscribed stock of some British chartered companies used to be transferred. After every such transfer, a new certificate must be issued by the company, and the old certificate must be cancelled; or the transfer must be noted on the old certificate together with the name, address, occupation and nationality of the transferor and the transferee.

The transfer of registered shares of companies listed on the Athens Stock Exchange within the administrative district of Athens takes place by the endorsement of the share certificate by the transferor in favour of the transferee in the presence of a broker, who certifies that the signature of the transferor is authentic, as well as the fact that the share certificate has been delivered to the transferee. The endorsement must be authenticated by the registrar of the Settlement Department of the Athens Stock Exchange, who must inform the company of the transfer within a prescribed time period, so that the company can enter the transfer in its register of registered shares. A notarial act is necessary for the transfer of shares in a listed company outside the administrative district of Athens. Particulars of the notarial act and the name of the transferor and transferee must appear on the share certificate. A copy of the notarial act must be sent to the company, after the receipt of which the company enters the transfer on its register of registered shareholders (Law 2190 of 1920, art 8b(2); Law 3330 of 1955, art 5(1)).

A company may not acquire its own shares (art 16(1)). This prohibition does not apply: (*a*) to the acquisition of shares for the purpose of cancellation; (*b*) to acquisitions made on a reduction of capital; (*c*) to acquisitions made as a result of a process of execution of a judgment, or for the purpose of satisfying a debt due to the company; or (*d*) to acquisitions made by banking companies on behalf of a third party (art 16(2)). Shares acquired under (*a*) and (*b*) must be cancelled immediately, whilst those acquired under (*d*) must be sold within the shortest period of time possible (art 16(3)). Shares held by a company in itself may not be voted on at the general meeting (art 16(4)). A company may not accept its own shares or the shares of its subsidiaries as security for a loan made by it (art 17(1)). A company is deemed to be the subsidiary of another if the latter company owns shares amounting to more than one-half of its paid up capital (art 17(4)). A subsidiary may not invest any part of its share capital in the shares of another company which exercises control over it (art 17(3)).

At least some part of the annual profits of the company must be distributed to the shareholders. A general meeting may resolve by a three-fifths majority to capitalise profits that have been transferred to revenue reserves other than the general reserve, or which have been credited to provisions or to reserves maintained for special purposes, and the company may then issue fully paid bonus shares of an equivalent nominal value to the company's shareholders in proportion to their existing holdings. It may only do so when its general reserve exceeds 30 per cent of its share capital and, irrespective of the amount of its reserves, when five years have elapsed since the last capitalisation (Law 148 of 1967, art 1(3)).

The articles of the company may provide that shares may be

issued carrying the right to a preference dividend payable before the first dividend of at least 6 per cent required by art 45 of Law 2190 of 1920 is paid to the ordinary shareholders, and also carrying the right to repayment of capital in priority to ordinary share capital. The preference dividend may be made cumulative by the terms of the articles, which may also stipulate that the preference shareholders shall be entitled to participate to any extent desired in the residual profits of the company (art 3(2)).

Preference shares may be issued without voting rights, in which case the holders of the shares may be granted, in addition to the rights explained above, the right to the payment of a fixed rate of interest in the absence or insufficiency of profits (art 3(4)). The rights attached to preference shares may be abrogated or restricted only by a resolution passed by a special meeting of such shareholders by the affirmative votes of the holders of at least three-quarters of the capital in respect of which votes are cast on the resolution (art 3(5)).

The articles may provide that shareholders may be repaid capital which they have contributed to the company by amortising shares held by them, on condition that such amortisation takes place by the drawing of lots. The repayment of capital must be made out of the company's profits. The shareholder is given new shares, called *actions de jouissance*, in place of those which have been reimbursed, and all the rights which attached to his old shares attach to these new shares, except that he loses his right to be paid the corresponding amount of the nominal value of his shares in the liquidation of the company and, it would seem, his right to a first dividend.

Founders' shares are also recognised by law. They are divided into ordinary and extraordinary founders' shares (art 15). Ordinary founders' shares do not represent any contribution to the capital of the company and are issued in consideration for services rendered in connection with the formation of the company. The number of ordinary founders' shares may not exceed one-tenth of the number of issued shares (art 15(1)). Ordinary founders' shares only carry the right for their holders to receive an amount specified by the articles, which may not exceed one-quarter of the company's net profits after the deduction of the amount allocated to general reserves and the amount required for the payment of the first dividend (art 15(2) and (3)). Extraordinary founders' shares may be issued at the time of a company's establishment or subsequently in return for contributions in kind. The company is entitled to determine the terms on which the holders of the extraordinary founders' shares participate in the company's profits, and the terms for their redemption, which must take place no later than the time when the company ceases to have the use of the assets contributed (eg the expiration of a patent or a lease). A special committee, constituted in accordance with art 9 of Law 2190 of 1920, must verify the existence of the contributions in kind, and the period for which they are to be utilised (art 15(5)).

(b) Bonds

The general meeting of the company has sole competence to decide on the issue of bonds (*homologa* (art 34(1)). A public issue of bonds may only be made by a company which has a fully paid up share capital of at least 10 m drachmae, and the amount of the issue may not exceed the paid up capital (art 8a(2)). The issue must be made either through the medium of a bank, or through the Office of Consignments, Deposits and Loans (a national banking institution), the Post Office Savings Banks, or the Athens Stock Exchange, or through stockbrokers who have been granted permission to place the bonds by a special committee (art 8a(3)). Bonds may be in registered form, or be payable to order or to bearer.

Companies are permitted to issue bonds secured as to principal and as to interest by a mortgage on one or more items of real property belonging to the company or to a third party (art 3c(1)). Such an issue is subject to the permission of the Capital Market Committee, which must examine the adequacy of the security to be provided on the basis of particulars furnished by the company and the Registrar of Mortgages, and the company must nominate a common representative of the bondholders, which must be a bank (art 3c(2)). The issuing company must publish particulars of the bond issue in two daily newspapers (art 3c(3)). The mortgage may be cancelled only after the approval of the Capital Market Committee has been given, which approval must be granted when the representative of the bondholders has certified that the principal and interest has been fully repaid, or that any amount remaining unpaid out of the principal and interest has been deposited in favour of the bondholders with the Office of Consignments Deposits and Loans.

Convertible bonds may be issued if a general meeting at which a quorum consisting of shareholders or their proxies representing two-thirds of the paid up capital so decides by a three-fifths majority of the votes represented at the meeting (arts 3a, 24(3) and 31(2)). The shareholders have a preferential right to subscribe for the convertible bonds (art 13(5)). The total value of the shares which would be issued if all the bonds were converted may not exceed one-half of the present paid up capital of the company (art 3a(1)). When shares are allocated to bondholders who exercise their conversion rights, the company's capital is treated as having been increased, and the directors are required at the end of the accounting period during which the conversion took place to alter the provisions of the articles governing the amount of the company's capital, and to publish notice of the increase in the Public and Private Limited Liability Companies Bulletin, which forms part of the official gazette (art 3a(3)).

A company may also issue bonds which carry the right to receive a share of the company's profits or a sum dependent on the company's turnover, in addition to the interest payable on them. Greek law does not contain any rules governing the common representative of bondholders except in the case of bonds secured by a mortgage on real property.

3 Management and control

(a) Board of directors

The board of directors must consist of at least three persons (art 21(1)). Any natural person having full legal capacity and any legal person is qualified for membership. The articles may provide that candidates for appointments must be shareholders, or must fulfil other requirements. The election of the directors is in principle within the competence of the shareholders in general meeting, which is the supreme organ of the company (arts 33 and 34(1)(b)). The necessary quorum at the meeting consists of shareholders or their proxies representing at least one-fifth of the paid up capital, and the appointment is made by an ordinary resolution passed by a majority of the votes cast at the meeting (art 31(1)). The articles may provide that a particular shareholder or shareholders shall have the right to appoint not more than one-third of the total number of the board of directors. This right must be exercised before any necessary appointments to the board of directors are made by the general meeting, which will only be required to make appointments in respect of the vacancies remaining unfilled (art 18(3)). A director's term of office may not exceed six years, and a retiring director may be reappointed (art 19)). The directors may be empowered by the articles to fill a casual vacancy resulting from the death or retirement etc of a director until the next general meeting is held (art 34(2)(c)).

Directors may always be dismissed by the persons who appoint them, and there is no need for there to be substantial grounds for such dismissal. If a director has a service contract with his company, his dismissal may give rise to an action for damages. A director may be removed from office for substantial reasons by the competent court of the district where the company's registered office is situated, on the application of shareholders holding one-tenth of the paid up capital (art 18(4)).

Unless the articles specify the amount of remuneration or compensation payable by the company to a member of the board of directors, the payment of such remuneration or compensation is only permitted if the general meeting passes a special resolution giving its approval (art 24(2)). If the articles provide that the directors shall be entitled to a fixed share of the profits of the company, the amount of profits out of which this share is payable is determined in accordance with the formula contained in art 24(1). The court may reduce remuneration or compensation which has been approved by the passing of a resolution in a general meeting if it seems that it is exorbitant and the persons holding at least one-tenth of the capital in respect of which votes were cast on the resolution voted against such approval (art 24(2)).

The board of directors represents the company for all purposes (art 18(1)), and is authorised to decide on every matter relating to the management of the company, the administration of its property, and the pursuance of its objects (art 22(1)). It appears that transactions which are outside the objects of the company, or which are beyond the powers conferred on the directors by the articles, are not binding on the company. The powers of the directors may be restricted by resolution passed by the general meeting, but no such restriction may be relied on by the company against a third party acting in good faith (art 22(2)).

Directors may not borrow from, or be granted credit by, the company or have the company give guarantees or security for their debts. This prohibition extends to their spouses and to their blood relatives by marriage up to the third degree (art 23(1)). All other agreements between the company and its directors and their relatives mentioned in art 23a(1) are null and void, unless they have been previously approved by a special resolution in general meeting. Such a resolution is defeated if the holders of at least one-third of the share capital in respect of which votes are cast vote against it.

This provision has no effect on agreements entered into by a company with its customers in the ordinary course of its business (art 23a(2)).

Unless the articles otherwise provide, the directors must exercise their powers of managing and representing the company collectively. However, the articles may permit one or more of the directors or the managing directors to exercise all or any of the board's powers, and the board may delegate any of its powers to one or more of its members or to other persons (arts 18(2) and 22(3)).

Directors are liable to the company for loss caused by their fault in managing the company's affairs (art 22a(1)). A director will not incur such liability if he can show that he has carried out his functions with the diligence of a good head of a family. The diligence required by the latter standard is greater than that which the director is expected to exercise in connection with his own affairs. This present rule does not apply to the managing director, who is responsible even for slight negligence (*culpa levis*) or an omission to use ordinary care: the directors do not incur any liability in connection with acts or omissions expressly authorised by law or by a resolution of a general meeting (art 22a(2)). An action by the company against its directors based on faults in their management is brought by the board of directors on behalf of the company. Such an action must be brought where the general meeting so resolves, and also on the requisition of the holders of one-third of the company's capital (art 22b(1)). The company may waive or accept a compromise of its claim for damages against its directors within two years after such claim came into existence, provided that the compromise is approved by an ordinary resolution passed by a general meeting which is opposed by the holders of less than one-quarter of the share capital in respect of which votes are cast on the resolution (art 22a(4)).

(b) Auditors

All Greek AEs must have at least two auditors (art 36(1)). The function of the auditors of a Greek AE are wider than those of the auditors of a British public company. The auditors of a company whose shares or bonds are quoted on the stock exchange and of an insurance company must be chartered accountants (Decree Law 3329 of 1955, art 2(4)). Other companies are free to appoint whom they wish as auditors, although art 36a expresses a preference for graduates of the Graduate School of Economics and Business Science. The auditors must be appointed by a general meeting (Law 2190 of 1920, art 34(1)(*b*)). When the auditors have to be chartered accountants, they must be chosen from a list drawn up by the Supervisory Council of the Association of Chartered Accountants (art 36(2)).

The auditors are required to verify the accounting position of the company throughout the accounting period. They have the right of access to any book, document or account, including the minutes of general meetings and of the board of directors. They must make any necessary suggestions to the board of directors, and report any violation of the law or the articles to the Minister of Commerce (art 37(1)). They may also require the chairman of the board of directors to call an extraordinary general meeting (art 38(1)). They must audit the company's balance sheet and profit and loss account at the end of each accounting period and submit a report on the results of their audit to the annual general meeting. This report must state clearly whether the financial position of the company at the end of the relevant accounting period is properly shown in the balance sheet, and whether the profit or loss of that period is properly presented in the profit and loss account (art 37(1)). The balance sheet must be laid before the general meeting for approval (art 34(1)(*c*)).

(c) General meetings

A general meeting of shareholders has sole competence to decide upon: (*a*) the alteration of the articles; (*b*) the increase or reduction of the company's capital; (*c*) the election of directors and auditors; (*d*) the approval of the balance sheet; (*e*) the appropriation of the annual profits; (*f*) the issue of bonds; (*g*) the merger of the company with another company and its consequent dissolution; (*h*) the winding up of the company and the appointment of liquidators. Limited exceptions to this rule apply in the case of certain increases of capital, and the appointment of the first directors, and the filling of casual vacancies in the board of directors (art 34). The general meeting may be granted additional powers under the articles, and it is also competent, as the supreme organ of the company, to decide all matters concerning the company; this power includes the adoption of resolutions relating to the company's management (art 33), and any general resolution of a general meeting in this connection overrides a conflicting decision of the board of directors.

The directors call general meetings, but an extraordinary general meeting must be called on the requisition of the holders of at least one-twentieth of the company's paid up share capital (art 39(1)), or on the requisition of the auditors (art 38). An ordinary general meeting must be called within the first six months of the company's financial year to approve the company's balance sheet, to declare dividends out of the previous year's profits, to resolve whether the directors shall be discharged from any liabilities for breaches of duty during that year, and to appoint auditors (arts 23, 34 and 35).

Profits remaining after the deduction of any expense, loss, depreciation or other charge are called net profits. Before any distribution can be made of the net profits, a sum fixed by law or the articles of the company, which must be at least one-twentieth of these profits, must be transferred to the general reserve until it amounts to at least one-third of the share capital of the company or the greater amount specified by the articles (art 44). A deduction is next made from profits of a sum necessary for the payment of the first dividend: this sum must be at least 6 per cent of the paid up capital or 35 per cent of the company's net profits, whichever is the greater (art 45(2)). The distribution of 35 per cent of the company's net profits may only be prevented by a resolution passed by a three-quarters majority vote at the annual meeting (Law 148 of 1967, art 2(1) and (2)). The balance of the profits is disposed of in accordance with a resolution passed in conformity with the provisions of the articles: the balance may be used in whole or in part to make a bonus issue of shares, to constitute free reserves, or to pay an additional dividend (art 45(3)).

Notices calling general meetings must be posted at a prominent place in the company's offices and be published in the Public and Private Limited Liability Companies Bulletin and in a daily financial journal at least twenty days before they are held. The notice calling the meeting must clearly define the items on the agenda of the meeting (art 26(2)). A shareholder is not entitled to speak or vote in a general meeting if he has not deposited his share certificate with the company, or with the Office of Consignments Deposits and Loans or with a bank established in Greece, at least twenty days before the date fixed for holding the general meeting (art 28(1)). Copies of the balance sheet together with the directors' and auditors' report thereon must be made available to any shareholder requesting them at least ten days before the annual general meeting is held (art 27(1)).

The quorum for a general meeting is the presence in person or by proxy of the holders of one-fifth of the paid up capital (art 29(1)); resolutions are passed by a majority of the votes cast at the meeting, and abstentions are treated as votes cast against the resolution (art 31(1)). However, a larger quorum is required for a general meeting which has to consider a resolution for the change of the company's nationality or its objects, or an increase in the shareholders' obligations, or an increase in or the reduction of the share capital, or the issue of bonds, or an alteration in the method of distribution of the profits, or the merger of the company with another company, or the extension of the period fixed for the company's duration, or its dissolution; the quorum for these matters is the presence in person or by proxy of the holders of at least two-thirds of the company's paid up capital (art 29(3)). Resolutions on such matters are passed by a three-fifths majority of the votes cast; abstentions are treated as votes against the resolution (art 31(2)).

Votes are cast at all general meetings in proportion to the nominal value of shares, and shares cannot be issued without voting rights or with diminished voting rights (art 30(1)). An exception is made in the case of preference shares, which can be issued without voting rights or with limited voting rights (art 3(4)). An official of the Ministry of Commerce is entitled to attend a general meeting, but he is not entitled to vote thereat, or to express any opinion on the items on the agenda (art 53(1)).

A resolution passed in general meeting is void if the resolution infringes a statutory prohibition, or is contrary to good faith, or if it contravenes the statutory requirements governing the composition of, or the quorum or majority at, a general meeting, or if it violates provisions of the articles which are exclusively or mainly intended for the protection of creditors (Civil Code, arts 174 and 178; Law 2190 of 1920, art 35a(1) and (2)). In addition, a resolution is void if it is inconsistent with the nature of a public company, or if it violates statutory provisions which are designed to protect creditors, or which are otherwise in the public interest. Where a resolution is void, the invalidity may be invoked by anyone, provided that he institutes proceedings within two years of the date on which copies of the minutes of the general meeting at which the resolution was passed are submitted to the Ministry of Commerce.

A resolution passed in general meeting rejecting a request for information which must be given by law (see art 39(4)(a) and (b)) or under the company's articles, may be annulled by the court (art 35(b)(1)). Furthermore, a resolution passed by a general meeting approving a balance sheet which does not comply with the requirements of Law 2190 of 1920 or the company's articles or with accepted commercial practice, or in which depreciation is calculated or assets are valued in a manner different from that permitted by law, or which conceals profits so that the first dividend specified by the articles is not distributed, may be annulled by the court on the application of shareholders holding one-twentieth of the paid up share capital (art 35b(2)).

4 Take-overs and mergers

There appears to be no voluntary or statutory regulation of take-overs in Greece. In Greek law a merger between AEs may be carried out in three different ways. Firstly, one or more public companies may transfer all their assets and liabilities to another public company (the transferee or acquiring company) in consideration of the issue of shares of the acquiring company to the shareholders of the transferor company. Secondly, two or more transferor companies may simultaneously transfer their assets and liabilities to a company newly formed by them in return for the issue of shares in the newly formed company to the shareholders of the transferor companies. Thirdly, the whole of the assets and liabilities of one or more companies may be transferred to another company in consideration for a cash payment: the transferor company is then automatically dissolved without a winding up being necessary, and the considersation paid by the transferee company is divided between the shareholders of the transferor company (art 68).

To be legally effective, a merger requires approval by general meetings of the transferor and acquiring companies. The necessary quorum is the presence in person or by proxy of the holders of at least two-thirds of the paid up capital of the relevant company. The resolutions must be passed by a three-fifths majority of the votes cast at each meeting, abstentions being treated as votes cast against the resolution (art 68(1)). If the merger takes place by means of one or more companies transferring all their assets and liabilities to one of those companies or to another existing company, the capital of the transferee company must be increased. A merger contract is necessary, and this contract must be appropriately authenticated by a notary. The value of the assets which are to be transferred or contributed to a company on a merger must be verified by a special committee constituted in accordance with the provisions of art 9; however, the Minister of Commerce may dispense with the requirement where the merging companies are large ones (art 68(2)).

The resolutions passed by the general meetings of the merging companies must be approved by the Minister of Commerce. These resolutions, together with the merger contract, the ministerial approval of the resolutions concerning the merger, and the report of the special committee must be published in the Public and Private Limited Liability Companies Bulletin (arts 9(6) and 69(1)). On the publication of the merger in the Bulletin, the merger is treated as being completed. Thereupon, all the transferor company's assets and its debts and liabilities vest by law in the acquiring company.

5 Dissolution and liquidation

(a) Dissolution

An AE is dissolved in the following circumstances:

(1) Upon the expiration of the period specified in its articles (art 47a(1)(a)); in this case the dissolution comes about automatically by law, but the existence of the company may be prolonged by a resolution passed by its general meeting either before or after its dissolution in accordance with the requirements of arts 29(3) and 31(2), provided that the distribution of its assets to its shareholders has not already begun.

(2) Upon the publication of a resolution for dissolution in the Public and Private Limited Liability Companies Bulletin after this resolution has been approved by the Minister. The resolution must be passed in conformity with the special quorum and majority requirements of arts 29(3) and 31(2) (art 47a(1)(b)). If it appears from the company's balance sheet that the value of the company's assets after the deduction of its liabilities is less than one-half of its paid up share capital, the board of directors must convene a general meeting to decide whether or not the company shall be dissolved (art 47(1)). A company which has been dissolved may be revived by the passing of a further resolution in accordance with the requirements of arts 29(3) and 31(1).

(3) When the company is adjudged bankrupt in bankruptcy proceedings (Law 1690 of 1920, art 47a(1)(c)).

(4) Upon the revocation of the ministerial decisions authorising the establishment of the company. The reasons for such revocation are enumerated exhaustively in arts 48(1)(a)–(d) and 48a: the most important of these is that it appears from the last balance sheet that the value of the company's assets after the deduction of its liabilities is less than one-twentieth of the company's paid up share capital.

The articles may provide for additional grounds for dissolution.

(b) Liquidation

Except where the company is adjudicated bankrupt, the dissolution of the company is followed by its liquidation. The company continues to exist as a legal person during the liquidation, and the provisions of Law 2190 of 1920 continue to apply. The general meeting is still the supreme organ of the company and retains all its powers during the liquidation (art 49(3)), but the board of directors is replaced by the liquidators, who are appointed by the shareholders in general meeting, or in accordance with the provisions of the articles (art 49(1)). The Law of 1920 contains few specific provisions governing the conduct of the liquidation, and the opinion has been expressed both by text writers and by the courts in their relevant decisions that the provisions of arts 780–782 of the Civil Code governing the liquidation of civil companies are applicable by way of analogy. The liquidators must, on assuming their duties, take an inventory of the company's assets and ensure that a balance sheet is published in the press and in the Public and Private Limited Liability Companies Bulletin (art 49(1)). The liquidators must terminate the carrying on of the company's business, convert the company's assets into money in order to satisfy its creditors and distribute its residual assets among its shareholders. It has been held in certain judicial decisions that the consent of the court and a public auction is necessary when immovable property and negotiable securities are sold during the course of a liquidation, whilst other courts have treated a public auction as not being essential in these circumstances.

If the liquidation lasts for more than one year, the liquidators must submit a report to the general meeting explaining the reasons which have prevented the earlier conclusion of the liquidation (art 49(3)). They must submit a final balance sheet in a general meeting on the conclusion of the liquidation (art 49(2)).

ETAIRIA PERIOSMENIS EFTHYNIS (EPE)

The EPE was introduced into Greece by Law 3190 of 9–16th April 1955, and is now in very common use in that country; many AEs have been converted into EPEs and many newly formed companies have been EPEs. The principal differences between an AE and an EPE are as follows:

(1) There must be at least two founders of an EPE and its articles

must be contained in a notarised deed. They must include (*a*) the name, surname, profession, domicile and nationality of the members; (*b*) the name of the company, which must indicate the nature of the company's business or the names of its principal shareholders, or contain both of these elements; (*c*) the registered office of the company, which must be in Greece, and its objects; (*d*) a statement that the company is an EPE; (*e*) particulars of the company's capital which must be not less than 200,000 drachmae (£1,790 approximately), each member being required to take at least one share having a nominal value of 10,000 drachmae or a multiple thereof (art 4(1)); (*f*) particulars of the number of shares held by each member and a declaration made by the founders that the company's capital has been paid up; (*g*) particulars of any contributions in kind and of their value, the name of each contributor, and the total amount of share capital paid up by contributions in kind (art 6(2)). The valuation of the contributions in kind must take place in accordance with the rules applicable to AEs.

Agreements between members of an EPE concerning certain matters are valid only if included in the articles. These are agreements for: supplementary contributions and other additional obligations of members beyond the payment of contributions in money or in kind; the prohibition of competition by the members; any absolute or conditional restriction on the transfer of shares; the withdrawal of members from membership; or the dissolution of the company for a reason not provided for by law (art 6(3)).

A copy of the company's articles must be deposited with the registrar of the court of first instance of the district where the company's registered office is to be situated, and a summary of the articles must be published in the Public and Private Limited Liability Companies Bulletin (art 8). The company acquires legal personality from the date of such publication (art 9). There is no provision for judicial or administrative measures suspending the incorporation of the company so as to ensure compliance by the founders with the rules governing its formation. However, if certain of the requirements for the formation of the company are not complied with, the court must declare the company to be null and void if an action for its annulment is brought by any interested person (art 7).

(2) Each share in an EPE has the same nominal value. Shares are freely transferable and transmissible on death and on the constitution of a dowry on marriage, unless the articles impose restrictions: the only restriction they may impose on transmission on death and on the constitution of a dowry is that the share belonging to the

deceased member or the donor shall be sold to a person designated by the company at a price determined by the president of the court of first instance, and that the proceeds of the sale shall be paid to the person otherwise entitled to the shares (arts 28 and 29). Transfers of a share must be effected by a written instrument attested by a notary. A transfer is only effective against the company's register of shareholders. A share in an EPE, unlike one in an AE, may not be represented by a share certificate (art 27(2)). Furthermore, a share may not be represented by a negotiable instrument in registered or in order or bearer form. In practice, the holders of shares in an EPE are often given a document containing a summary of the company's articles (including a statement of the capital held by them) and containing a statement that it does not constitute a negotiable instrument.

(3) The managers of the company are normally appointed by its articles or by a resolution of its members and they may be appointed for any length of time. In default of such appointment, all the members of the company are treated as being its managers. Unless the articles otherwise provide, the managers must act jointly (arts 16 and 17). The managers represent the company in dealings with outsiders, and perform on its behalf any acts of management or disposition which fall within the company's objects (art 18(1)). Limitations on the authority of managers to bind the company imposed by the articles may not be invoked against outsiders dealing with the company. A manager may not on his own behalf, or on behalf of another person, enter into any transaction in the company's name which falls within the objects of the company. A manager may not be a member of a general partnership, or of a limited partnership, or of another EPE pursuing the same objects, unless he is so authorised by a unanimous resolution passed by all the members in general meeting (art 20). A member of the company who is appointed to be a manager by the articles for a fixed period may only be dismissed if there are substantial grounds for his dismissal; a resolution for this purpose must be passed in general meeting by a majority comprising more than one-half of the company's members holding more than half the company's capital; the dismissal then takes place if the competent court so orders, after having established the existence of substantial grounds for the resolution (art 19(1) and (3)). A manager appointed by the articles who is not a member of the company or who is appointed for an unlimited period of time, or who is appointed by a general meeting, may be dismissed by a resolution passed in general meeting by a

majority consisting of more than one-half of the company's members holding more than one-half of its capital. If there is no substantial cause for such dismissal, the manager will be entitled to damages (art 19(4)). Since the general meeting is the supreme organ of the company, and is competent to make decisions concerning any of the company's business affairs (art 14(1)), it would appear to be entitled to give directions to the managers concerning the performance of their functions.

(4) General meetings of the members of an EPE are called by the managers (art 10(2)), and a general meeting must be held each year within three months after the end of the company's accounting period (art 10(3)). Members who hold one-twentieth of the company's capital may require a general meeting to be called and specify the matters to be discussed (art 11). Each member is entitled to vote at a general meeting, and the number of votes which he may cast is equal to the number of shares which he holds (art 12(1)). Except where the articles otherwise provide, resolutions are passed by a majority consisting of more than one-half of the company's members holding more than half its capital (art 13). Resolutions for the alteration of the articles (including increases and reductions of capital) and for the dissolution of the company must be passed by a majority consisting of at least three-quarters of the members holding three-quarters of the company's capital (arts 38–40 and 44). Unanimity is required for a change in the nationality of the company, or for an increase in the members' obligations towards the company, or for the imposition of restrictions on the rights accorded to them by the company's articles (art 38(3)). An annual balance sheet must be drawn up by the managers and submitted to the members in general meeting for approval (art 23). There is, however, no requirement that the annual accounts shall be audited. Dividends on shares may only be paid out of profits, and they are declared by resolution of a general meeting (art 14(2)(c)).

(5) An EPE is dissolved (a) when the law or the articles so provide and upon the occurrence of any of the causes common to all companies and partnerships; (b) unless the articles otherwise provide, when a majority consisting of three-quarters of the members holding three-quarters of the company's capital so resolves at a general meeting; (c) if the court so orders, having determined that there are substantial reasons for it to do so, upon the application of one or more members holding at least one-tenth of the company's capital; (d) if the company is adjudged bankrupt in bankruptcy proceedings; (e) if the court so orders upon the application of any

person having a legal interest, where all the company's shares are held by a single member (art 44). In the event of the loss of one-half of the company's capital, the managers must call a meeting of the members for the purpose of passing a resolution for the dissolution of the company or for the reduction of the company's capital, which may in no case be reduced to an amount below the prescribed minimum (art 45(1)). The dissolution of the company is followed by its liquidation. The company continues to exist and has corporate personality for the purpose of the liquidation. The liquidation of the company is carried out by the managers, unless the company's articles otherwise provide, or unless the general meeting otherwise resolves (art 47(1)). The rules governing the liquidation of the company are in general similar to those governing the liquidation of an AE.

CHAPTER 7

DENMARK

The main types of business associations which may be formed under Danish law are the partnership (*interesseselskab*), the limited partnership (*kommandetselskab*), the cooperative society (*andelsforening* or *andelsselskab*), the public company (*aktieselskab*), the public company some of whose directors are personally liable for the company's debts (*kommandetaktselskab*), and the private company (*anpartsselskab*). The public company has been in use in Denmark since the seventeenth century, and is at present regulated by the Public Companies Law (*lov om aktieselskaber*) No 370 of 13th June 1973, as subsequently amended. The private company was introduced into Denmark by the Private Companies Law (*lov om anpartsselskaber*) No 371 of 13th June 1973, which has been subsequently amended by later legislation. Private companies are now of considerable economic importance in Denmark.

The First and the Fourth Directives of the Council of Ministers of the European Communities have been implemented by legislation in Denmark. The latter directive was implemented by Law No 284 of 10th June 1981 on the preparation of annual accounts by certain types of companies. This law is applicable to all public and private companies and to limited partnerships, but not to banks and insurance companies. The provisions of the new law are much more detailed and comprehensive than the previous accounting rules in the Companies Law of 13th June 1973, but in many respects the new law puts into statutory form rules that are already followed in current Danish accounting practice.* Only limited advantage is taken of the provisions of the Fourth Directive enabling member states to make concessions in respect of the form of accounts of small and medium sized companies (Law No 284 of 10th June 1981, arts 25 and 49).

The paragraphs (§§) referred to by number in the part of the chapter which deals with the *aktieselskab* are paragraphs of Law No

---

* For an English language text of the Law, see *Commercial Laws of Europe* (European Law Centre), Vol 5, Part 48, pp103 *et seq* (March 1982).

370 of 1973 as amended, unless otherwise stated. The paragraphs referred to in the same way in the part which deals with the *anpartsselskab* are paragraphs of Law No 371 of 1973 as amended.

AKTIESELSKAB (A/S)

1 Formation

The first step in the formation of an *aktieselskab* (A/S) is for the founders, who must be at least three in number, to prepare and sign a memorandum of association, which must contain draft articles of association (*vedtaegterne*) (§ 3). At least two of the founders must be resident in Denmark (§ 3). The Ministry of Industry may grant an exemption from this requirement, and it has done so for Community nationals residing in other member states (§ 176 and Decree No 476 of 10th August 1973).

The memorandum must state the price at which the company's shares (*akties*) are offered; the dates by which the shares must be subscribed and paid for; the time at which the statutory meeting will be held (§ 5); and whether the share capital is to be subscribed by payment in cash or by assets other than cash (§ 6(1)).

The articles must specify:

1 The name of the company, which must contain the word '*aktieselskab*', or an abbreviation thereof such as A/S, but not necessarily at the end of the name (§ 153).

2 The municipality in Denmark where the company has its registered office.

3 The objects of the company, which need be stated in general terms only.

4 The amount of the company's share capital, which must be at least 100,000 Kr (£6,925 approximately).

5 The nominal value of the shares, and the voting rights of the shareholders.

6 The number, or minimum and maximum numbers, of members of the board of directors and their deputies (if any), the number of auditors, and the terms of office of the members of the board of directors and of the auditors.

7 The length of notice for convening general meetings and the notification of meetings to members.

8 The matters to be dealt with at ordinary general meetings.

9 The dates of the company's financial year.

10 Whether the company's shares are to be in registered or bearer form.

11 Whether the company's shares are to be represented by non-negotiable instruments.

12 Whether the shareholders are to be bound to permit the company or any other persons to redeem their shares wholly or partly and, if so, the rules governing such redemption.

13 Whether the transferability of shares in the company is to be restricted and, if so, the rules applicable thereto.

14 Whether certain shares are to have special rights and, if so, the scope of those rights.

15 Any restrictions on the authority of members of the board of directors and the general managers to bind the company by their signatures (§ 4).

The founders are required either to subscribe for all the share capital themselves, or to invite other parties to subscribe for shares at a statutory meeting (§ 9): the latter method of formation has now fallen into disuse. At least one-half of the nominal capital (including any share premiums) or at least 100,000 Kr, whichever is the larger amount, must be contributed before the company can be registered (§ 11(2)). The final resolution for the formation of the company must be passed at a statutory meeting held in accordance with the provisions of the articles governing general meetings, notice of which must be given to all subscribers. A statutory meeting must be held even though the whole of the share capital has previously been subscribed in the memorandum (§ 9(1) and (2)). After a resolution for the formation of the company has been passed, the statutory meeting proceeds to the election of a board of directors and auditors (§ 10(4)).

After the statutory meeting has been held the board of directors applies for the registration of the company by notifying the Companies Registry in Copenhagen of its formation not more than six months after the date of the signature of the company's memorandum (§§ 11(1), 154 and 155). If the Registrar is not notified within this period, the company cannot be registered, and the subscribers will be relieved of their obligation to subscribe the share capital (§ 11(1) and (3)). An A/S only acquires legal personality when it is registered in the register (§ 12).

The Chief Registrar arranges for the publication of the registration of the company in the Official Gazette (*Statstidende*). Certain further particulars, including the names of the directors, are published in a special registration gazette (§§ 154 and 158 and Notice No 1477, § 7).

In practice it is more common to form new companies as private companies (ApSs) initially, and to convert them into A/Ss only when the need arises, than to form them as A/Ss. It takes a considerable period of time to complete the formalities necessary for the formation of an A/S, and in order to save time, lawyers frequently make use of shelf companies which they have already formed and registered. Such companies are bought by persons wishing to begin or develop a business enterprise in the form of an A/S or an ApS. After the shares in these companies have been bought, an extraordinary general meeting will be called for the purpose of making necessary amendments to the articles and electing the board of directors.

2 Shares and bonds

(a) Shares

The shareholders of an A/S are not personally liable for its debts or obligations (§ 1(3)). The uniting of all the company's shares in one hand is not a cause of the dissolution of the company.

Contributions to the capital of the company may be made in cash or in kind. Where shares are allotted for a consideration in kind, full particulars, including the basis of the valuation of the consideration, must be given in the memorandum on formation, or in the resolution of the general meeting if shares are issued in consideration of kind on an increase of capital (§§ 6(2) and (3), and 33).

Shares subscribed at the time of the formation of a company must be fully paid up not later than one year after the registration of the company. Where notice that the share capital has been fully paid up has not been submitted one month before the expiration of the year, the Chief Registrar of Companies prescribes an appropriate period within which full payment must be made. If such payment is not made within this period of time, the company is dissolved (§ 15). Twenty-five per cent of the total amount of any increase of capital (which for this purpose is determined in accordance with the issue price of the shares) must be paid before the increase of capital can be registered (§ 36(2)). The shares subscribed on an increase of capital must be fully paid up not later than one year after the increase of capital has been registered. Where notice that the new shares subscribed for have been fully paid up is not submitted one month before the expiration of the year, the Chief Registrar prescribes an appropriate period within which full payment must be made. If it is not made within this period, the increase in capital is cancelled (§ 16).

Shares may not be issued at a discount, and when a call or instalment capital falls due for payment a subscriber may not exercise any right to set off a claim he has against the company unless the directors consent thereto. No such consent may be granted if the set off may be detrimental to the company or its members (§ 13). If a shareholder fails to pay a call or instalment of capital he is, unless the articles otherwise provide, liable to pay interest on the amount due at a rate equal to the discount rate fixed by the Bank of Denmark at the relevant time plus 2 per cent. The company may sue the shareholder for the unpaid capital, or, after giving him a certain length of notice, sell the shares on his account (§ 14).

An A/S must issue share certificates (§ 21(2)). Share certificates are negotiable except where the articles otherwise provide, and in that case each individual share certificate must contain a clear and conspicuous statement to the effect that it is not negotiable (§ 21(1)). Shares may be in registered or bearer form, but bearer certificates cannot be issued in respect of shares that are not fully paid, or shares which are redeemable or the transfer of which is subject to restrictions (§§ 21 and 23). Shares may be bearer shares without being negotiable, or they may be negotiable and in registered form. Bearer shares may be converted into registered shares (§ 24(1)), but a registered share does not become a bearer share by delivery to bearer. A bearer shareholder is entitled to have his name entered in the company's register and his shares are then converted into registered shares (§ 24(1)).

The transfer of shares is governed by the Bonds Law 1938. Registered shares are transferred by the registered holder endorsing the share certificate, and delivering it to the transferee. The transferee cannot exercise his rights as a shareholder until he is entered in the share register. The entry in the share register must be noted on the share certificate or a new certificate must be issued to the transferee (§§ 25 and 27). Bearer shares are transferred by delivery, and a person who takes delivery of bearer shares obtains a good title to them, unless he was aware that his transferor's title was defective, or unless he would have discovered that fact if he had exercised due diligence.

Any restrictions imposed on the transferability of the shares on the formation of the company or on an increase of capital (§ 32(2)), or later by a unanimous resolution of all the shareholders, must be included in the company's articles and must be set out in all the company's share certificates; a requirement that a share transfer shall be subject to the company's consent is treated as a restriction for this purpose (§§ 19(1) and 20(1)).

Where the articles of the company provide that certain persons shall have preemptive rights on the sale of shares, they must state in what order these rights may be exercised; the time within which they must be exercised, which must be not more than two months from the date when notice of the intended sale is given to the board of directors; and the time within which the purchase price must be paid, which must be not more than two months from the date when its amount is determined. When the articles do not contain any provisions governing the method of determining the purchase price, or where the provisions they contain concerning this matter are manifestly unreasonable, the purchase price is fixed by valuers appointed by the court. Any of the parties may refer the decision of the valuers to the court, and an action challenging its validity may be instituted within three months after the notification of the decision (§ 19).

Where the articles provide that any transfer of shares shall be subject to the company's consent, the company's decision is given by the board of directors, unless the matter is referred to the general meeting for decision. The decision must be made as soon as possible after the receipt of the request therefor. The party requesting such consent must be notified of the decision without delay. If he is not so notified within two months of the date of his request for consent it is deemed to be given (§ 10).

A company may not purchase or take a mortgage of its own shares if after the acquisition the shares so acquired, together with the shares of the company held by it and its subsidiaries, will exceed 10 per cent of the company's subscribed capital. The latter rule applies correspondingly to the acquisition by a subsidiary of shares in the parent company. Exceptions exist in the case of the take-over of another company or its undertaking, on a reduction of share capital, or on a redemption of shares, or on a purchase at a sale by way of execution of a judgment to satisfy claims of the company. Shares acquired under any of the exceptions must be disposed of as soon as possible. If they are not disposed of within two years, they must be cancelled, and the company's capital must be reduced accordingly (§ 48). Shares in the company held by the company itself or by its subsidiary carry no voting rights (§ 6).

Dividends on shares may only be paid out of the company's net profits and free reserves (§ 110). A general meeting may, by a majority comprising two-thirds of the votes cast as well as of two-thirds of the voting capital represented at the meeting, resolve to capitalise profits and reserves, or amounts resulting from the revaluation of assets, or amounts transferred from the statutory reserve to free reserves, and to issue bonus shares to the company's shareholders accordingly in proportion to their existing holdings (§§ 30(1), 39, 78 and 110(1)).

The articles may make provision for different classes of shares. The commonest types of shares met with in practice are ordinary shares and preference shares. All shares must confer voting rights. However, the voting rights given to preference shareholders may be restricted to certain matters. The articles may also provide that the voting rights attached to certain shares shall be increased in certain specified circumstances, although not in excess of ten times those given to other shares of the same nominal value (§ 67). The articles may also provide that certain shares shall be redeemable compulsorily (§ 21). Such redemption may take place only if the company's share capital and the statutory reserve corresponding thereto (this is one-quarter of the share capital: § 111(1)) will be fully represented by the company's net assets after the shares have been redeemed (§ 47).

(b) Bonds

The issue of ordinary bonds is governed by the Bonds Law of 1938, and the Companies Law No 370 of 1973 does not contain any provisions regulating the issue of bonds. No government authorisation is necessary for the issue of bonds. Bonds may be issued in favour of a named person or to bearer.

Companies may issue bonds which entitle their holders to convert them into shares. The amount of such an issue must not exceed one-half of the company's share capital. A resolution of the general meeting passed by a majority comprising two-thirds of the votes cast as well as two-thirds of the voting capital represented at the meeting is necessary for the issue of convertible bonds. As in the case of a subscription for new shares on an increase of capital, shareholders have a preferential right of subscription for convertible bonds (§ 51). Companies may also issue bonds bearing interest at a rate which is wholly or partly dependent on the dividends paid on the company's shares, or on the profits earned by the company. The issue of such bonds requires an ordinary resolution of the general meeting passed by a simple majority of the votes cast. The directors of the company may be authorised by the general meeting to carry out the issue of convertible bonds (§ 63).

The rules for the transfer of bonds are contained in the Bonds Law 1938, and are the same as for the transfer of shares.

3 Management and control

(a) Board of management

Public companies which have a share capital in excess of 400,000 Kr must have a board of management (*direktion*), whose members are approved by the board of directors (*bestyrelse*). The board of management consists of one or more members (§ 51), who must be natural persons of full age and capacity and resident in Denmark (§ 52). The board of management is responsible for the conduct of the day-to-day business of the company, and decisions which in the circumstances of the company are unusual or of far reaching importance to the company must be referred to the board of directors. However, the board of management may act on its own initiative if it is not possible to await the decision of the board of directors without causing considerable inconvenience to the company's business (§ 54(2)).

Transactions and contracts entered into by any of its managers bind the company. However, the articles may provide that the company may be bound only by one or more particular managers acting individually, or by several managers acting jointly. Such a restriction can only be invoked against third parties if it is entered in the register of companies and published. No other kind of restriction is permitted (§ 60). A contract or transaction entered into on behalf of the company by any person or persons authorised to represent it, including a manager or managers, is binding on the company even though it is outside the objects of the company, unless the company proves that this fact was known to the third party, or that he could not have been ignorant of it in the circumstances. Mere publication of the articles is not sufficient for this purpose (§ 61).

Managers must notify the board of their shareholdings in the company and any other company in the same group, as well as of any sales or further purchases of shares. Managers may not participate in speculative transactions in the shares of the company or of another company belonging to the same group (§ 53). They may not take part in the discussion of matters at management or board meetings if they have a substantial interest in the matters that might conflict with the interest of the company (§ 58). Loans may only be made to a manager against good and valuable security, and the loan must be provided out of assets in excess of those required to represent the company's share capital and statutory reserve (§ 115). Managers are liable for loss which they deliberately or negligently cause to the company in the execution of their duties. The general meeting may resolve to institute proceedings against the managers. An action may be brought notwithstanding that the general meeting has previously resolved to exonerate the managers if, before the resolution was passed, correct and complete information was not given to the general meeting. Where the holders of at least 10 per cent of the company's share capital vote against a resolution of the general meeting exonerating the managers, any shareholder may institute proceedings against them (§ 144).

(b) Board of directors

All public companies must have a board of directors consisting of at least three persons if the company has a share capital of 400,000 Kr or more or if it has had an average of fifty employees or more over the last three years. This number is exclusive of those directors who may be appointed by public authorities or others, or elected by the employees. Where the company has a share capital of less than 400,000 Kr, and has less than fifty employees, the board may consist of only one or two members (§ 49(1)).

Members of the board representing the shareholders are elected by the general meeting: they may also be appointed by the shareholders' committee where, which happens infrequently, one has been established (§ 49(1)). The articles may give public authorities and other persons (eg bondholders) the right to appoint one or more members of the board (§ 49(2)). In companies which have had an average of at least fifty employees for the last three years, the company's employees have the right to elect a number of members of the board equal to half the number of directors elected by shareholders and appointed by public authorities or other persons, subject to the proviso that the directors elected by employees must be at least two in number. Special rules are applicable to groups of companies (§ 49(3) and (4)). The majority of the directors must be elected by the general meeting or appointed by the shareholders' committee (§ 49(6)).

The election of the employee directors is governed by § 177. The company's employees must first of all take a vote in order to decide whether they wish for board representation. If at least half of those entitled to vote do so in favour of such representation, a ballot is held to elect the employee directors.

The directors must be natural persons of full age (eighteen years) and capacity, and at least half of them must be resident in Denmark (§ 52). The majority of members of the board of directors must consist of persons who are not managers of the company (§ 51), and the chairman of the board may not be a manager (§ 56). There is no limitation to the number of boards of directors on which any one person may sit.

Directors may resign. They retire upon the expiry of their period of office, which may be up to four years in the case of directors elected by the shareholders, and two years for employee directors (§§ 49(7) and 50(1)). Directors who have been appointed by the general meeting may be removed by that body at any time. Directors appointed by another body or person may be removed by that body or person at any time. Employee directors may be removed by the employees at any time (§ 50(1)).

The board of directors and the board of management are together responsible for the management of the company. The principal task of the board of directors is to supervise the board of management. As has been pointed out above, transactions of an unusual nature or of far reaching significance to the company must in principle be submitted by the board of management to the board of directors for its approval. The board of directors must ensure that the company's accounts and the management of the company's assets are examined and supervised satisfactorily in accordance with the company's position (§ 54). The articles may define more particularly the transactions for which the approval of the board of directors must be obtained. The practical internal division of powers between the two boards is dependent on the actual circumstances of the company and, in particular, on the nature of its business, its size and its tradition of management.

In principle, transactions and contracts entered into on behalf of the company by the entire board of directors, or by a single director, are binding on the company. However, the articles may provide that the company shall be bound only by one or more directors acting individually, or by several directors acting jointly. Such a restriction is only effective against third parties if it is entered in the register of companies and published. No other type of restriction is permitted (§ 60). A transaction or contract entered into on behalf of the company by a director or directors authorised to represent it is binding on the company even though it is outside the objects of the company, unless the company proves that this fact was known to the third party, or that in the circumstances he could not have been unaware of it. Mere publication of the articles is not sufficient for this purpose (§ 61).

The rules discussed above which are applicable to managers' shareholdings, conflicts of interest between the managers, the company, loans to managers, and the liabilities of managers, apply equally to directors (§§ 53, 58, 115, 140 and 146).

(c) General meetings

The general meeting of shareholders (*generalforsamding*) is the company's supreme organ, and it may in principle pass resolutions giving instructions to the board of directors. The general meeting must, however, respect the limitations imposed on it by law and by the company's articles.

An ordinary general meeting must be held within six months after the end of each financial year of the company to receive and approve the annual accounts, to decide on the application of the profits (if any) and to decide on other matters in accordance with the provisions of the articles (§§ 49(1), 69 and 82). An extraordinary general meeting must be held whenever the board of directors or the auditors or the shareholders' committee (if any) thinks fit (§ 70(1)). Shareholders owning at least 10 per cent of the company's capital may require that an extraordinary general meeting shall be held for the purpose of deciding on a particular matter (§ 70(2)).

General meetings are called by the board. If the board fails to call a meeting, the Chief Registrar of Companies will do so on the request of a director, a member of the shareholders' committee (if any), a manager, an auditor or a shareholder (§ 72).

Not more than eight and not less than four weeks' notice must be given of the general meeting, unless the articles provide otherwise. Registered shareholders must be given written notice of the meeting; bearer shareholders must be notified thereof in accordance with the provision of the articles; if the employees have passed a resolution in favour of representation on the board of directors and have notified the board accordingly, notice of the general meeting must be given to the employees in accordance with regulations made by the Ministry of Industry. The notice of a general meeting must contain an agenda of the meeting. Where the meeting is an annual general meeting, copies of the annual accounts and of the auditors' report (and if the company is a parent company, consolidated accounts) together with the text of any proposed resolutions must be made available for inspection at the company's registered office before the meeting, and must be sent to registered shareholders on request (§ 73).

The articles may require a shareholder to notify the company not more than five days in advance if he intends to participate in the meeting (§ 63). Any shareholder may appoint another person to act as his proxy; such an appointment is valid for a year (§ 66). A shareholder may require a resolution proposed by him to be placed upon the agenda of a general meeting (§ 71).

Each share carries the right to cast at least one vote: the question of multiple voting rights has been discussed above.

A shareholder may request the board of directors and the board of management to provide the general meeting with available information on matters of significance for the evaluation of the annual accounts or the general position of the company, or in respect of items to be decided upon at the general meeting or relations with companies belonging to the same group. The board of directors must give this information, unless it considers that to do so would cause serious detriment to the company. If the information is not available at the meeting, it must be given within ten days (§ 76).

A shareholder may not participate in a vote at the general meeting relating either to any legal proceedings against himself or to his own liability to the company; nor may he participate in a vote relating to legal proceedings against other persons or relating to other persons' liability if, in respect of any such proceedings, he has a significant personal interest which conflicts with the interests of the company (§ 67).

Resolutions amending the articles, or increasing or reducing the share capital (§ 78), or waiving the preferential right of shareholders to subscribe for new shares (§ 30(3)), or for the issue of convertible bonds (§ 41), or for the winding up of the company (§ 116(2)) must be passed by a majority of two-thirds of the votes cast and of the share capital carrying voting rights. The resolution must conform with any additional requirements contained in the articles. A resolution for the amendment of the articles whereby the shareholders' right to dividends or to other distributions of assets is restricted must be passed by the votes of the holders of more than three-quarters of the share capital entitled to vote who are present or represented at the meeting (§ 39(2)). Amendments of the articles whereby: (*a*) the right of shareholders to dividends or to other distributions of assets is restricted for the benefit of persons other than shareholders, except where new shares are to be allotted to employees; (*b*) the obligations of the shareholders are increased; (*c*) the transferability of shares is restricted, or (*d*) shares are made redeemable compulsorily, must be unanimously approved by all the shareholders (§ 79(11)).

A general meeting must not adopt any resolution which is clearly likely to procure for certain shareholders or others undue advantages at the expense of other shareholders or the company (§ 80). Resolutions which are contrary to the law or the articles, or which have not been adopted in the prescribed manner, may be annulled by the court (§ 81).

Every A/S must prepare annual accounts comprising a balance sheet, a profit and loss account, and notes on the accounts (Law No 284 of 10th June 1981, § 2). These accounts must be submitted to the auditors for examination and report (§§ 88–91). At least one of the auditors must be professionally qualified, and there must be at least two auditors if the company's shares or bonds are listed on the stock exchange (§§ 83 and 84). Shareholders representing 15 per cent of the capital may request the Chief Registrar of Companies to appoint a special auditor to participate in the audit of the company's accounts together with the ordinary auditors (§ 82). The auditors' report must be made available to the board of directors not later than two weeks before the date of the annual general meeting which has to decide whether to approve the accounts (§ 69(2) and 91). The accounts must give a true and fair view of the company's assets and liabilities, its financial position and the profit or loss for the accounting period (Law No 284 of 10th June 1981, § 4).

Ten per cent of the profits shown in the annual accounts must be transferred to statutory reserve until it amounts to 10 per cent of the company's capital before the general meeting can use profits to declare a dividend or to make transfers to other reserves. After the statutory reserve has reached 10 per cent of the company's capital, 5 per cent of the profits shown in the annual accounts must be carried to it annually out of profits until it reaches 25 per cent of the total of the company's capital plus share premiums, less preliminary expenses incurred on the formation of the company. After an increase of capital, additional transfers of a fraction of profits to statutory reserve must be made annually as though the increase in capital were the original capital of the company (§ 111). A dividend exceeding 6 per cent of the paid up share capital may not be declared by a general meeting until the statutory reserve amounts to one-tenth of the share capital (§ 110(1)).

Danish law contains a number of provisions applicable to parent and subsidiary companies. If an A/S holds shares carrying the majority of votes in another A/S or in an ApS, the former company is deemed to be the parent company (*moderselskab*) and the latter the subsidiary (*dotterselskab*). The same rule applies where the A/S and its other subsidiaries hold shares which taken together carry controlling voting rights in the company whose status as a subsidiary is in question, and this is so also if all the shares carrying control are held by one or more subsidiaries of the same A/S. If an A/S exercises a controlling influence over another A/S or ApS in any other manner by virtue of shareholding or of an agreement and is entitled to a significant share of 'ts profits, the former company is likewise deemed to be a parent company, and the latter to be its subsidiary. Parent and subsidiary companies together constitute a group (§ 2). The most important consequence of the existence of a group under Danish law is that the parent company must prepare consolidated accounts for itself and its subsidiaries which must be laid before the ordinary general meeting (Law No 370 of 13th June 1973, § 69, and Law No 284 of 10th June 1981, §§ 1 and 57–61).

4 Take-overs and mergers

No statutory code exists governing take-over bids and no government permission is required for them. However, the Copenhagen Stock Exchange endeavours to secure compliance with a recommendation of the Danish Ministry of Industry based upon the proposals of the Commission of the European Communities of 25th July 1977 concerning a European code of conduct relating to transferable securities (OJ 1977 L212/27).

A merger may be effected by an existing A/S or ApS taking over all the assets and liabilities of one or more A/Ss, or by the creation of a new A/S which takes over the assets and liabilities of two or more companies, which may include ApSs, and at least one of which must be an A/S. Resolutions for the dissolution of the transferor companies must be passed by general meetings of each of these companies by a majority of two-thirds of the votes cast as well as of the share capital represented at the meetings: the articles of the transferor companies may impose additional requirements (§§ 134(1) and 135(1)). When the merger is by absorption of one company's undertaking by another company, the approval of the general meeting of the absorbing company is necessary if the merger involves an increase of capital for the purpose of issuing shares to the shareholders in the company to be dissolved. An audited statement of the accounts of the merging companies showing the assets and liabilities of each of them and a draft initial balance sheet of the acquiring company must be presented to the general meeting of the transferor companies.

Shareholders in a transferor company who have opposed the merger at a general meeting are entitled to demand that their shares be purchased by the acquiring company. The phrase 'have opposed' does not necessarily mean that the shareholders in question have voted against the proposed merger: an indication of opposition thereto is sufficient. If the purchase price cannot be agreed upon, it is fixed by an expert appointed by the court (§ 136). If a parent company owns 90 per cent of the shares in a subsidiary, the parent company may purchase the remaining shares in the subsidiary, and in addition the owners of those shares can require it to do so. If the purchase price cannot be agreed on, it is fixed by an expert appointed by the court (§ 139).

5 Dissolution and liquidation

Both solvent and insolvent companies may be wound up. A solvent A/S may be placed in voluntary liquidation. The winding up resolution must be passed by a majority of two-thirds of the votes cast and of the share capital entitled to vote represented at the meeting (§§ 78 and 116). The court may order the liquidation of an A/S on the application of the holders of one-tenth of the share capital if it finds that they have been oppressed or disadvantaged (§ 119). A company must be liquidated in accordance with the special rules applicable to insolvent companies where the company becomes or is discovered to be insolvent during a voluntary liquidation. A company must also be put into liquidation if it has not submitted annual accounts to the Chief Registrar of Companies for three years; or if it does not have the board of directors or the board of management prescribed by law and fails to remedy the situation within a period fixed by the Chief Registrar (§ 118). In these circumstances, the company is liquidated by the bankruptcy court at the request of the Chief Registrar, unless the general meeting passes a winding up resolution or requires the directors to file a petition in bankruptcy (§ 117).

If the company is solvent, the liquidation is carried out in accordance with the provisions of the Public Companies Law. The liquidation of an insolvent company is carried out in accordance with the provisions of the Bankruptcy Law No 298 of 8th June 1977.

ANPARTSSELSKAB (ApS)

Private companies are governed by the provisions of Law No 371 of 13th June 1973, whose provisions are identical or very similar to those of Law No 370 of 13th June 1973 governing public companies in respect of a considerable number of matters. The principal differences between an A/S and an ApS are as follows:

(1) An ApS need have only one founder. The founders must sign a memorandum of association, which must contain draft articles of association (§ 3(1)). The memorandum must contain information and provisions relating to: (a) the names and addresses of the founders, managers and auditors of the company and, where a board of directors is elected, of the first board members; (b) a statement whether shares in the company will be paid up in cash or in kind; (c) the price of the shares subscribed for; (d) the time within which full payment must be made for the shares; and (e) whether the company will pay the promoters' expenses (§ 5). The articles must contain provisions which are, in general, very similar to those required in the case of a public company (§ 4). Before the company can be registered, all the shares (anparts) must be subscribed, and at least half of their nominal value plus the premium (if any) amounting in total to not less than 30,000 Kr (£2,090 approximately) must be paid up. In addition, the first managers and auditors and the first board members (if any) must be appointed before registration (§ 5).

Once the above steps have been taken, the board or the managers are required to apply to the Registrar of Companies for registration. The company is incorporated as an ApS when it is entered in the register.

(2) Unless the articles otherwise provide, the rights attached to the shares are proportional to their nominal value (§ 13). Shares may carry multiple voting rights. All shares must be entered in the share register in the name of a member (§ 16). Share certificates may be issued: they are required to show the name of the member. Such certificates are not negotiable instruments, and they have an evidential value only (§ 15). Shares are transferred in accordance

with the Bonds Law of 1938; the procedure is the same as that for registered shares in an A/S. The articles may impose restrictions on the transfer of shares. Where the restriction takes the form of preemption rights in favour of members or other persons, § 19(2) of the Public Companies Law is applicable, *mutatis mutandis*. Where the restriction takes the form of the requirement of the company's consent to a transfer of shares, § 20(2) is applicable in the same way (§ 14).

An ApS is on principle not allowed to acquire its own shares. However, a number of exceptions exist to this general principle; these are the same as apply to an A/S, apart from the fact that no general exception is made for acquisitions which do not exceed 10 per cent of the share capital (§ 30). An ApS can issue ordinary bonds, but the public may not be invited to subscribe for its bonds. An ApS may also issue convertible and participating bonds. A resolution passed in general meeting by a majority of at least two-thirds of both the votes cast and of the paid up voting capital represented at the meeting is required for such an issue (§ 25).

(3) The business of an ApS which has a share capital of at least 400,000 Kr, or which has had an average of at least fifty employees for a period of three years, must be conducted by a management board and a board of directors, to which the employees may exercise their right to appoint directors (§ 31). An ApS which has a share capital of less than 400,000 Kr, and which has not had an average of at least fifty employees for a period of three years, need only have a board of management, which will carry out the tasks normally assigned to the board of directors (§§ 31 and 32). The rules applicable to the board of management and the board of directors of an ApS are generally the same as those applicable to the boards of an A/S. The rules governing employee representation on the board of directors (§§ 32 and 136) and the authority of members of the board of directors and of managers to bind the company are also the same as for an A/S (§ 41–44).

(4) The rules for general meetings of an ApS are in general the same as those for an A/S. The general meeting is the company's supreme organ, and the right of the members to take decisions is exercised thereat. However, if all the members agree, a resolution may be passed in writing without a general meeting being held (§ 46(1)). The business of an ordinary general meeting of an ApS is the same as for an A/S. An extraordinary general meeting must be called within two weeks at the request of members holding 25 per cent of the paid up capital or such smaller fraction as may be

provided for in the articles (§ 51). Written notice of a general meeting must be given to each member. Each member must be sent a copy of the accounts before the annual general meeting (§ 54). The rules governing the majorities required for the adoption of resolutions at a general meeting are the same as those for an A/S, with the exception that resolutions for the amendment of the articles, the increase or reduction of capital, the waiver of the shareholders' preferential right to subscribe for new shares, the issue of convertible or participating bonds, and for the voluntary winding up of the company must be passed by a majority consisting of two-thirds of the votes cast and of the paid up voting capital represented at the meeting, unless the articles provide otherwise (§ 59). The rules governing the accounts and dividends of an ApS are generally the same as those for an A/S. However, an ApS is not required to have a professionally qualified auditor unless the holders of 25 per cent of the company's paid up capital so require (§ 65). An ApS is not required to establish a statutory reserve (§§ 79–82).

CHAPTER 8

REPUBLIC OF IRELAND

The Republic of Ireland retained its common law heritage after partition in 1922, and it continued to apply United Kingdom law as of the date of partition. However, a considerable amount of new legislation has been introduced, including the Irish Companies Act 1963 (hereafter referred to as the Irish Act) which, although implementing many of the proposals contained in the Report of the Jenkins Committee, generally corresponds to the British Companies Act 1948. None of the provisions of the later enactments in Great Britain (ie the Companies Acts 1976, 1980 and 1981) have been enacted in the Republic of Ireland. The European Communities (Companies) Regulations 1973, which were made under the Irish European Communities Act 1972, are broadly similar to those of s 9 of the United Kingdom European Communities Act 1972, which implemented the First Directive of the Council of Ministers of the EEC on Company Law (OJ 1968 L 65/8). The term 'United Kingdom Act' is used in the present chapter to denote an act which was extended to the whole of the United Kingdom, as constituted at the time of its enactment.

None of the provisions of the Second, Third or Fourth Directives on company law has yet been implemented in the Republic of Ireland. However, it is anticipated that the necessary legislation will be introduced in the near future.

The same kinds of commercial associations are recognised in the Republic of Ireland as in the United Kingdom. General partnerships are regulated by the United Kingdom Partnership Act 1890, and limited partnerships by the United Kingdom Limited Partnerships Act 1907. Public and private companies, limited and unlimited companies, and companies limited by guarantee have the same meaning as under the Companies Act 1948 (Irish Act, ss 5 and 33). All private companies, even where they are wholly owned subsidiaries of public companies, are exempted from the obligation of delivering a copy of their accounts to the Registrar of Companies (s 128(4)). In addition, a private company which is a holding company need not prepare group accounts, although shareholders in the holding company are entitled to request that copies of the accounts of each subsidiary belonging to the group be supplied to them (s 154).

The discussion of public and private companies below is restricted to companies which are limited by shares.

PUBLIC COMPANIES

1 Formation

The rules governing the formation of an Irish public company are in substance the same as those that were applicable to the formation of a British public company before the passing of the Companies Act 1980. The form prescribed for the memorandum of association (*meabhrán chomlachais*) of a company limited by shares follows that of Table B of the First Schedule to the Companies Act 1948, except that it contains no registered office clause. However, the registered office must be in the Irish Republic and its situation must be notified to the Registrar within fourteen days of incorporation (s 113). The memorandum must be subscribed by at least seven persons (s 5), each of whom must write opposite his name the number of shares he takes (s 6). The memorandum must be printed (s 7).

The first clause of the memorandum states the name of the company. When the name is in the Irish language, the Irish form '*teoranta*' or '*teo*' may be used as an alternative to 'limited' as the last word of the name (s 6). A company may not be registered in a name which, in the opinion of the Minister, is undesirable, but an appeal lies to the court against a refusal to register (s 21). A company, when incorporated, must exhibit its name outside every place where it carries on business, and must mention its name in all business letters and publications and in all bills of exchange, promissory notes, endorsements, cheques and orders for money or goods purporting to be signed by or on behalf of the company and in all invoices, receipts and letters of credit of the company (s 114).

The second clause of the memorandum is the objects clause. Section 8 of the Irish Act, which follows the recommendations of the Jenkins Committee, provides that an act which is *ultra vires* the company shall nevertheless be effective as against the company in favour of a third person relying on it, unless the company can prove that the third party knew that the act was not within the powers of the company at the time when he relied on it. The directors are liable to the company for any loss suffered by it in consequence of the *ultra vires* act.

The third clause states that the liability of the members is limited. The fourth clause states the capital of the company: no minimum capital is at present required. As in the United Kingdom, the shares must have a nominal value.

A public company limited by shares is not required to have its own articles of association (*airtegail chomlachais*), but in practice always has such articles. It would seem that if any company having seven or more members has no articles of association of its own, the regulations contained in Part I of Table A of the First Schedule to the Act constitute its articles (s 13(2)). All articles of association must be printed, and must be signed by the same seven or more subscribers who signed the memorandum; their signatures must be attested (s 14). The company and its members are bound by the memorandum and articles once they have been registered (s 25). The Irish Table A follows its British counterpart in most respects.

In addition to the memorandum and articles of the company, a statutory declaration by the solicitor engaged in forming the company, or by a director or secretary named as such in the articles, that all the requirements of the Companies Act 1963 have been complied with must be filed with the Registrar in order to obtain the incorporation of the company (s 19(2)).

After the Registrar has satisfied himself that the documents filed with him are formally in order, that the company's name is unobjectionable and that its objects are lawful, he issues a certificate under his hand which certifies that the company is incorporated, and that its liability is limited (s 18). The certificate of incorporation is conclusive evidence that all the requirements of the Companies Act 1963 in respect of registration and matters precedent or incidental thereto have been complied with, and that the company is a company authorised to be registered and duly registered under the Act (s 19).

A company which is incorporated as a public company may not commence any business or exercise any borrowing powers unless it has complied with certain conditions which are the same as those which were formerly applicable to companies which were incorporated as public companies under the Companies Act 1948 (which was repealed by Schedule 4 to the Companies Act 1980) and has obtained a certificate from the Registrar that it is entitled to commence business (s 115). A company so incorporated is also bound to hold a statutory meeting within a period of not less than one month nor more than three months from the date at which it is entitled to commence business, and the directors are required to forward a statutory report to each member of the company not less than fourteen days before the date of the statutory meeting (s 130).

The above requirements do not apply to private companies, and for this (and other) reasons, public companies are usually initially incorporated as private companies, and are converted into public companies by altering their articles later on.

A company may ratify a contract or other transaction entered into prior to its formation (s 37(1)). Until the contract is so ratified, the persons who purported to act for the company are personally liable on the contract in the absence of express agreement to the contrary, and are entitled to the benefit of the contract (s 37(2)).

2 Shares and debentures

(a) Shares

An Irish public company has a separate legal personality from its shareholders, and its assets alone are liable to satisfy its obligations. However, if the number of members of the company falls below seven, and remains less than that number for six months, every person who becomes or remains a member while that situation continues after the period of six months has expired is personally liable for the debts of the company incurred while he remains a member and is aware of the position (s 36).

The issue of shares at a discount must be authorised by a special resolution of the members (this must be passed by a majority of not less than three-quarters of the votes cast: s 141), and must be sanctioned by the court (s 63). If shares are issued at a premium, a share premium account must be established, and the provisions of the Act relating to the reduction of the share capital are applicable to the share premium account (s 62).

Shares may be in registered or in bearer form, provided that, in the latter case, they are fully paid (s 88). Bearer shares are transferred by delivery of the warrant (s 88(3)). Registered shares are transferable in the manner provided for by the company's articles (s 79). Table A of the 1963 Act does not provide for any form of transfer, but the Irish Stock Transfer Act 1965, which contains provisions similar to those of the British Stock Transfer Act 1963, authorises simple stock transfer forms in the case of fully paid shares.

A company may not give financial assistance for the purchase of its own shares (s 60(1)). A number of specific and limited exceptions exist to this rule (s 60(3)) which are the same as those under s 54(3) of the Companies Act 1948. In addition, s 60(2) provides for a general exception under which financial assistance may be given for any acquisition of shares if authorised by a special resolution passed by a general meeting, provided that a statutory declaration made by the directors has been forwarded to the members and filed with the Registrar stating the form, purposes and intended beneficiaries of the assistance, and affirming that the declarants are of the opinion that the company will be fully solvent after the giving of such assistance.

The share capital may be divided into different classes of shares. Companies may, if so authorised by their articles, issue redeemable preference shares (s 64(1)). The rules of law governing the variation of class rights would seem to be the same as those that were applicable in Great Britain before the enactment of s 32 of the Companies Act 1980. If provision is made by the memorandum or articles of a company for the variation of the rights attaching to any class of its shares with the consent of a specified portion of the holders of shares of that class, or with the sanction of a resolution passed at a separate meeting of that class of shareholders, and the rights of that class are varied, the holders of not less than 10 per cent of the issued share capital of that class, being shareholders who did not consent to or vote for the variation, may apply to the court to cancel the variation, and where any such application is made, the variation does not have effect unless it is confirmed by the court (s 78(1)). An application to the court must be made within twenty-eight days after the consent to the variation is given on behalf of the class, or after the resolution of the class meeting is passed (s 78(2)).

The rules governing the raising of capital and the allotment of shares are very similar to those applicable under the Companies Act 1948. Where there is reason to believe that the creation or issue of shares is invalid, the court may declare the shares to have been validly created or issued if it is satisfied that it is just and equitable for it to do so (s 89).

An unrealised capital surplus arising on the revaluation of fixed assets may not be distributed by way of dividend, or be used to pay up debentures or partly paid shares; however, if a revaluation of all the company's fixed assets takes place, the surplus may be capitalised and issued in the form of fully paid bonus shares (s 149(6)).

(b) Debentures

The rules governing the issue of debentures, and the creation of fixed and floating charges and the registration of mortgages and charges at the Companies Registry are very similar to those in the British Companies Act 1948. There are some differences, however, in the rules applicable to registration with the company. A company is under no obligation to maintain a register of charges at its registered office, but it is required to maintain a register of debenture holders. This requirement is not applicable, however, to a debenture which does not form part of a series ranking *pari passu* nor to bearer debentures (s 91(1)).

3 Management and control

(a) Directors

Most of the rules governing directors are the same as under the British Companies Act 1948. The company must have at least two directors (s 176). There is no maximum age for directors. Where a person is convicted on indictment of any offence in connection with the promotion, formation or management of a company, or any offence involving fraud or dishonesty whether in connection with a company or not, there is no time limit on the disqualification which the court may impose on him being or acting as a director of any company, and the court may therefore disqualify him for such period as it thinks fit (s 184).

The company's annual accounts must state the aggregate amount of the directors' emoluments, the aggregate amount of pensions payable to present or past directors, and the aggregate amount of compensation for the loss of office paid by the company to directors during the period to which the accounts relate. No further particulars of the directors' salaries and other emoluments have to be disclosed in the accounts (s 191). There is no provision for the inspection of directors' service contracts by members. Every public company must keep a register at the place where its register of members is kept showing the interests of each of its directors in its shares and debentures and in the shares and debentures of its holding and subsidiary companies and of other subsidiaries of its holding company (s 190).

There is no prohibition or restriction on loans to directors. Details of such loans must be included in the accounts, unless the loan is made in the ordinary course of the business of a banking or similar company, or unless the director is also an employee of the company and the loan does not exceed £4,000, and the directors certify that the loan is consistent with the company's practice governing loans to employees (s 192(2)).

Subject to the provisions of the Companies Act 1963, which require that certain powers shall be exercised by the members in general meeting, the division of power between the board and the members of a public company is determined entirely by the articles. Table A, Article 80, of the Companies Act 1963 is the same as Table A, Article 80, of the British Companies Act 1948.

The rules relating to the kinds of meetings and resolutions, and the convening of, and proceedings at, general and other meetings are very similar to those contained in the British Companies Act 1948. All annual general meetings, other than the first such meeting, must be held in the Republic of Ireland, unless all the members entitled to attend and vote at such a meeting give their written consent to its being held elsewhere and the articles do not provide that the meeting shall be held in Ireland (s 140). A general meeting may be held even though it is called by less than the required period of notice, if the auditors and all the members entitled to attend and vote thereat agree (s 133(3)). A general meeting called to pass a special resolution may be held even though less than twenty-one days' notice of it has been given, if the shorter notice is accepted as sufficient by a majority in number of the members entitled to attend and vote at the meeting who between them hold at least 90 per cent of nominal value of the shares carrying voting rights thereat (s 141(2)). If so authorised by the articles, a written resolution signed by all the members entitled to attend and vote at a general meeting is as valid and effective for all purposes as a resolution passed at a properly convened general meeting (s 141(2)). This rule applies to a special resolution as well as to an ordinary resolution (s 141(8)).

The holders of not less than one-tenth of the paid up capital of the company carrying voting rights may require the directors to call an extraordinary general meeting (s 132). Shareholders have no right to require the inclusion of resolutions on the agenda of a general meeting or the circulation of statements to the members.

The company's annual accounts (balance sheet and profit and loss accounts and, if the company is a holding company, so far as not incorporated in the balance sheet or profit and loss account, any group accounts) in the form specified in the Sixth Schedule to the 1963 Act together with the auditors' report thereon and the report of the directors must be laid before the annual general meeting (ss 157, 158 and 163). The directors' report must contain particulars of the activities of the company and its subsidiaries (if any) and of any significant changes therein during the year, the amounts recommended to be paid as dividend and the amounts proposed to be carried to reserve, and a list of all subsidiary companies and other bodies corporate in which the company has a beneficial interest of more than 20 per cent of the shares carrying voting rights. The auditors' report must state the matters set out in the Seventh Schedule.

(b) Judicial control over directors

A winding up order may be made by the court if the company's affairs are conducted, or the powers of the directors are exercised, in a manner oppressive to any member, or in disregard of his interests as a member. The court will dismiss a petition for winding up if it is of the opinion that proceedings under s 205 would, in all the circumstances, be more appropriate (s 213(g)). The alternative relief under s 205 (which corresponds to s 210 of the British Companies Act 1948, now replaced by s 75 of the Companies Act 1980) is available when the affairs of the company are being conducted or the powers of the directors are being exercised in an oppressive manner, or in disregard of the interests of any of the members. There is no need to show that the facts would justify the making of a winding up order, or that such an order would not be appropriate. The relief which may be granted includes the prohibition of any act, or the cancellation or variation of any transaction (s 205(2)).

The rules governing the appointment of inspectors to investigate the affairs of the company contained in ss 165 and 166 of the Irish Companies Act 1963 are very similar to those contained in ss 164 and 165 of the British Companies Act 1948. However, s 165(1)(a) provides that an inspector may be appointed on the application of 100 members, as opposed to the 200 members that are required under the corresponding s 165(1)(a) of the Companies Act 1948. The Irish Act does not provide for the appointment of an inspector to investigate the beneficial ownership of a company's securities. The powers and duties of inspectors and of the Minister of Industry and Commerce on receipt of their report are the same as in the case of an investigation by the Department of Trade under the Companies Act 1948.

4 Take-overs, mergers and reconstructions

The City Code on Take-overs and Mergers applies to companies incorporated in Ireland which are listed on the Stock Exchange. The notes for Irish companies published by the Stock Exchange in January 1980 as an addendum to 'Admission of Securities to Listing' have proved to be most helpful in clarifying the position of Irish listed companies, and the following statement appears in the introduction: 'The members of the Irish Unit as members of The Stock Exchange do subscribe to the aims of the Council for the Securities Industry and, having due regard to the laws and practices of the Republic of Ireland, adhere to these guidelines.'

Mergers and reconstructions may take place in a voluntary winding up (s 260) as well as with the sanction of the court (ss 201–203), as is the case under the British Companies Act 1948. The offeror company is empowered by s 206 of the Irish Act (which generally corresponds to s 209 of the Companies Act 1948) to acquire compulsorily the shares of shareholders of the offeree company who have not accepted an offer for their shares which has been accepted by the holders of four-fifths in value of the shares for which the offer has been made.

5 Liquidation and dissolution

Companies may be wound up by the court, or placed in voluntary liquidation, as under the Companies Act 1948. A company which is in voluntary liquidation may be compulsorily wound up (s 282). A special resolution must be passed to put the company into a members' voluntary winding up (s 251(1)(b)). An ordinary resolution passed by a simple majority of members suffices to put the company into a creditors' voluntary winding up where the company is insolvent (s 251(1)(c)).

The procedure in voluntary and compulsory liquidation is very similar to that under the Companies Act 1948. However, the Official Receiver has no Irish equivalent; in a compulsory liquidation the court may appoint a provisional liquidator at any time before the appointment of liquidators at the first meeting of members and creditors (s 226).

PRIVATE COMPANIES

A private company is defined in s 33 of the Irish Companies Act 1963 solely by reference to the contents of its articles of association. A company is a private one if its articles: (a) restrict the right to transfer its shares; (b) limit the number of its members to fifty, excluding employees and former employees of the company who are members of it; and (c) prohibit it from issuing any invitation to the public to subscribe for its shares or debentures.

The principal differences between Irish public and private companies are summarised below:

(1) A private company limited by shares which has no articles of association of its own, is governed by the articles in Table A, Part I, as modified by Table A, Part II, whereas a public company in a similar situation is governed by the articles in Table A, Part I, alone. A private company must in practice have articles of its own containing the restrictions required by s 33(1) or expressly incorporating Table A, Parts I and II, in order to show that it is a private company. A private company limited by shares which has articles of its own is governed by the articles in Table A, Parts I and II, insofar as its own articles do not expressly or impliedly exclude them, whereas a public company is governed only by the articles in Table A, Part I, in that situation.

(2) A private company's memorandum and articles of association need only be subscribed by two persons (ss 5(1) and 11), and the members of a private company only incur personal liability for its debts if its membership falls below two (s 36).

(3) A private company may commence business on its incorporation (s 115(7)); it does not hold a statutory meeting or issue a statutory report (s 130(11)), and it may issue shares and debentures without delivering a statement in lieu of prospectus to the Registrar of Companies (s 48(2)).

(4) A private company may not issue share warrants or freely renounceable letters of allotment in respect of its shares.

(5) Unless its articles otherwise provide, the quorum at a general meeting of a private company is two persons present in person (s 134(c)). A member may appoint only one proxy to represent him at such a meeting unless the articles permit the appointment of more than one, and any proxy may speak as well as vote at the meeting (s 136(1)).

(6) A private company in which all the members are directors is not required to maintain a register of directors' interests in the shares and debentures of the company (s 190(12)).

(7) A holding company which is a private company is not required to prepare group accounts, but a member is entitled to request to be supplied within fourteen days with copies of the accounts of each of the subsidiaries (s 154). A private company is not required to file copies of its annual accounts and the directors' and auditors' report with its annual return (s 128(4)).

(8) with its annual return a private company must send to the

Registrar of Companies a certificate signed by a director and the secretary that the company has not since the date of the preceding annual return, or in the case of the first annual return, since the date of its incorporation, issued an invitation to the public to subscribe for its shares or debentures, and, if the company's membership exceeds fifty, a further certificate that the excess consists of members who are employees of the company, or former employees who became members while employed by it (s 129).

(9) A private company may be wound up by the court on the ground that its membership has fallen below the statutory minimum only if it has less than two members, whereas a public company may be wound up if its membership is less than seven (s 213(*d*)).

The rules governing the loss of privileges of a private company and the conversion of such a company into a public company are the same as those contained in ss 29 and 30 of the British Companies Act 1948, which were repealed by Sched 4 to the Companies Act 1980.